RECREATIONAL DRUGS

LAWRENCE A. YOUNG

LINDA G. YOUNG

MARJORIE M. KLEIN

DONALD M. KLEIN

DORIANNE BEYER

MACMILLAN PUBLISHING CO., INC.
NEW YORK
COLLIER MACMILLAN PUBLISHERS
LONDON

Macmillan Publishing Co., Inc.
866 Third Avenue, New York, N.Y. 10022
Collier Macmillan Canada, Ltd.

Library of Congress Cataloging in Publication Data
Main entry under title:
Recreational drugs.
   1. Psychopharmacology. 2. Hallucinogenic drugs.
I. Young, Lawrence A.
BF207.H66   615'.78   77–11867
ISBN 0–02–633310–4

First Printing 1977

Printed in the United States of America

To our children—

Jeffrey, Allison, Peter, and Kenny—

with the hope it enlightens your world.

CONTENTS

CONTENTS

FOREWORD

In any healthy society, irresponsible use of drugs can never be encouraged or condoned. Virtually every physician has had an opportunity to observe personally the damage, destruction, and despair drug abuse can cause.

The full scope of the subject, including both legal and illegal substances, has rarely been viewed objectively or presented openly. Lacking facts, the public for the most part has had little choice except to choose sides emotionally, damning all drugs as the panacea of hell or praising them as manna from heaven. *Recreational Drugs* does neither. It is written so people can clearly understand what most commonly used and abused drugs are about, providing readers with truth in place of misinformation and fable.

Although drug research is still in its infancy, and much remains to be learned in the months and years ahead, I have reviewed *Recreational Drugs* for medical accuracy and find it a thorough reflection of current knowledge in this vital area. I believe it provides a wealth of valuable information for interested lay people and professionals alike.

Harold L. Deutsch, M.D.
Miami, Florida

INTRODUCTION

The evolution of humanity was marked by man's realization that his mind separated him from all other forms of life. Equally enlightening was the revelation that the mind could be manipulated by ingesting certain substances, creating new levels of reality. These inner glimpses, sometimes considered spiritual, formed the basis of many religious and philosophical beliefs.

As civilization progressed, mind-altering substances were often condemned as evil. Pleasure quotas were devised, mandating who should have how much pleasure, and in what manner. Pleasure providers were approved or disapproved in a scatter-shot, arbitrary, uninformed way.

Alcohol and nicotine, responsible for thousands of deaths each year, are legally and socially accepted. Relatively harmless substances, such as marijuana, can still send the otherwise law-abiding pleasure seeker to jail.

People have always used drugs. Like it or not, legal or not, history has consistently shown man's occasional need to bend his mind in an effort to bring it to a better place. Whether nirvana is reached by prayer, meditation, or chemical reaction, he seems determined to get there.

Many non-drug-using Americans tend to think of drugs as a matter of past history—a temporary phenomenon of the 1960s, the days of Timothy Leary and Haight-Ashbury. Nothing could be further from the truth. Consider the statistics:

According to government surveys, half the bicentennial graduating high school class has smoked marijuana, and 32 percent consider themselves to be regular users.

Department of Defense figures indicate half the enlisted men in our armed forces regularly use drugs.

Almost 750,000 Americans are habituated amphetamine users.

Eight million Americans have experimented with cocaine.

The bottom line is simple and obvious: More people are using drugs recreationally than ever before. Ask any high school student, anywhere in the country, what is floating around his school and he'll start to bombard you with a list of natural and synthetic exotics including "windowpane," "reds," "blotter," "purple microdot," "714s," and a host of other drugs.

This book does not attempt to take a position on drug use. Neither pro nor con, we do realize one thing: Drug experimentation and use is booming. The likelihood that the trend will lessen in the months and years ahead is virtually nil.

If we can accept this fact, it should be apparent that the best way to deal with our national recreational-drug problem is not by creating and enforcing stricter laws. That approach, obviously, has not worked. Rather, it is time to take an honest, objective look at what these drugs are all about: which ones are harmful, and which ones are relatively harmless; which ones can lead to serious problems or addiction, and which do not. Warnings of any type will not lessen drug use or abuse, but knowledge and awareness can help put the subject of drugs into some sort of rational perspective. The uninformed drug user plays a dangerous game of mind-and-body Russian Roulette. The uninformed parent, educator, spiritual adviser, and community-at-large chance further alienation of an increasingly larger segment of the younger population by refusing to look at drugs truthfully and instead responding to often fallacious drug-scare stories.

Recreational Drugs is meant to provide nontechnical, understandable information needed by users, abusers, experimenters, and non-users alike. It is based on the premise that one who knows the truth about drugs will be better able to deal with them. Drugs can kill, but often they do so merely through lack of information. We have tried to provide this information in the form of a complete, accurate, up-to-date, and honest picture of the drugs making the recreational rounds. Some of it may be surprising and contrary to long-held beliefs.

This book is based on research, not experience. In our search for factual information, many of our own concepts and opinions were changed. Some drugs we had considered acceptable were discovered to be dangerous; the horrors of certain other drugs were found to be gross exaggerations. We have attempted to be as thorough in our research as we could, cross-checking sources and information whenever possible.

Drugs are part of man's attempt to explore his inner space. We hope this book will help him chart his way.

Miami, Florida
July 1977

RECREATIONAL DRUGS

ALCOHOL

Alcohol is the most widely used and abused drug in our society. One hundred million Americans, 70 percent of the adult population, consume in excess of 300 million gallons every year—roughly 3 gallons per drinker. The price we pay is staggering.

Alcohol misuse is responsible for 250,000 deaths in the United States annually. Only cancer and heart disease kill more.

Half our prison population is incarcerated because of alcohol-related crimes, and 50 percent of arrests in America are alcohol-connected.

One out of five of those in mental institutions is there because of alcohol misuse. Alcohol is also directly or indirectly responsible for one-third of all suicides and is a major factor in the nation's growing child-abuse problem. Half the auto deaths on our roads can be credited to alcohol, along with a majority of sex offenses.

Alcohol drains the economy of more than $25 billion each year, including $10 billion in lost work time, $8 billion for welfare and for the treatment of alcoholism, $6 billion for automobile accidents and property damage.

Yet, in spite of these frightening statistics, alcohol remains something of a social enigma. On the one hand, it is the biggest killer drug in America, taking more lives and causing more damage than all other drugs, legal and illegal, combined. On the other hand, when used responsibly in moderation, it can be a relatively pleasant, safe intoxicant for the majority.

The "problem" lies not with alcohol, but rather with its misuse—misuse due to ignorance and a false sense of security stemming from the simple fact that it is legal to anyone deemed to be of age. Because it is so available, we tend to forget that alcohol is a drug, and a potentially dangerous one at that. As with any other drug, information is essential if we are to avoid problems.

Alcohol is the oldest drug known to man. Recorded history indicates evidence of its use in Egypt almost six thousand years ago. Indeed, alcoholic beverages were probably consumed by prehistoric man, simply because the juice of any fruit left open to the air inevitably undergoes fermentation.

Throughout the ages alcohol has played a wide variety of roles: social, medical, and religious. Socially, it has always served as an intoxicant to be shared by friends—one seemingly capable of producing a spirit of conviviality and euphoria by clouding over life's stresses. Medically, alcohol has been prescribed in the treatment of many ailments, in addition to having been used widely as an early anesthetic. Most medical "benefits" have proved to be largely imaginary, however. Religious use dates to Bacchus. Wine is still an integral part of Holy Communion, not to mention weddings, bar mitzvahs, and other religious festivals of the Western World.

Use of alcohol in America dates back to pilgrim times, when drinking in moderation was generally accepted. During the 1800s, however, western migration and the industrial revolution brought many to stress-filled areas, greatly accelerating alcohol consumption. As a result, citizens began to regard drinking and drunkenness as a social problem. The drunk became an object of shame and scorn and drinking was looked upon as a serious vice. This negative attitude peaked with Prohibition in 1920, a total ban that remained in effect until 1933.

Prohibition was a failure. Despite the law, people continued to drink. Speakeasies—illegal drinking parlors—soon abounded, and where alcohol of quality was not available, people turned to substitutes such as ether and marijuana.

Since the repeal of Prohibition, public attitudes about alcohol have changed significantly. Alcohol is now an accepted part of our way of life; it is no longer looked down upon, although most of us are aware of the problems caused by the drug. While what we do "accept" is drinking in moderation, drinking to excess is also largely ignored today. We sometimes do it to celebrate (as on New Year's Eve) and we often find the comic "drunk" a million laughs. But alcohol is no laughing matter.

Contrary to popular belief, alcohol is not a stimulant. The drug is actually a downer—a sedative-depressant of the central nervous system similar to a fast-acting barbiturate. Ethyl alcohol (or ethanol) should not be confused with methyl alcohol (or wood alcohol), which is potentially deadly when ingested in even moderate amounts. When ethyl alcohol is unavailable, desperate alcoholics may turn to methyl alcohol, with such serious effects as blindness and brain damage, if they survive.

In pure form, alcohol is a colorless liquid with a burning taste and slight odor. Usually consumed in beverage form in varying strengths, it is one of the most powerful drugs legally available. Alcohol content varies in different beverages: Beer has about 4 percent, wine about 12 percent, and whiskey up to 50 percent. Don't let these figures fool you: A bottle of beer, a glass of wine, and a shot of whiskey all have about the same alcohol content and inebriation potential.

Alcohol is a fast-acting drug. Effects usually appear within minutes, varying widely from person to person, depending upon one's physical and psychological makeup, the setting, and tolerance levels. Some experience the drug as a stimulant, others as a tranquilizer-sedative. High enough quantities can produce hallucinogenic effects. Generally, the more a given person drinks, the less control he will have—physically, socially, psychologically, and occupationally.

Three ounces of 90-proof whiskey can reduce the user's anxiety, his sense of unknown fear. He relaxes, his self-confidence grows; he becomes talkative, believing his conversation to be brilliant and scintillating. This sense of well-being may be accompanied by slightly reduced reflexes, but with this quantity driving skills are not yet significantly impaired.

After 6 ounces, the imbiber's mood may decline; self-confidence generally starts to crumble and collapse. He usually becomes unsteady, fumbling for his keys, finding it difficult to handle routine tasks. Memory control dwindles, as does concentration. Self-restraint is weakened, sometimes causing the drinker to become hostile. Speech is slurred, movements become awkward, and inhibitions disappear along with emotional control. Driving becomes hazardous, with the chance of accidental death or injury increasing sixfold.

Nine ounces can produce gross intoxication. Judgment becomes distorted; rage may alternate with tears. If the user can stand, his gait will be markedly impaired. Thinking and memory become clouded, emotions can run amok. The drinker is easily involved in quarrels and no longer cares about normal responsibilities such as being on time.

Beyond the 9-ounce level, the chance of coma and death from respiratory depression becomes a distinct reality for some, especially after 18 to 30 ounces have been consumed.

For the vast majority of users, moderate drinking is not upsetting and does not prove to be habit-forming. Moreover, alcohol's effects are not cumulative, unless the drug is consumed excessively.

Most common "cures" for overimbibing are of little or no benefit. Coffee, cold showers, and home remedies will not significantly affect the rate at which alcohol is oxidized. Emptying the stomach may help, but time is the chief factor in removal of alcohol from the body.

If alcohol is consumed too rapidly, particularly if the user has not eaten, the stomach may reject it by vomiting. The drug is quickly absorbed into the bloodstream through the stomach wall and promptly distributed to every organ. Effects begin once the drug reaches the brain.

One popular misconception about alcohol is that it can warm you if you are chilled. Actually, it has precisely the opposite effect, causing the user to feel even colder by increasing perspiration and loss of body heat.

Alcohol is a dangerous drug when misused, having a high potential for physical and psychological dependence. It increases violent or homicidal behavior and is the major cause of motor-vehicle accidents because it impairs coordination, reflexes, and judgment. It is capable of producing major irreversible body damage; it can rupture veins, cause vitamin deficiencies and deteriorate the brain, liver, kidneys, and stomach. As few as four drinks a day can cause organ damage. Overuse of alcohol can seriously interfere with the liver's ability to process fat, and is definitely responsible for cirrhosis of the liver, a very serious and potentially deadly disease common to alcoholics. It can also be a killer in combination with other drugs. Just one bout of alcohol intoxication may give rise to mild withdrawal symptoms, along with the effects of hangover.

Alcohol used beyond moderation produces tolerance; more and more is needed to produce the same effects. This trend is reversed at alcoholism levels, when the liver has been so damaged that the drug is not broken down before going to the brain.

Alcohol has high addiction potential. We politely call alcohol dependence "alcoholism" rather than "addiction," perhaps because the drug is legal and so widely used. Becoming an alcoholic takes time, usually three to fifteen years of prolonged use. There are approximately ten million alcoholics in the United States. Eighty percent do not believe they are addicted.

Alcoholism is still a cloudy subject area. Experts have not agreed on the reasons why some people become alcoholics while others do not. Some see it as an illness; others think it has hereditary roots (54 percent of all alcoholics and 36 percent of all narcotics addicts had alcoholic parents). There is no standard definition of alcoholism. Although 2 to 3 ounces per day is generally considered "safe," it does not depend upon the number of drinks consumed, but rather on one's physical and psychological makeup. Experts contend that some people are more prone to alcoholism than others. Those who cannot react well to serious life stress situations, such as the illness or death of a loved one, may be prime candidates. The angry, destructive personality with an excessive need for power may be a serious contender before he touches his first drink. Other experts suggest that alcoholics' bodies cannot break down sugar the way most people's do, and they may unknowingly crave alcohol as an energy source. This may explain why alcoholics often drink alone, rather than with groups, as social drinkers do.

Although there is much speculation and argument regarding the causes of alcoholism, no debate exists about the serious consequences of this condition. Heavy users are subject to a wide variety of problems. Proper diet is often neglected, resulting in serious vitamin and mineral deficiencies. Alcohol, more than any other factor, causes impotence, family problems, and child abuse. Insanity can result from excessive use over a long period of time because of the severe beating it administers to the nerves and organs. The chronic alcoholic often experiences delirium tremens (the DTs), a frightening, screaming state that can accompany one to the alcoholic ward. The heavy drinker can look forward to a greatly reduced lifespan.

If the alcoholic goes just a few hours without a drink, he can expect withdrawal symptoms, including tremors, jitters, anxiety, nausea, sweating, vomiting, cramps, frightening hallucinations, convulsions, exhaustion, coma, circulatory and heart failure, and even death. Withdrawal from alcohol is serious business, similar to that from barbiturates and other depressant substances. It is more dangerous than withdrawal from heroin, since heroin withdrawal is never fatal, while alcohol withdrawal can be. Delirium is difficult to control and reverse. Attempts to detoxify and withdraw an alcoholic should be made only by those with professional medical training, and withdrawal can take several weeks to achieve.

True "cure" of alcoholism is rare, with only a handful of ex-addicts remaining abstinent. Research continues for a medical method to reduce craving, but so far the results have been less than satisfactory.

One approach to treatment was discovered in the late 1940s by two Danish scientists who had been searching for a cure for worms. The drug they developed was tetraethylthiuram disulfide, or disulfiram, now marketed under a variety of trade names including Antabuse, Refusal, and Aversan. Antabuse alone is harmless, but when alcohol is taken by an Antabuse user the combination produces a harrowing set of effects, including nausea, flushing, dizziness, vomiting, weakness, disorientation, and chest pain—enough to stop even hardened drinkers from further imbibing. This drug, which must be taken daily, is a serious one and should only be prescribed by a physician.

LSD has been another experimental treatment. While some initial success had been reported in alcoholism-cure experiments with LSD, research in this area was discontinued when the drug was outlawed in the late 1960s.

Megavitamin therapy has also been tried, because large amounts of injected B and C vitamins can help repair damaged nerve cells.

Some amethystic agents, such as L-Dopa (often used by those with Parkinson's Disease), have been the subjects of experiments in recent years. Amethystic agents do not reduce the amount of alcohol in the user's system; rather, they stimulate the manufacture of chemicals in the brain that reverse the effects of alcohol and help to sober up the overindulger.

Perhaps the most famous, accepted, and successful approach to alcoholism is that of Alcoholics Anonymous. AA does not believe there is a cure for alcoholism, but seeks to control the condition through abstinence. What the organization provides for its members is a powerful form of group therapy, with emotional security and support for the alcohol-troubled. Constant vigilance is maintained over members to prevent any return to drinking. For some, the AA approach works; for others, it does not. Perhaps the greatest weakness in AA's philosophy is its refusal to believe in psychotherapy for alcoholics. While abstinence may be the most immediate need for many, psychotherapy has the best potential for getting to the root of the problem—the reason why drinking to excess began in the first place.

As is the case with all recreational drugs, alcohol should not be consumed by expectant mothers. Since alcohol is at one point absorbed through the placenta, fetal damage can occur. Alcohol-related birth defects have been known to physicians for more than a century. Studies show that alcoholic mothers can pass the problem on to their babies, who often suffer withdrawal symptoms soon after birth. Alcoholic mothers have eight times the number of stillbirths as normal mothers. Birth defects resulting from alcohol outweigh those caused by all illegal drugs combined.

Mixing alcohol with other drugs can be a deadly practice. Many drugs relate to alcohol in a synergistic fashion, which means that small, ordinarily "safe" quantities of each, when taken together, can combine to cause death from central-nervous-system depression. Specific drugs that should *never* be mixed with alcohol include barbiturates, PCP, MAO inhibitors (e.g., Ritalin, Elavil, etc.—ask your physician if you are taking any of the drugs in this category), methaqualone (e.g., Quaalude), tranquilizers, opiates, and synthetic narcotics.

Other recreational drugs should not be mixed with alcohol, either, since at least half of all street drugs tested are not what they are purported to be.

Used properly in moderation, alcohol tends to do most people very little harm. Misused, its potential for damage is mind-boggling. Good or bad, it is here to stay.

Although there has been a national slowdown in hard-liquor sales, due in part to the increase in marijuana smoking, alcohol use is still widespread. Estimates indicate 85 percent of teenagers have their first drink before reaching legal age. Alcohol is used at elementary-school levels as well as in upper grades. For many youngsters, the first drink is associated with a rite of passage into adulthood. Children are subject to strong peer pressure when it comes to alcohol and, as with tobacco, often feel its use makes them look grownup. Because they can afford and obtain it more easily, some children use alcohol in place of less harmful drugs such as marijuana. Unfortunately, parents often feel unconcerned and even relieved when they discover their children using alcohol instead of other drugs.

With all of alcohol's negatives, one thing is certain: It cannot be banned or controlled to any great degree. The only hope for control lies within ourselves and our attitudes. Early childhood education would seem to offer the most logical answer. If children are instructed about responsible use of alcohol before they develop uncontrollable habits of misuse, the problems it produces may be minimized in the future.

Alcohol: harmless intoxicant, or deadly killer? The choice is yours.

AMANITA MUSCARIA

COMMON NAMES: *death's head, fly agaric, the woodpecker of Mars*

"One side will make you grow taller, and the other side will make you grow shorter."

One side of what? The other side of what? thought Alice to herself.

"Of the mushroom," said the Caterpillar, just as if she had asked it aloud; and in another moment it was out of sight.

Lewis Carroll
Alice's Adventures in Wonderland

Out of sight, indeed. As little Alice (soon to be big Alice, thanks to the Caterpillar's culinary suggestion) discovered, the lowly mushroom can make you high. Lewis Carroll, a known dabbler in psychedelia, evidently had more than lunch in mind when he portrayed Alice eating her way through a mind-bending buffet.

It is now believed that what Carroll had in mind was the powerful *Amanita muscaria* mushroom.

Although the *Amanita muscaria* has been used as a hallucinogen for more than six thousand years, it is today rapidly dropping in popularity because of significant dangers. In fact, some mushrooms of the genus *Amanita* are so highly toxic that they account for virtually 90 percent of all cases of lethal mushroom poisoning.

Amanita muscaria picked up the nickname "fly agaric" because the poison in the mushroom was, at one time, used by Europeans on flypaper. Just as it spelled disaster for the unsuspecting housefly, it can end a drug sampler's career permanently.

The six- to eight-hour journey has been described as a kind of marijuana high and alcohol drunk combined. But *Amanita muscaria* is more complex and potentially dangerous than that, full of good and bad news.

First, some bad news: Initial effects of the drug begin to take hold fifteen to twenty minutes after ingestion. These may include dizziness, confusion, dryness of the mouth, rapid breathing, nausea, vomiting, diarrhea, and muscular twitching, along with a general feeling of numbness in the limbs.

Now the good news: Once these feelings have passed, a period of peacefulness follows, including a twilight sleep lasting about two hours. From behind closed eyelids, mildly euphoric dreamlike sounds and visions are heard and seen. Upon waking, vivid, psilocybin-like hallucinations and size distortions may be experienced, along with physical agitation and a sense of overall joviality.

Back to the bad news: In some cases, users of *Amanita muscaria* have been known to become both paranoid and aggressive during their trips. Red-faced, they have exhibited high levels of violence and self-destructiveness, even to the point of self-mutilation. Because things may be seriously distorted, accidents of all sorts are not uncommon on this trip. Prolonged use can be debilitating mentally. For those who have consumed too much, raving madness may result. Overdose can cause delirium, convulsions, deep coma, and death as a result of heart failure. The only known antidote for overdose is atropine, but the effectiveness of this drug on *Amanita muscaria* "poisoning" is now being seriously questioned. Some profess that adding atropine may increase the chance of serious illness or death.

Most important, one must know which mushroom to pick. A small mistake in this regard can be deadly.

In Europe and Asia, the *Amanita muscaria* mushroom can be found growing wild on forest floors underneath and among fallen leaves. It has a large flat bright-crimson or red cap and is mottled with white warts. In North America it also grows on the floor of spruce, birch, or pine forests, but has a white, orange-red, or yellow cap, and white, red, or yellow warts.

Please don't let these brief, sketchy descriptions suffice. Many varieties of *Amanita* and similar mushrooms exist, and some of them are very deadly. Only an expert can harvest with any degree of certainty. For example, one close relative of *Amanita muscaria* is *Amanita phalloides*, also known as "destroying angel," "avenging angel," "white amanita," "death cup," and "deadly amanita." This, the most lethal member of the *Amanita* genus, is 60 percent to 100 percent fatal when eaten. Growing to 8 inches in height, with caps that are 2 to 5 inches wide, it ranges in color from yellow to green to white to green-brown. The stem is white. The most distinguishing characteristic of *Amanita phalloides* is the mushroom's bulbous base, or volva, called the "death's cup." Other members of the species, such as *Amanita pantherina* and *Amanita verna,* are equally dangerous. Beware, beware!

Once the collector is absolutely certain that the mushrooms gathered are really *Amanita muscaria,* they should be thoroughly dried, either outdoors or in a 200-degree oven, to reduce possible toxicity.

A starting dose should be limited to no more than one medium-size mushroom, until individual tolerance level is determined. Tolerance varies widely from person to person just as dosage of active ingredients varies widely from mushroom to mushroom. One to three mushrooms is considered an average dose, but under no circumstances should more than three ever be consumed.

Amanita muscaria actually contains a number of psychedelic substances, including muscazon, ibotenic acid, muscimol, and bufotenine.

Interestingly enough, the main psychoactive ingredients of *Amanita muscaria* pass unchanged into the user's urine. Siberian natives and other primitive users save urine excreted while tripping for reuse by themselves and their friends later. Urine can be recycled four or five times before losing potency. Though the thought of drinking urine may not be very appealing, even if it is psychoactive, it is not only the thriftiest way to keep the party going but the safest as well, since it is easy to tell if the previous user is still alive.

As *Amanita muscaria*'s dangers can far outweigh its pleasures, it is a drug to be avoided by those who value life and well-being.

AMPHETAMINES

COMMON NAMES: *A, beans, bennies, benz, benzies, black beauties, blackbirds, black mollies, bombida, bombido, bombita, bottle, browns, bumblebees, businessman's trip, cartwheels, chalk, chicken powder, coast-to-coasts, co-pilots, cranks, crystal, crossroads, dexies, double-cross, eye-openers, fives, footballs, forwards, greenies, hearts, jelly babies, jelly beans, jolly beans, jug, L. A. turnabouts, lidpoppers, lightning, meth, minibennies, nuggets, oranges, peaches, pep pills, pink and green amps, rhythms, roses, skyrockets, sparkle plenties, speckled birds, speed, splash, sweets, tens, thrusters, truck drivers, turnabouts, uppers, ups, wake-ups, water, West Coast turnarounds, whites*

Common as coffee in the wake-up world of truckers and students, amphetamines are as sinister as the shiny red apple that put Snow White away. As near as your doctor's prescription pad, they have acquired a veneer of respectability and acceptability because of their primary purpose as a supposed medical aid. Hospitals, mental wards, and prisons are populated with those folks who have been "helped" by this medical miracle—amphetamines.

The proliferation of brand-name amphetamines on the market can be grouped into three categories: amphetamines, dextroamphetamines, and methamphetamines. Chemically, these synthetic drugs differ in structure. All create similar, long-acting, cocaine-like effects on the central nervous system.

The amphetamines are represented by Benzedrine and Biphetamine. Dexedrine, Synatan, and Appetrol are dextroamphetamine sulfate, similar in structure to the hormone epinephrine, secreted by the adrenal gland during moments of fright. Dexamyl is a combination of dextroamphetamine and amobarbital. Biphetamine-T combines dextroamphetamine with its mirror image, levoamphetamine, and methaqualone, a tranquilizer. Eskatrol is yet another combination capsule, containing dextroamphetamine and Compazine, an antinausea drug.

Methamphetamine, the most powerful of the amphetamines, includes Methedrine, Desoxyn, and Ambar. Desbutol is a combination of methamphetamine and pentobarbital, a sedative barbiturate.

Obedrin combines methamphetamine with pentobarbital, and Amphaplex combines all three: methamphetamine, amphetamine, and dextroamphetamine. Ionamin, Preludin, Didrex, Plegine, Pemoline, Tenuate, Tepanil, Voranil, Pondimin, and Ritalin differ chemically from the amphetamines but are considered amphetamine-like both pharmacologically and in effect. Their sale is less restricted legally than amphetamines.

Not only have the drug manufacturers presented us with a variety of amphetamines from which to choose, they also offer them in decorator colors. From basic white tablets with a simple but elegant cross etched on top, to the green of Dexamyl, the orange of Dexedrine, and the rose of Benzedrine—all romantically heart-shaped. Biphetamine comes in basic black. Long-acting spansules are available in multiple hues including green and white, orange and white, and pink and white.

Generally taken by mouth in bitter but odorless tablet or capsule form, amphetamines may also be sniffed or injected. In pure form, amphetamines appear as yellowish crystals with a harsh chemical taste. Oral dosage in medical use is either short-acting 5-mg tablets (four hours) or long-acting spansule capsules (eight to twelve hours). Mini-whites, or white crosses, are usually bootleg amphetamine, either homemade or "imported" from Mexico. The dosage of whites can range from 2.5 to 10 mg, making them particularly dangerous because the quantity ingested is unknown.

Injection, the most damaging form of amphetamine abuse, is preferred by many "speed freaks" because of the instantaneous rush it produces when entering the bloodstream. Thus "speed" is an appropriate name for amphetamines used in this manner.

"Speeding" refers to a series of injections, each followed by an intense climax of feelings and bodily sensations.

America's preoccupation with obesity is largely responsible for the glut of amphetamines on the market. Doctors have doled out diet pills by the millions to chubby patients. Temporarily effective in suppressing the appetite center, amphetamines soon lose dietary power as the patient develops tolerance and needs higher and higher doses to accomplish the same purpose.

At one time, amphetamines were considered a blanket drug, used to treat not only obesity, but depression, epilepsy, Parkinsonism, narcolepsy, and hyperkinetic reactions in children. Today, only narcolepsy and hyperkineticity are regarded as valid areas for amphetamine usage. The remaining medical problems can be treated by other drugs or nondrug treatments.

Some disagree that there is justification for using Ritalin, originally developed as a mind elevator without the drawbacks of amphetamines, in hyperkinetic children. Causing an opposite reaction in children from that seen in adults, Ritalin may calm down the hyperactive child. Controversy exists as to whether use of such a drug is necessary, or if other methods would be equally effective.

Until recently, fifty 5-mg doses of amphetamines were produced each year for every man, woman, and child in the United States—20 percent of all prescriptions. Statistics show that six million people have used amphetamines, 750,000 of whom are regular users. Pressure is being placed on both drug manufacturers and doctors to cut down the deluge of these multicolored mind-rotters. Medical justification for capriciously prescribing amphetamines no longer exists.

Amphetamines stimulate the central nervous system by potentiating the effects of norepinephrine, a neurohormone which activates parts of the sympathetic nervous system. Adrenalin-like effects are produced at the brain's synaptic sites, causing the heart and bodily systems to race at high speed. Blood pressure rises, along with the pulse pressure and heart rate. Appetite is suppressed because of the drug's action on the control centers of the hypothalamus and the depression of gastro intestinal activity. The effects may last from four to fourteen hours, depending on dosage. Amphetamines may be detected in blood and urine by lab tests up to seventy-two hours after ingestion.

Amphetamines are quickly assimilated into the bloodstream. The roller-coaster ride begins with a tremendous rush accompanied by feelings of elation and confidence. Unlimited power seems to be at the speeder's fingertips. The pupils dilate, the heart pumps frantically, breathing is rapid, and the mucous membranes get dry. Speech becomes rat-a-tat-tat gibberish. The user may focus in on one thing to the exclusion of everything else. But the speeder doesn't care because he feels he is at the height of his intellectual powers. This initial flash of brilliance is succeeded by a euphoria, an elevated mood, as the body continues to release stored energy from its reserves. Physically as well as mentally charged up, he feels capable of superman feats. Life is a cartoon and the speeder is the road runner.

The high level of vitality begins to decline as the body's energy stores are depleted. Restlessness, nervousness, and agitation replace nirvana. The speeder's irritability progresses to paranoia, fatigue, and depression as the ride comes to an end. The roller coaster has hit bottom. Headache, palpitations, dizziness, agitation, apprehension, and confusion have replaced ecstasy.

Over? So soon? Well, that's easy to correct, reasons the speeder. All I have to do is pop another upper. So the roller coaster chugs into action once again, setting into motion the vicious cycle known as the amphetamine jag. Since tolerance develops rapidly with use of amphetamines, the user needs to increase the dosage each time just to keep up. Feeling down? Pop an up. And so it goes, until the speeder is into a "run," staying up for four or five days at a time, unable to eat or sleep until he "crashes," falling into a deep sleep that can last for eighteen hours.

The sleep of the speeder is hardly refreshing, however, since the dream cycle is interrupted by the drug. True dreams are not experienced. When he awakens, he's ready for another run, and it's *déjà vu* time, up and down on the carnival ride. If the amphetamine is injected, the effects become more intense, and the jag is shortened to days instead of weeks. Methedrine is a favorite for this form of self-abuse, called "speeding."

Other patterns of abuse involve barbiturates, either alternating with amphetamines or combined. If the user can't sleep after he pops an upper, he may take a barbiturate to knock him out. To bring back his high, he takes another upper, thereby establishing an upper-downer cycle. "Goofballs," combined amphetamine-barbiturates such as Dexamyl, are for those who get off on the stimulant-depressant combination. The heavy goofball user can unknowingly become addicted to barbiturates.

Escalation of dosage, whether through repeated low doses over a period of time, high doses in sequence, or a single large dose, may create a toxic reaction known as amphetamine psychosis, lasting from a few days to a few weeks. The short-term reactions to the drug are magnified, leading to an exaggeration of effects.

Loss of appetite may become anorexia, a state in which it becomes difficult for the user to eat at all. Extreme weight loss occurs, and even the act of swallowing becomes difficult. Speed freaks aware of this phenomenon may force themselves to eat and take vitamins, but malnutrition can still occur.

Insomnia, lasting a day or two for moderate users, extends into days or even weeks during a "run," before the heavy user crashes. Hallucinations, misperceptions, and inability to function accompany insomnia, and may persist even with abstinence. Consciously aware that he is slipping into a world of delusion, the speeder can do little more than watch as anxiety and suspicion fill the vacuum that was once occupied by reality.

Sooner or later, the high-dose user will experience paranoia, with its feelings of persecution. He skulks about, certain the little old lady with the wrinkled stockings is following him. He is positive the kids on the corner are talking about him, his best friends are plotting behind his back, and his girlfriend is poisoning his toothpaste. "Crank bugs," the feeling of insects under the skin (formication), harass him, and he has begun compulsively picking at his now-delicate skin, forming ulcerations. Hypomania, a form of repetitive action, overcomes the speed freak, producing behavior often considered bizarre, such as foot-tapping, coin-flipping, or construction of elaborate, useless mechanical devices. Jaw grinding, tremors, abscesses, and tooth loss are common symptoms of heavy amphetamine use. Several years of aging can occur in just a few months. Sexual performance is impaired and the user can't find words to describe how he feels. His vocabulary drops to a few hundred words, including such pithy quotes as "far out" and "gotanyspeed?"

"Speed kills" is the warning, scary but inaccurate. In fact, amphetamines themselves rarely kill, even in enormous doses. Some of the long-term side effects may kill, but death, when it occurs, usually comes from violence, common to the speed freak. Paranoia, mood shifts, hyperactivity, and the resulting intensification of emotions, combined with the inevitable change of lifestyle—the hustling, the dealing, the cheating necessary for survival in the chaotic community of speed freaks—leads to a high level of violence, including rape, homicide, and assaultive behavior. When the speeder combines the mainlining of barbiturates along with amphetamines, results can be disastrous. Irrational and dangerous, this variety of speed freak has not only the downer-induced compulsion for violence, but the upper-induced energy to do it.

The long-term effects of amphetamine abuse may kill. Malnutrition can lead to an increased susceptibility to disease and bacterial infection. Although pill-poppers are susceptible to most of the same detrimental reactions as needle freaks, injection may lead to even further complications. Needle-related diseases such as viral hepatitis, leading to liver damage, occur, and the shooting of impure amphetamines containing materials not dissolvable in water may lead to blockage or weakening of small blood vessels, causing kidney and lung damage. A correlation exists between heavy users and strokes, aneurisms, hematomas, destruction of the brain by picnosis of the brain cells, and other cardiovascular disruptions.

Illegally obtained amphetamines are genuine about 70 percent of the time. Common antihistamines, inducing some of the effects of speed, are often passed off as the real thing. The insecticide Rotenone, sometimes offered, may cause nausea, vomiting, muscle tremors, increased respiration, and numbness.

Street speed, the home-cooked stuff, may include ingredients such as lactose, Epsom salts, quinine, baking powder, ether, insecticides, MSG, photo developer, and strychnine. Heavy freaks may even prefer these additives because they have developed a tolerance to the weaker solutions and the impurities may produce a more intense flash. Poisonous adulterants can cause death, since the intravenous use of these will bypass natural bodily rejection, such as vomiting.

Amphetamine psychosis is considered by some to be a manifestation of pre-existing paranoid tendencies, a latent amphetamine personality which blossoms with the taking of the drug. Emotionally troubled before he enters the speed scene, dependent on other drugs or alcohol, the user's sense of insecurity and ineffectiveness vanishes with the euphoria of speed. Others feel that anyone given a large enough amount of amphetamines will eventually become psychotic.

Overdosing, or "over-amping," is rare. The lethal dosage is unknown. Habitual users may ingest from 200 to 1,000 mg a day without the overdose symptoms of chest pains, muscle or joint pain, unconsciousness, aphasia, paralysis, convulsions, coma, or cerebral hemorrhage. More commonly, the victim will remain conscious, but his mind races full speed beyond his control, while he remains immobile, unable to move. Speed doesn't create energy; it mobilizes adrenalin. While the speeder may be thinking, "Feet, don't fail me now," they might.

Overdose may be treated with niacin (vitamin B_3), which acts as a mopping-up agent, ridding the bloodstream of impurities and restoring energy levels. Doses of 2,000 or 3,000 mg with equal amounts of vitamin C after meals throughout the day will help the speeder avoid a hard crash, although he may experience a harmless heat flash lasting fifteen to thirty minutes. Tranquilizers such as Thorazine, Mellaril, Librium, and Valium are effective. Barbiturates are not advised because of their toxicity and the possibility of developing a speed/downer habit.

Abstinence is the most effective method of withdrawal, but is often the most difficult because of the extreme fatigue, lethargy, anxiety, and depression which inevitably ensue. The combined problems of the hooked amphetamine user and the paranoid personality lead to a low cure rate. Although the body needs a full day to recover from each day of speed abuse, withdrawal does not have to be gradual. In addition to tranquilizers, treatment includes a nutritious diet stressing milk and yogurt to replace the calcium lost, plus liquids, vitamins, and psychotherapy. Complete recovery is slow, but possible. Confusion, memory loss, and delusions may remain up to a year after use is discontinued.

Abstinence, the key to cure, is often almost impossible because of the strong psychological dependence acquired. Contrary to the official medical establishment's original opinion, amphetamines *are* addicting —but psychologically, not physically. Amphetamine addicts outnumber heroin addicts by ten to one. The damage they inflict on both themselves and others is far out of proportion to that resulting from other drugs.

The Controlled Substances Act of 1970 resulted in government placement of amphetamines in Schedule II of the act. It places severe restrictions on the manufacture, distribution, and use of both amphetamines and amphetamine-barbiturate preparations, prohibits refilling of prescriptions, and empowers the Justice Department to impose production quotas. Only firms licensed by the government are permitted to deal in amphetamines, and violations are punishable by a maximum term of ten years' imprisonment. Paradoxically, this has inspired drug firms to devise an elaborate array of methods for circumventing the law.

It is alleged that one world leader in the manufacture of amphetamines has produced large amounts of amphetamines at its U.S. plant for shipment to its Mexican subsidiary. There the amphetamine is packaged and reshipped back across the border, where it is sold illicitly. Under investigation by the Justice Department, this corporation has developed supposedly "new" drugs, under new names, identical in effect to the illegal drugs.

Bowing to the omnipotent dollar, both the American Medical Association and the Pharmaceutical Manufacturer's Association have opposed federal legislation controlling amphetamines, arguing that amphetamines do not produce physical dependence and should not be stigmatized by labeling them "Dangerous drugs: Habit-forming and psychotoxic." When, in 1971, AMA's Council of Drugs attacked speed as a treatment for obesity, the council was summarily dissolved under pressure from the drug industry. The AMA receives over $10 million in advertising revenue from the drug industry each year, leading us to the obvious question: Who watches the watchdogs?

Senate hearings may ultimately lead to the banning of all further manufacture and sale of amphetamines. Whether this dries up the speed market or not remains to be seen. Past efforts at inhibiting legal distribution have resulted in a backlash of illicit "speed labs."

The anti-speed campaign by the FDA in 1962, in tandem with exaggerated anti-grass and anti-LSD propaganda, had the reverse effect of turning kids *on* to speed. Knowing from experience that the properties of grass and LSD had been misrepresented, they assumed that the same was true of speed. The publicity paid off for the amphetamine manufacturers. Turning away from the milder intoxicants, users turned to the more legal danger, speed, available by prescription from their friendly doctors.

The first amphetamine was synthesized in 1887 by German pharmacologist L. Edeleano, who regarded it simply as phenylisopropylamine. Not until 1927, when Gordon Alles discovered that this substance alleviated fatigue, enlarged the nasal and bronchial passages, and stimulated the central nervous system, was it considered to have any medical use. Smith, Kline and French first marketed it in inhaler form as Benzedrine in 1932. By 1937 it was marketed, in pill form, as the new AMA-approved wonder drug. Sales climbed to over fifty million units in the first three years after Benzedrine was introduced in tablets.

From the countries that brought you World War II came speed freaks, regardless of race, creed, or national origin. Amphetamine usage boomed, legally and illegally, as both Allied and Axis powers systematically fed their troops speed to combat fatigue, heighten endurance, and elevate mood. Methedrine was used by the German Panzer troops and Benzedrine by American Army Air Corps personnel stationed in Britain, although the United States did not officially authorize the issuing of amphetamines until Korea.

Postwar Japan was the site of the first epidemic of amphetamine psychosis, thanks to its feverish production of amphetamines for the German Luftwaffe. Japanese munitions-factory workers popped uppers at an alarming rate as the war neared its end. Drug companies advertised amphetamines for the "elimination of drowsiness and repletion of the spirit," enabling them to clean out their stockpiles, thereby creating 500,000 new Japanese addicts.

Until the introduction of Methedrine in 1945, Dexedrine and Benzedrine were the main amphetamines being sold. By this time there were seven different nonprescription benzedrine inhalers on the market, each containing the equivalent of 500 mg of Dexedrine. Users smashed the containers, soaked the cotton fillers in water, alcohol, or coffee, and drank the solution, perhaps chewing the bits of cotton—good to the last drop. Injection of the solution was first reported in 1959, the same year many drug firms dropped the manufacture of the inhalers. The last inhaler was not removed from the market until 1971.

The armed forces introduced another "first" to the drug world—the intravenous use of amphetamines. Servicemen stationed in Korea and Japan in the early 1950s invented the "speedball," an injectable mixture of amphetamines ("splash") and heroin.

When amphetamines were made available through the Swedish health plan in 1965, another country fell victim to amphetamine madness. Thousands of abusers took advantage of the free ride on speed, and when amphetamines were finally restricted, turned to the black market or used substitutes such as cocaine and Preludin.

The U.S. black market was also readily available to supply truck drivers, the original upper-poppers, and students and athletes with speed. By the late 1960s many San Francisco flower children had metamorphosed into a pack of speed freaks.

What hath amphetamines wrought? Not much beneficial to mankind aside from the few instances where they help alleviate symptoms of diseases such as narcolepsy. Economically, they have been a boon to the drug industry. Sociologically, they have destroyed the lives of thousands of people, from housewives to kids to businessmen. Morally, they have taught us all that the alchemy combining business and government can transform even an intolerable wrong into an acceptable right, as long as it makes money.

AMYL NITRATE

COMMON NAMES: *amys, pearls, poppers, snappers*

If sex is your thing, you may have already heard about amyl nitrate, or "poppers" as they are called in illicit circles.

This substance has been used legally for more than a century for the treatment of angina pectoris (heart spasm). When taken it quickly dilates blood vessels leading to the heart. The drug has also been used, less frequently, for the relief of certain types of asthma attacks.

A prescription drug, amyl nitrate is a clear yellow volatile liquid, with a fruity odor not unlike that of rotten apples. It is marketed in glass ampules, containing .2 milliliter, which have to be broken open immediately before use. Once the ampule is broken, the drug must be inhaled immediately. For potential reuse the ampule is often placed in an airtight container to capture its potent fumes. Its effect, which lasts only two to three minutes, begins in about thirty seconds.

The first feelings the user experiences are those of relaxation and a breakdown of normal inhibitions. The drug is usually inhaled during sex, particularly at the point immediately preceding orgasm. Users claim that orgasm can be lengthened and strengthened with the help of a popper. At the very least, a great euphoric feeling of warmth and thrilling sensuousness generally occurs. Visual and perceptual distortions, as well as alterations in consciousness, may result.

Still another effect resulting from the use of amyl nitrate is the relaxation of the involuntary muscles, including the sphincter, which has made it popular among gays.

While there are no really dangerous aftereffects from amyl nitrate, some users do experience headache, flushing, nausea, and/or vomiting. Death from nitrate poisoning is virtually nonexistent. Glaucoma sufferers should not use amyl nitrate. People with low blood pressure should avoid the drug because one of its effects is the further lowering of blood pressure.

A number of enterprising manufacturers are currently marketing butyl nitrate, similar to amyl nitrate in effect but different in chemical rings, under a variety of brand names such as Aroma, Locker Room,

Rush, and Bullet. They are sold in liquid form as room deodorizers to avoid problems with the Food and Drug Administration, but reports indicate most have vapors capable of producing the same disoriented, flushed, short-lived high as amyl nitrate.

ASPIRIN

Even if you don't consider yourself a "drug user," do yourself a favor and read this chapter about aspirin. There's a lot about these little white tablets that may surprise you.

Aspirin is the most widely used drug in the world today, and certainly in the United States. Just consider these statistics: Americans use more than 50 billion aspirin tablets and compound aspirin preparations annually. That's roughly 40 million pounds of aspirin, or some $600 million worth. In fact, if most people had to choose just one drug with which to stock their medicine cabinets it would, in all probability, be aspirin.

Aspirin is a relatively safe drug when it is used correctly. But, as is the case with many other drugs, it not only can make sick people feel healthy but can, when abused, make healthy people feel pretty sick. Some people just can't handle aspirin, particularly large doses, which can cause a variety of adverse reactions and can even be fatal. Yet no prescription is required for the drug. You can buy aspirin almost everywhere; at the supermarket, at gas stations, in drugstores, or at your favorite newsstand.

Aspirin's generic name is acetylsalicylic acid. As far back as 2,500 years ago, Greeks boiled the bark of the willow tree (a member of the Salicaceae family with a high salicin content, a natural relative of acetylsalicylic acid) to prepare medicines to deal with fever and aches. Aspirin was first synthesized by an Alsatian chemist named Charles Frederick von Gerhardt during the mid-1800s. It was not used by physicians until around the turn of the century, when a chemist working for the Bayer Company, Felix Hofmann, discovered it helped bring relief to his father, who was suffering from arthritis.

Today, Bayer is the best-known brand name in the aspirin world. In the United States, where aspirin has become as American an institution as hot dogs and apple pie, the biggest manufacturer of the drug is Glenbrook Laboratories, a division of Sterling Drug Company. Its brand name: Bayer. Bayer originally owned the generic name "aspirin" exclusively. Now any company can use that name in the United States. In most other countries of the world you'll find the name "aspirin" still the exclusive property of Bayer. Knowledge of one fact alone can easily repay the cost of this wonderful book many times over: all aspirin is basically the same. For example, you can buy 100

Bayer tablets for about $1.49 or you can buy 250 Norwich tablets for 98 cents. The choice is yours.

Our recommendation: Don't believe misleading advertising. Aspirin is aspirin, as long as it is made and marketed by any reputable source. Just make sure the bottle is fresh before buying. Check by removing the cap and sniffing. If the contents smell similar to acid or vinegar, the drug is deteriorating and losing strength. Periodically check aspirin bottles in your medicine cabinet the same way. Buy the least expensive brand and you'll be way ahead of the game over the years without any sacrifice in quality. Don't be like all those other consumers who assume that anything costing more must be better. It just ain't so!

While on the subject of economy, we might as well point out the fact that none of the aspirin-plus-extra-ingredients products has ever been proven to be any more effective than aspirin alone for those illnesses requiring simple aspirin treatment. You're just paying extra for extra ingredients that don't do anything extra in most cases. Learn to tune out those TV ads and their false promises. If you need a medicine in addition to aspirin, buy it separately. You'll be doing your pocketbook a big favor.

Most adults take aspirin in the form of a 5-grain (325-mg) white tablet, although the drug also comes in liquid, powder, and capsule form, particularly when combined with other ingredients. These pills contain mostly aspirin (content is government-regulated) mixed with some filler to hold the tablet together. While no one is quite certain how the drug works, we've been popping them down for the better part of this century. We do know that aspirin is absorbed in the stomach and small intestine after oral ingestion. First effects generally occur within thirty minutes to two hours. One recent theory is that aspirin halts the production of prostaglandins. Prostaglandins are hormonelike substances that are found in menstrual fluid, semen, and many human tissues. They relate to the functions of the stomach, blood vessels, heart, and bronchial tubes.

Aspirin generally has three types of effects:

Antipyretic (fever reducing): Reduces body temperature by increasing sweat production, which, in turn, has a cooling effect. This is accomplished, researchers believe, by affecting the hypothalamus, the body's thermostat. Aspirin will not, however, lower normal body temperature.

Anti-inflammatory: Aspirin is of help to people who suffer from rheumatic fever and mild arthritis. While it helps to minimize or eliminate minor pains caused by these illnesses, the exact reason it does so is still a scientific mystery.

Analgesic (pain relieving): Aspirin will work better for some types of pain than for others. It is most effective in dealing with somatic pain (headache, arthritis, sprains, toothache, etc.), and less effective when dealing with visceral pain (colic, gastric disturbance, cramps, etc.).

Some research has indicated that in not too many years aspirin may be used to help prevent such problems as heart attack, stroke, miscarriage, and hardening of the arteries.

But, contrary to popular belief, there are some things that aspirin will not do. For one thing, aspirin definitely will not work as a sedative or relaxant. Surprisingly, that is one of the primary reasons people use the drug. They think they'll get a better night's sleep or have a calmer day as a result of taking aspirin. So they'll pop a couple every few hours in their vain quest for mental tranquillity. Don't consider yourself foolish for having tried. Commercials, again, are really to blame. They've just promised us too much over the years and, as a result, we've downed a lot of extra aspirin we could have easily lived without.

We might as well mention the common cold, too. Again, despite popular belief, aspirin will not influence the course of existing colds to any real degree, nor will it help to prevent the symptoms of colds. The drug simply does not have any effect whatsoever on bacteria or viruses. So skip the extra aspirin if you're trying to prevent a cold.

We're not just cautioning you against excessive use of aspirin so you can save a few cents. While aspirin can be valuable, it can also do extensive physical damage if misused. Believe it or not, aspirin overdose accounts for more hospital admissions in the United States each year than any other drug—10 percent of all adverse drug reactions in U.S. hospitals are caused by aspirin. Aspirin also causes hundreds of deaths in this country annually. Many of these deaths occur among children simply because the drug is so available and easy for them to get at in the home. Treat aspirin like any other drug. Keep it out of the reach of children. It is by no means a harmless substance.

Be very careful about aspirin dosage. Follow package directions. If they say take two aspirins, don't think you'll get twice the relief by taking four. The drug doesn't work that way. And don't take it any more often than the package recommends. Unless your doctor has told you differently, don't take more than a few doses of aspirin in any given day, and don't take even the recommended dosage more than a couple of days in any week.

If you do take too much you may be in for a variety of unpleasant surprises. Overuse of aspirin, and even more particularly aspirin-plus-extra-ingredients products (usually those "extra" ingredients are caffeine and/or phenacetin), can cause such problems as gastritis, peptic ulcers, migraine headache, anemia, intestinal nephritis, and a shortening of your lifespan. Aspirin intoxication may be caused by the use of just fifteen to twenty tablets a day. Symptoms can include dizziness, headache, shock, ringing in the ears, disorientation, internal-tissue bleeding, hallucinations, incoherent speech, asthma attacks, gastric disturbances, convulsions, and coma. Prolonged use can cause serious problems such as irritation of the stomach lining, potassium depletion, and abdominal bleeding. If you really overdo it, you can take a lethal dose. For most adults, 20 to 30 grams (60 to 90 adult-strength tablets) will stop your headache permanently. Naturally, a fatal dose for children or the elderly will be significantly lower.

If you are with someone who has overdosed on aspirin, rush him to the nearest hospital. There is no dependable quickie home remedy. The patient's best chance for survival is at the hospital. Inform them that his condition is due to aspirin overdose.

Aspirin has a tendency to prolong bleeding time. If you suffer from abdominal bleeding, stay away from this drug. One study recently showed that 80 percent of people suffering from abdominal bleeding had taken aspirin within forty-eight hours of their attacks. Most people lose about a teaspoonful of blood in their stools after taking just two aspirins. Taking your aspirin with some food or a full glass of milk or water may help to minimize such loss. While this quantity of blood loss is not significant, iron-deficiency anemia may result in some cases where aspirin is taken too often. Persons suffering from acute illnesses that involve bleeding (stomach cancer, varicose veins of the esophagus, ulcers, etc.) face a greatly increased chance of excessive bleeding if aspirin is used. Keep away from aspirin for at least a week before any surgery (including childbirth), since aspirin does inhibit blood clotting. Don't use the drug if you suffer from hemophilia, for obvious reasons.

If you're pregnant, don't use aspirin during your first three months. Some studies have indicated a slight possibility of malformed babies resulting from aspirin use. This is not yet completely proved, but there is no point in taking chances.

If you do feel the need for aspirin, but any of these warnings worry you, try using acetaminophen, an aspirin substitute that contains no aspirin. It will be perfectly safe for you.

Aspirin is not an addictive drug. It carries with it no problems relating to tolerance or withdrawal, although some people do seem to develop a perceived psychological need for aspirin to deal with real or imagined pain. Perhaps that's just another result of all that TV brain-washing.

Recently, researchers have noted that some people, about one in every five hundred, suffer from a condition called aspirin intolerance. These folks sometimes experience a variety of undesirable effects within fifteen minutes to three hours after using aspirin. These effects may include asthma, gastrointestinal bleeding, and skin rashes, and can continue even after use of the drug has been discontinued. Aspirin intolerance seldom occurs in children or teen-agers. In adults, it usually develops suddenly, even in people who have used aspirin for years with no ill effects. Not an allergy, it is a metabolic disorder that most commonly affects people with sinus infections, bronchial asthma, nasal polyps, and recurring stuffy noses. Aspirin intolerance can't be predicted or prevented. Sometimes people have it for years before they even notice it. Almost a quarter of the people who suffer from chronic hives experience outbreaks after taking aspirin (although researchers are not sure if it is the aspirin that causes hives or the contaminants in aspirin tablets, which vary from brand to brand). Our advice: If in doubt about aspirin intolerance, use Tylenol, Datril, or any other acetaminophen.

Aspirin and other aspirin-containing products can also interact negatively with a variety of substances. When taking aspirin, be careful about the following categories of drugs:

Alcohol: Do not mix alcohol and aspirin, or products containing aspirin, including products such as Alka-Seltzer. Forget what the commercials tell you. Alcohol will make your stomach very sensitive, and in such a state aspirin can cause a serious amount of bleeding from the stomach wall.

Anticoagulants: If you're on blood thinners of any sort, don't mix in aspirin or you might find yourself suffering from massive hemorrhaging. Generally, anticoagulant doses must be reduced if you are taking aspirin. Ask your doctor about the combination if you are taking this type of drug.

Anti-cancer medication: The toxic effect of Methotrexate can be increased if you are taking aspirin. Again, consult your doctor if you are on this drug.

Arthritis medicines: If you are taking any strong arthritis medication to reduce inflammation, don't combine it with aspirin or you may end up with ulcers or serious, uncomfortable, and dangerous stomach irritation.

Diabetes medication: If you are diabetic and are taking oral medication, be wary of aspirin, as it can lead to too drastic a decrease in blood sugar. To avoid such problems, check with your doctor.

Gout: Don't combine aspirin with any medication for gout unless your doctor specifically advises it. You may be blocking the beneficial effects of these drugs if you do.

The bottom line: Don't let us scare you away from aspirin. It's not our intent to do so at all. It is a fine drug for most people if used properly and intelligently for the right things. Just be aware of what it can't do for you and the potential harm it can cause when abused. Follow package directions carefully and watch for any adverse symptoms you may experience. If you don't feel aspirin is treating you right, discuss use of the drug with your physician.

BANANA SKINS

Mellow yellow is simply dried scrapings taken from the inside of fried banana skins.

Ever since it was first introduced in the late 1960s (when druggies would try anything), some people have claimed that, when smoked alone or mixed with tobacco, mellow yellow will bring on the same type of high as marijuana.

Analysis shows that mellow yellow has no psychoactive ingredient. While some experts contend that the smoking of banana will convert some of its chemistry into a DMT-like substance, the reality is that as many as four mellow yellow joints will produce little more than a slight buzz, and that's probably more a result of hyperventilation than the banana itself.

Any high experienced from this one will be virtually imaginary. Mellow yellow won't do much at all except waste good bananas.

BARBITURATES

As the pace of contemporary life accelerates, our ability to refresh ourselves with natural, uninterrupted sleep is often diminished. Anxiety and sleeplessness have always plagued mankind; they were alleviated in the past by various remedies such as opiates, bromides, chloral hydrate, paraldehyde, and alcohol, all with various drawbacks. The development of barbiturates seemed, at first, to be the panacea. Now, it appears, the cure is worse than the disease.

A greater health hazard than the opiates, barbiturates are as addicting as heroin and even more dangerous during withdrawal. Barbiturate-related deaths average over three thousand annually; almost half of these are suicides. Although they constitute a major drug-abuse problem in schools, barbiturates are still considered "soft" drugs because they may be obtained legally, by prescription.

Three hundred tons of barbiturates are produced annually in the United States, and may be found in one out of three medicine chests. Of 2,500 barbiturates synthesized, only about a dozen are commonly used. The five top barbiturate "sleepers" (sleeping pills) accounted for nineteen million prescriptions in one recent year, costing the public $16 million. The drug industry churns out an annual ten billion doses of "downers," including both barbiturates and nonbarbiturate sedative-hypnotics—or fifty for each man, woman, and child in the United States. One million people are habitual barbiturate abusers.

Barbiturates are central-nervous-system depressants containing barbituric acid, or malonylurea. Three categories of the drug exist: long-acting, short-to-intermediate-acting, and ultra-short-acting.

The long-acting drugs (eight to sixteen hours) are used as anticonvulsants in the treatment of epilepsy, and for controlling peptic ulcers and high blood pressure. Veronal (barbital), Luminal (pheno-barbital), Mebaral (mephobarbital), and Gemonil (methabarbital) are in this group.

The short-to-intermediate-acting drugs (four to six hours) are sleeping pills, the most commonly abused barbiturates. These include Alurate (aprobarbital), Amytal (amobarbital), Butisol Sodium (butabarbital), Dial (diallybarbituric acid), Nembutal (pentobarbi-tal), Seconal (secobarbital), and Tuinal (amobarbital and seco-barbital).

Ultra-short-acting barbiturates (immediate but brief), used either as intravenous anesthetics or as a sedative in conjunction with in-halants such as nitrous oxide, include Pentothal Sodium (thiopental), Brevital (sodium methohexital), and Surital (sodium thiamylal). Most barbiturates have generic names ending in "al."

Unlike amphetamines, barbiturates have many legitimate medical uses: as a hypnotic (sleep inducer), sedative, anti-convulsant, minor analgesic (pain reliever), stress reliever, and as a treatment for alco-holics. They do not relieve severe pain, however, and paradoxically may cause hyperalgesia, or an increase in reaction to pain. After a few weeks, barbiturates lose their hypnotic power for many and thus their effectiveness as sleeping pills. They also disturb REM sleep, the dream portion, which may have psychological ramifications. As a result, tranquilizers have replaced barbiturates in many areas.

Aside from legitimate medical use, the production of enormous quantities of barbiturates fills another need, by feeding the insatiable habits of "downer" abusers. The short-to-intermediate-acting versions are popular for their effect, speed, and duration. Favorites include blue-capsuled Amytal (amies, blues, bluebirds, blue devils, blue heav-ens), red-capsuled Seconal (reds, pinks, redbirds, red devils, seccies), red-and-blue Tuinals (rainbows, tooies, double trouble), and yellow-capsuled Nembutal (yellows, nembies, yellow jackets, yellow bullets). Longer-lasting phenobarbitals, such as Luminal, are also widely abused.

Mexican reds are homemade pink capsules sold on the street; their content and strength are variable, and therefore they are dangerous.

Cheap enough by prescription—a penny to 15 cents each—barbiturates claim a higher price on the street. The drug is usually sold as a white powder, either in colorful capsules, tablets, and supposi-tories, or dissolved in liquid for injection. Oral ingestion is usually preferred over injection, since results occur quickly enough with the short-acting capsules. Some "barb freaks" prefer the surging rush that comes with mainlining, however, and ignore the possibilities of severe infection and abscess that may result if the vein is missed and the drug is injected under the skin. Gangrene can occur if an artery is hit, and may necessitate amputation of the affected part.

Barbiturates affect the central nervous system by depressing or inhibiting nerve signals in the brain, altering chemical balance and decreasing functions of some organ systems. Heart rate, blood pressure, respiration, and neurological action are all depressed, and general relaxation of the skeletal muscles occurs. Effects of the drug increase according to dosage, as body functions decelerate: from anxiety relief to sedation to hypnosis to anesthesia to coma to death.

Once ingested, the drug enters the bloodstream and is distributed throughout the body, with the highest accumulation in fat deposits and organ tissues. Barbiturates are ultimately metabolized and eliminated through the kidneys and liver. Rate of effect depends on how quickly the drug moves through the body and is metabolized. Laboratory tests can indicate the presence of barbiturates in the body.

Dosage, type of barbiturate, metabolism, and method of administration, along with the circumstances under which it is taken, all affect the drug's result. Barbiturates affect different people in different ways, and even the same individual may experience a variety of effects. Sensitivity reactions may range from serenity to hostility.

Short-term effects of barbiturates resemble those of their CNS-depressant cousin, alcohol. Anxiety and tension melt into peaceful, calm relaxation. Cares vanish into a blurry intoxication, where nothing really matters. The user staggers through his altered universe, speech slurred, muscles like rubber. Reaction time slows to a zombie pace. If sleep overcomes him, he may wake up with a hangover.

Long-term, regular use of barbiturates may lead to chronic symptoms: continual drowsiness and sluggishness, shortened memory and attention span, loss of coordination and awareness, emotional instability, rashes, nausea, anxiety and nervousness, involuntary eye movements, staggering gait, slurred speech, and trembling hands. Paranoid delusions and increased hostility may lead to a barbiturate trademark —violence. Either alone or in combination with other drugs such as amphetamines, barbiturates account for a high percentage of drug-related assaults.

With repeated use over a period of time, tolerance will occur. More of the drug becomes necessary to produce the same effects, resulting in both physical and psychological dependence. While tolerance develops, lethal dosage nevertheless remains the same; as a consequence, the higher dosage a habituated user needs may be enough to kill him. For most, a lethal dose is considered to be ten times the prescribed dose.

The usual therapeutic dose, 100–200 mg per day, will not produce dependence over a short period of time. When habitually ingested in dosages exceeding 600 mg a day for two months, or 800 mg a day for one month, tolerance will occur. Unlike the opiates, however, tolerance develops gradually and may disappear after one to two weeks of abstinence. If heavy dosages are taken for three months or more, the user may become addicted, and will experience withdrawal symptoms if use is terminated.

Withdrawal from chronic, heavy use of barbiturates is more severe and life-threatening than withdrawal from heroin. Untreated, "cold-turkey" withdrawal can last up to two weeks—an eternity to the victim, who suffers increasingly violent symptoms as abstinence continues. Loss of appetite, anxiety, insomnia, sweating, agitation, nausea, vomiting, hyperactivity, tremors, severe cramps, increased heart rate, and muscle twitches accelerate until hallucinations, delirium, paranoia, high temperature, convulsions, and epileptic-like seizures overcome the addict. Alcoholic-like DTs may occur, resulting in a psychotic state, exhaustion, cardiovascular collapse, kidney failure, and even death. Untreated withdrawal symptoms peak within two to three days for the short-acting barbiturates, and within seven to eight days for the long-acting types. Withdrawal should never be attempted alone. Medical supervision, preferably in a hospital, is essential.

Medically supervised withdrawal is accomplished gradually, over a period of several months; the actual length of time depends on the severity of addiction. The addict is first administered his usual intoxicant dosage, then is withdrawn by reducing this level 10 percent daily until he is drug-free. This process is accompanied by other aids such as careful diet and psychiatric help. Alcohol is often used to relieve withdrawal symptoms, since it has a cross-tolerance to barbiturates. This substitution of one CNS depressant for another helps cancel the most severe effects of barbiturate withdrawal. Proper diet, vitamins, fluids, and long-term psychiatric care are necessary for the complete rehabilitation of the addict.

Addictive when used alone, barbiturates' dangers are multiplied when they are used in combination with other depressant drugs. Alcohol, opiates, tranquilizers, antihistamines, and nonbarbiturate hypnotic sedatives greatly increase overdose potential. This synergistic effect may result in depression of the central nervous system, causing the heart and respiratory systems to slow down and possibly fail.

The deadly barbiturate-alcohol combination must be emphasized. Alcohol potentiates the effects of barbiturates, multiplying their depressant power; the combination causes hundreds of deaths annually. In tandem with alcohol, a small amount of barbiturates may cause overdose. While the liver is busily processing alcohol first, barbiturates wait their turn, touring the body and saturating the organ systems. By the time they are eventually metabolized and eliminated, they have done their damage.

Heroin addicts often use barbiturates as a substitute when heroin is unobtainable. Those on methadone may use downers as a means of getting the high otherwise prevented by methadone maintenance. Heroin should never be combined with barbiturates. Most deaths attributed to heroin overdose result from multiple drug use—the combination of heroin, barbiturates, and alcohol.

Barbiturates plus amphetamines equals one of the most dangerous of all forms of drug abuse. Taken in combination—as in the amphetamine-barbiturate Dexamyl, or in an alternating pattern of stimulation and sedation—the two drugs may create separate addictions. Combined, they produce a higher degree of euphoria than when either is taken alone. The speed freak often uses them alternately: first, amphetamines for several days of speeding, followed by barbiturates for rest. This vicious cycle can be a deadly one, both for the addict and for potential victims of his resulting psychosis.

Downers should be avoided by those suffering from heart defects, low blood pressure, depression, or anxiety. Since barbiturates penetrate the placental walls, causing babies of addict mothers to be born addicted, the drug should be avoided by pregnant women.

Driving under the influence of barbiturates can be as dangerous as drunk driving once the 100-mg dosage level is exceeded.

Street-obtained downers are often cut with indeterminate quantities of unknown drugs or with poisons such as arsenic or strychnine. Homemade capsules may look legitimate, since it is simple to empty a capsule partially and refill it with another powder.

Overdose deaths from barbiturates are estimated at more than three thousand annually; of these, 42 percent are suicides, the remainder accidental, either from ingestion of lethal amounts or from combination with other drugs, such as alcohol. Lethal amounts may be consumed unknowingly by an already-sedated person unable to remember how much he has previously ingested. This confused mental state is called "drug automatism." Death comes quickly to those who overdose on short-acting barbiturates; the victims of longer-acting downers die in hospitals.

Severe central respiratory depression is the usual cause of barbiturate death. Overdose is indicated by shock syndrome—sweaty cold skin; weak, rapid pulse; and either painfully slow or rapid, shallow breathing. Deep coma, as well as respiratory and kidney failure, follow. Since barbiturates reduce the amount of oxygen reaching the brain, the overdoser who survives may be left with brain damage.

While overdose should always be treated in a hospital, in an emergency and until medical aid arrives, avoid letting the victim fall asleep. Keep him walking and, if possible, force him to throw up by sticking a finger down his throat. Do not give him coffee, as this breaks up barbiturates in the stomach, causing the drug to disperse even more quickly into the system. Do not give the victim amphetamines; the combination may kill him. Contrary to popular belief, amphetamines are not the opposite of barbiturates and will not reverse or cancel out their effects.

Hospitalization may involve pumping the stomach. However, this is often ineffective because it does not remove enough of the drug, which by that time has already been distributed throughout the body. Treatment also includes maintenance of heart functions, blood transfusions, oxygen administration, and kidney dialysis—hooking up the overdoser to a kidney machine and washing the drug from his blood. Pharmacological methods of treatment—including the use of stimulants, blood-pressure elevators, and diuretics to promote excretion—are controversial. Some feel that these agents put too much pressure on an already weakened system and thus mask important symptoms.

Barbiturates were first synthesized in Belgium in 1684, but not until 1903, when Veronal was introduced, was the search for the ideal sedative-hypnotic considered over. Luminal, in 1912, was the next popular barbiturate, followed by the synthesis of over 2,500 barbituric-acid derivatives since. Tasteless, odorless, easily prescribed and dispensed, the drug at first seemed the perfect answer to anxiety and sleepless nights.

Evidence began accumulating in the 1930s that this insomniac's delight had many of alcohol's negative side effects. Attendant publicity and warnings had a reverse effect: Barbiturates became known in the forties as "thrill pills"—capsulized benders. Today, although the dangers of barbiturates are acknowledged, official action to curtail their abuse has been minimal. Misinformation, inadequate clinical testing, incomplete labeling, and misleading promotional claims all combine to convince the public and government of the drug's safety.

Many addicts are introduced legally to the drug through therapeutic prescriptions. Easily obtainable, either by real or forged prescriptions, from friends, or on the street, the drug is everywhere. Black-market barbiturates are produced in the United States by drug manufacturers, shipped to Mexico, and smuggled back into the United States.

Short-acting barbiturates are currently classified under Schedule II of the Comprehensive Drug Abuse Prevention and Control Act of 1970. For all the controversy about their effectiveness and dangers, sleeping pills have not been formally re-evaluated by the FDA since 1969.

Under proper medical supervision, barbiturates can be helpful to some, but the dangers of misuse and abuse cannot be denied. Child of the drug industry, panacea of the seventies—they have earned the name of "downers."

BELLADONNA

COMMON NAMES: *banewort, beautiful lady, deadly nightshade, death's herb*

Atropa belladonna, a plant member of the potato family, is sometimes peddled as a surefire method of blowing your mind. If potatoes are your thing, we'd suggest that you stick to french fries and keep away from this one.

In Roman times, enlarged pupils were considered a mark of great beauty. Since one of the side effects of this drug is pupil dilation, the Italians long ago christened it belladonna—"beautiful lady." Beauty is, however, very much in the eye of the beholder, so you might want to look a bit further into belladonna before the name begins to sound too attractive.

For you chemists, the active ingredients in this plant are the alkaloids atropine, scopolamine, and hysoscyamine. When abused, this combination has a very high overdose potential.

Peddlers tout belladonna as being a mind-altering drug, and that it can be. Unfortunately, the mind alterations may turn out to be permanent.

Take it and it'll certainly get you stoned. Take a little more and you'll start to act in a somewhat bizarre manner. During the Middle Ages these effects made it one of the more popular potions for use by those into witchcraft and devil worship. Take too much and you'll end up with serious brain damage or maybe even dead.

Belladonna has been around since ancient times. The roots and leaves of this herb could originally be found in wooded areas of Southern and Central Europe. Today the plant is also cultivated in Asia, Algeria, and the United States.

In native areas, dosage is in the form of dried, crushed leaves (30–200 mg) or belladonna root (30–120 mg). Both can be eaten or smoked. Both can also be fatal, particularly the plant root, which contains apoatropine, lethal in even small doses.

In our country, belladonna can be found in a number of legal medicines, including some nonprescription sleeping pills. It is sometimes used as a preanesthetic in surgical situations. When mixed with other ingredients, tinctures of belladonna leaves and root, as well as pure atropine, can act as a treatment for certain types of ulcers and stomach problems by inhibiting gastric secretions. Some asthma drugs such as Asthmador also contain belladonna. Overdo Asthmador, or any other potent form of balladonna, and you'll find yourself on the way to a severe case of overdose—not a very pleasant trip.

While the trip may start out with some pleasant hallucinogenic and hypnotic sensations, before long a babbling, dry mouth, hot skin, and a rash may develop. The eyes will probably experience blurred vision, and a high degree of light sensitivity in addition to those "beautiful lady" enlarged pupils. Even if you survive this trip, there is a chance that your eyes will never be quite the same again. Permanent brain damage is possible.

Beyond its earliest stages, the trip will also consist of a good deal of fear, restlessness, and confusion. If really overdone, vomiting may progress to convulsions and even death from heart failure. Trip length may vary from several hours to several days, depending on how much belladonna has been consumed.

If you've got even a few smarts, by now you're probably convinced that belladonna isn't your bag at all. Before you take any oaths that you'll never touch the stuff, though, be reminded that you've probably had it already. Because belladonna helps dry up mucous membranes, small quantities can be found in a variety of cold remedies, including Contac capsules. Unless you refuse to follow package directions and over-pop these, the chances for encountering any problems are almost nil.

BETEL NUTS

COMMON NAMES: *areca nut, betel morsel, ping lang, supari*

Believe it or not, you are now reading about one of the most widely used drugs in the whole world. Literally hundreds of millions of people in Asian countries chew betel nuts regularly.

Betel nuts are usually consumed in the form of betel morsels. The recipe for morsels might not excite Julia Child, but here it is anyway: Take a piece of the nut from an areca palm tree (*Areca catechu*), a bit of catechu gum from a Malaysian acacia tree, add a pinch of burnt lime, and wrap the whole business in a betel leaf (*Piper chavica betel*). For gourmet tastebuds, a little bit of nutmeg, tumeric, or cloves will enhance flavor. The betel morsel can then be placed in the cheek or under the tongue and sucked on for a few hours much the same way as one would do with a sourball. It may not be candy, but to Asians it's dandy.

The effect of this concoction is primarily due to the oily, volatile arecoline contained in the areca palm nut. Saliva, when mixed with the lime in betel morsels, releases the arecoline, which in turn excites the central nervous system. Respiration increases while the work load placed upon the heart is decreased. The betel leaf contributes to the mix by adding several other mild stimulants such as chavicol, chavibetol, and cadinene.

A side effect of arecoline is that it increases salivation markedly. Before you start worrying about ruining your new T-shirt with dribble, however, take comfort in the fact that the catechu gum in the recipe for morsels will effectively inhibit the excess saliva flow.

Asians have long recognized that betel morsels, sold openly in streets and marketplaces, can lift the spirit, stimulate the nervous system, and generally work as an effective aphrodisiac. They are often included in an Eastern bride's dowry. Adolescents who harvest the nuts and munch while they work often take lovemaking breaks in much the same way as we take coffee breaks.

The aphrodisiac quality of betel nuts does not result from a direct effect upon one's sexual organs. Rather, it is due to the stimulating properties of the drug, its elevation of mood, and a general increase in the chewer's available energy.

As with many substances, for those interested in betel nuts, moderation would seem to be the answer. While a little may be harmless or even beneficial, a lot can actually weaken one's sexual potency and bring on undesirable side effects. Ingestion of too much arecoline, or the use of unripe betel nuts, can cause a feeling similar to being drunk. Dizziness, vomiting, diarrhea, or even convulsions may occur. Regular use will also result in a telltale dark-red staining of the mouth, teeth, and gums.

BROOM

For those who find marijuana to be in scarce supply, or are just interested in trying something new for their heads, broom may well be the answer.

Broom is a member of the bean family. Actually, there are three varieties, and all have much the same potency: Canary Island broom (*Genista canariensis*), Spanish broom (*Spartium junceum*), and Scotch broom (*Cytisus scoparius*).

Today broom is grown legally in the United States in nurseries and home gardens. It can also be found running wild in vacant lots and on country hillsides.

To prepare broom, a supply of the plant's colorful blossoms are collected and then aged for about ten days in a sealed jar. By the end of that time, they should be moldy and dry. The blossoms are then ground to a marijuana-like consistency and rolled into joints for smoking.

Normal dosage is one joint, and provides intoxicated, euphoric feelings for about two hours. Smoking a second joint stretches the broom trip to about four hours. Awareness of color is heightened and an even deeper state of relaxation is experienced. Mexican Indians often smoke broom when they want to get into heavy, contemplative thinking. A basically safe, semi-psychedelic relaxant, broom will not cause hallucinations or visual distortion.

The drug usually has no bad side effects. It doesn't produce any hangover afterward, although in some instances a slight headache may be experienced right after smoking.

Broom's active ingredient is the toxic substance cytisine, which isn't toxic when smoked. Under no circumstances should broom be eaten. Cytisine, which comes from the same pharmacological family as nicotine, is very toxic when ingested and will cause a disturbing level of excitement, followed by a heavy, drunk feeling or even unconsciousness. Cytisine also acts as a heart stimulant, much like digitalis. Eating any quantity may put unnecessary strain on the heart.

CAFFEINE

COMMON FORMS: *coffee (100–180 mg per cup); instant coffee (70–177 mg per cup); tea (50–70 mg per cup); cocoa (50 mg per cup); cola and diet-cola drinks (25–57 mg per 12-ounce can); compound headache tablets (15–30 mg per tablet); No-Doz tablets and similar brands (100 mg); chocolate (25 mg per small bar)*

Feeling nervous? Irritable? Not sleeping well? Suffering from pounding headaches or stomachache? Don't despair. The problem might be a lot simpler to solve than you think. Just pause for a moment to add up the amount of caffeine you are consuming (the above table will be a help).

If, when you add up those cups of coffee, tea, cocoa, and cola, along with those couple of aspirin, you come up with a total exceeding 250 mg per day (considered to be a large amount), watch out! You could be heading for serious problems.

Caffeine has become part of the American way of life. In fact, half the world's entire coffee supply is consumed by people in the United States, to the tune of some 16 pounds per year per person.

Think about it. Maybe you start the day out with a cup of coffee for breakfast. That's 100 mg. You get to the office and have a cup from the office percolator. You're up to 200 mg. You lay off until lunchtime, when you have a cola drink to wash down your sandwich, then two cups of coffee with dessert to brace yourself for what promises to be a dull afternoon's work. You're now up to over 500 mg. In midafternoon you take a coffee break (almost a contractual obligation for most of the working population) and add another 100 mg. Dinner wouldn't seem complete without a couple of cups of coffee, bringing the sum to at least 800 mg for the day. Wow! You've just consumed a lot of something . . . something called caffeine.

Caffeine, a member of the xanthine family, is a cheap, legal drug that comes from natural plant sources such as coffee beans and kola nuts. It acts as a powerful central-nervous-system stimulant, with first effects generally appearing thirty to sixty minutes after ingestion.

Used in moderation, beverages containing caffeine can offer some pleasant breaks in the day and can even have some rewarding benefits. Caffeine has a direct effect on the brain. As late-night drivers and exam-crammers have discovered, reasonable quantities can rapidly sharpen the senses, minimize drowsiness and fatigue, provide quick energy, improve muscular and mental efforts, and provide a high level of clarity and alertness.

High doses of caffeine can produce symptoms that are virtually identical to those found in people suffering from anxiety neurosis. These can include nervousness, lethargy, insomnia, irritability, pounding headaches, dizziness, trembling limbs, high blood pressure, elevated pulse, lightheadedness, breathlessness, and digestive disorders. Such symptoms may temporarily occur with more frequency in weakened or nervous adults as well as in children when they consume quantities of caffeine. So, you might want to skip Junior's extra cup of cocoa before bedtime. And you might want to watch those chocolate bars he keeps popping down. Each "small" one contains 25 mg of caffeine. A child's body weight is far less than that of an adult, thus the amount of caffeine he consumes may easily be excessive.

Excessively high doses can cause more serious problems: cardiovascular reactions such as rapid and/or irregular heartbeat, circulation difficulties, palpitations, flushing, nausea, diarrhea, and vomiting. If you are consuming more than five cups of coffee per day, some studies have indicated you may have twice the chance of experiencing myocardial infarctions (heart attacks) than those of us who drink no coffee at all. Overindulgers take years off their lives. If you suffer from gout or ulcers, the consumption of caffeine can promise you additional discomfort.

"But I like my coffee!" you are probably thinking (not to mention cokes, cocoa, and tea). Sure you do. If you drink any excessive quantity you're probably a caffeine addict, for the drug is mildly habit forming. Stopping "cold turkey" will result in withdrawal symptoms in about twelve to sixteen hours: irritability, headache, and restlessness —all signs of physical dependence.

Never fear. "Cold turkey" doesn't have to be the route for coping with caffeine excess. Cut down slowly over a period of days to allow your body to adjust comfortably without excessive shock. You'll find it an easy transition. Consider ordering decaffeinated coffee the next time you feel like having a cup. Coax whoever is in charge of the coffee pot in the office and at home to use decaffeinated coffee. It tastes almost as good. When it comes to aspirin-compound headache tablets, look for brands that do not contain caffeine (most do). It doesn't make sense to try to cure a headache with something that causes one.

If you are a heavy tea drinker, cut down to a reasonable level and find substitute beverages. Add a bit of milk or cream to your tea to cut the tannic-acid content. Your stomach will certainly thank you for it.

Cola freaks: Just cut down, period! It's not just the caffeine. Your body will appreciate the reduced consumption of sugar, too. Moderate use of caffeine is harmless for most people. Just don't overdo.

CALAMUS

COMMON NAMES: *flag root, rat root, sweet calomel, sweet flag*

A favorite psychedelic of the Cree Indian tribe of northern Alberta is calamus (*Acorus calamus*), more commonly referred to by the unappealing name "rat root." High enough doses can produce an experience similar to that of a light dose of LSD.

Calamus is a tall plant found in streams, marshes, and on the edges of ponds in North America, Europe, and Asia. Its fragrant, swordlike leaves have been a folk-medicine staple for many years. Often used by natives in low doses as a stimulant or tonic because of its energizing properties, calamus has also been used to treat a wide variety of ailments, including asthma, bronchitis, diarrhea, fevers, toothache, headache, and hangover.

The main active ingredient in calamus is a substance called asarone, chemically related to mescaline and amphetamines, but with significant differences. The drug provides users with an "up" feeling, but, unlike the tense up of amphetamines, the calamus trip produces a feeling of relaxation.

Calamus is unique in that it can simultaneously act as a sedative, stimulant, and hallucinogen. The experience that dominates largely depends on dosage and individual tolerance.

The plant is harvested in the late spring or fall. The calamus root, containing the psychedelic ingredient, is thoroughly washed to eliminate bitter fibers and dried with moderate heat.

With its similar appearance, blue flag can easily be mistaken for calamus. Blue flag is a highly poisonous plant, so the mistake could be deadly. Calamus leaves have a sweet smell when scratched; blue flag leaves do not. Calamus roots, in addition, have a pleasant aroma and a sharp taste, while roots from blue flag have no smell and a nauseating, bitter flavor. Pickers uncertain as to which is which should skip the whole idea. Better to miss out on a plant high than to end up as plant fertilizer.

Calamus root will deteriorate and lose potency if kept more than a few months. Chewed, or brewed into a tea, the fresh root is consumed on an empty stomach, since high doses may cause vomiting.

Because people have varying levels of tolerance, only about a 2-

inch length of pencil-thin root should be used for starters. The effect at that dosage level is one of energetic stimulation and euphoria. A 10-inch length of root will produce light LSD-like sensations.

Sale of calamus is presently legal in the United States, although the Food and Drug Administration has requested herb marketers not to sell it to the general public.

While there are no known negative side effects related to calamus use, it should not be taken with MAO inhibitors, including hydrazines such as Iproniazid, Marplan, Catran, Parnate, Eutonyl, Eutron, Nardil, Niamid, and Marsilid. Avoid yohimbine, harmala alkaloids, tryptamines, nonhydrazines such as cyclopropylamines, aminopyrazine derivatives, propargylamines, carbolines, and indolealkylamines. MAO inhibitors, in general, should not be used at least a week before and after taking calamus.

CALEA

COMMON NAMES: *bitter grass, leaf of God, Mexican calea*

Scientists claim *Calea zacatechichi*, a sunflower-family shrub which grows from Central Mexico to Costa Rica, to be one of the "latest" psychedelic discoveries. Not so, say the Chontal Indians of Oaxaca. For centuries, this drug, called Thle-pela-kano, has been used as a tea to induce hallucinations and clarify the senses, as well as to treat fevers and mild cases of diarrhea.

To prepare a dose, two tablespoons of dried leaves are brewed for about five minutes in a pint of boiled water. After straining, the resulting two cups of tea are sipped slowly. Indians often lie down in a peaceful spot after their sipping is done and top off their drink with a few tokes from a joint of dried calea leaves.

Within a short time, a sense of restfulness and drowsiness is experienced. The user knows he has had enough when he hears the throb of his pulse and heartbeat.

No one knows exactly what the chemical properties of *Calea zacatechichi* are, but research is underway. At the moment, the drug does not appear to have any negative side effects.

One problem—the leaves can be purchased inexpensively only at the Oaxaca marketplace. Not too convenient, but if you're in the neighborhood . . .

CALIFORNIA POPPY

The California poppy is an abundant West Coast wild flower whose leaves and orange petals can be dried, rolled into joints, and smoked when pot is hard to come by. It is not an opium poppy but does contain several opium-related alkaloids: chelerythrine, sanguinarine, protopine, a- and b-homochelidonine, as well as several glucosides.

A joint of this stuff will produce a mild, euphoric marijuana-like buzz for about thirty minutes or so. Light one up a little later in the day and it'll do next to nothing for your head. About one joint per day is all that anyone will find effective.

It is not addictive, nor does it have any negative side effects, and no laws prohibit the smoking of California poppy. There is a California statute against plucking or mutilating this plant, the official state flower. Those caught harvesting their stash in the wild will be faced with a small misdemeanor fine.

CAMPHOR

Real camphor has nothing to do with the moth flakes or moth balls (paradichlorobenzine) Mom has stored in the closet to protect her woolens. So, if camphor experimentation is to be your game, be sure you don't confuse the two. As deadly as mothballs and mothflakes are to moths, so can they be to you.

At one time the eating of real camphor (*Cinnamomum camphora*) enjoyed some degree of popularity. Today, when it is used, camphor tincture or powdered camphor is mixed with grass and smoked in a joint or pipe.

Ingestion of one gram of the stuff will produce a slight stimulating effect, since camphor irritates nerve endings. Users will experience a pleasant, tingly feeling on the skin, some mild restlessness, and a highly excited mental state.

Overdone, camphor can be a real bummer. Two grams of the stuff and your head becomes a swirling mess for about three hours. Accompanying this mental merry-go-round will be possible vomiting and amnesia. Delirium or convulsions are possible with an overdose.

CANNABINOL

Next time a "friendly" dealer tells you he can get some cannabinol, find yourself another dealer.

Cannabinol doesn't even exist. It's a cover name for PCP, which dealers try to pass off as pure THC, the active ingredient in marijuana. Want to know more about cannabinol? Turn to our section on PCP.

CATNIP

Does it or doesn't it?

The debate as to whether or not catnip can get one high has been going on among potheads for many years. Many teen-agers, particularly in times of grass or allowance shortage, have even given it a try. After all, it can be legally bought in any pet store and costs less than a dollar for an ounce. But just because Tabby does flips over the stuff, don't expect to be doing the same if you indulge.

Catnip is an herb member of the mint family. Chemically, it includes mepetalacton, nepetalic acid, and metabilacetone. Its active ingredient, which has not yet been identified, lies in its volatile oil.

Catnip can be taken in a variety of ways. Occasionally it is brewed into a tea. Most often, catnip leaves are smoked in a pipe or in the form of a joint. Catnip liquid extract may be sprayed directly onto tobacco and smoked that way.

The most effective way to use catnip is to smoke it in a 50/50 mixture with tobacco. This makes the mild euphoric feeling it produces slightly longer-lasting and more intense.

Catnip is significantly weaker than marijuana, thus large quantities must be smoked to bring on even a mild buzz. It doesn't have any mind-altering effects, nor does it have any dangerous or unpleasant side effects. If you smoke a lot, remember: The tobacco with which it is mixed is addictive and a danger to your health.

CHLOROFORM

Chloroform, a heavy, colorless liquid with a sweet, burning taste, gives off potent ethereal fumes at room temperature.

Chloroform was discovered simultaneously in Germany, France, and the United States in 1831. Recreational use of the drug began soon after and enjoyed a brief period of popularity. Both liquid and vapor forms were first thought to be "safe" alcohol substitutes since small quantities produced intoxication and euphoria without morning-after hangover.

In 1847, chloroform was used for the first time as an anesthetic for childbirth and surgery. As a general anesthetic, it acts faster, and eight times more powerfully, than ether. However, the overdose hazard, related to sudden death from circulatory depression, as well as the growth in popularity of other anesthetics eventually caused chloroform to fall into medical disfavor.

Because of its strength, chloroform can be highly dangerous in amateur hands. For some, large quantities, when ingested orally, can be lethal.

Use of chloroform as a recreational intoxicant is rare today.

CIMORA

Cimora is a hallucinogenic drink that Indians in Peru and Ecuador have been swallowing for centuries. Tribal witch doctors have used it for a variety of purposes, including foretelling the future and diagnosing disease in their patients.

The drink is actually a brew of several ingredients, but the ones that make it do its stuff are San Pedro and datura. Read through the information we've provided about these two and you'll have a pretty good fix on cimora.

COCAINE

COMMON NAMES: *Bernice, Bernies, big C, blow, burese, C, Carrie, Cecil, Cholly, coke, Corine, dream, dust, dynamite, flake, gin, girl, gold dust, happy dust, heaven dust, joy powder, lady, leaf, nose, nose candy, nose powder, paradise, rock, snow, snowbird, speedball (mixed with heroin), stardust, superblow, toot, white, white girl*

If you are rich, hedonistic, and willing to jeopardize your nose for a few brief moments of ecstacy, cocaine could be your pleasure. You may pay, however, both literally and figuratively through the nose. Cocaine's reputation as a rare and expensive drug has catapulted it into glamour status among such celebrities as Freud, Pope Leo XIII, Sir Arthur Conan Doyle, and the multitude of rock stars whose collection of neck paraphernalia invariably includes a custom-made coke spoon.

Cocaine comes in three forms: rock, flake, and powder. Rock is available, flake is considered a delicacy, but powder is the form that most people see. Powder is easily diluted, and that is what street coke is: diluted or cut. The stuff peddled by pushers is rarely more than 60 percent pure cocaine hydrochloride, and more often ranges from 5 to 35 percent. The rest is the "cut," which is there either to make the coke seem of a higher quality or to dilute it. The local anesthetics procaine, lidocaine, benzocaine, tetracaine, and butacaine are often added to enhance quality, as are stimulants such as amphetamine, ephedrine, and caffeine. Sugars such as lactose, inositol, and mannitol are used to dilute. Some unscrupulous dealers don't bother to add cocaine to the recipe at all.

The finished product is a white, flaky powder: bitter, odorless, and numbing to the lips and tongue. The privilege of stuffing this up your nose will cost from $10 to $40 a stuff. Cocaine may be purchased by the gram, or $\frac{1}{28}$ ounce, but is most commonly sold in the quantity of a "spoon," a nebulous measurement roughly equivalent to $\frac{1}{4}$ teaspoon. Depending on the cut, the dealer may pocket a neat profit of 500 percent. The drug may arrive in the United States nearly 100 percent pure, but by the time it is cut and reaches the street consumer it may skyrocket to over $1,200 an ounce.

The cost of coke became exorbitant once it left the realm of legality. Medically, synthetic drugs have taken over where cocaine left off, but it was once the drug of choice, used as local anesthetic, stimulant, and anti-depressant. Still used for local anesthesia in oral-nasal surgery, it has the effect of reducing mucous-membrane swelling, thus enlarging the nasal and bronchial passages.

The primary drug properties of cocaine are that it blocks impulse conduction in nerve fibers when applied externally, producing a numb, freezing sensation; it is a vasoconstrictor and inhibits excessive bleeding; is a local anesthetic; and, taken internally, works on the peripheral nervous system, inhibiting norepinephrine from being reabsorbed by the nerve, thus potentiating the effects of nerve stimulation. Coke is a stimulant of the central nervous system, similar to the amphetamines.

Snorting, via spoon, straws, or rolled currency, is the usual method of taking coke, since it is absorbed quickly through the mucous membranes of the nose into the bloodstream. Other body orifices can also be used. By mixing it with a liquid or semi-solid, it may be taken orally, or by direct application to the gums, palate, or underneath the tongue. Lesser-known and more hazardous is placing it on the inside of the eyelid. Applying it to the genitals may prevent premature ejaculation or serve to prolong sexual performance for both men and women. There are even folks who indulge in cocaine enemas.

Cocaine may be injected, preferred by some because of the intense initial rush. This is the most dangerous method because it introduces the drug directly into the bloodstream. Shooting also causes one to become more dependent. Heavy cokeheads may shoot from twenty to thirty times a day. Coke smoking, which causes temporary numbness in the lungs, is less common.

Proponents of cocaine consider it the champagne of drugs. Coke is an upper. Research on human responses to cocaine began in 1974, 115 years after cocaine's discovery, and indications are that in moderate use it is a mild euphoric drug, similar to the amphetamines in action but without their serious side effects. It is legally classified as a narcotic.

For some cocaine produces feelings of intense sexuality, psychic energy, and self-confidence, without the mind-bending qualities of the hallucinogens. The drug's powers are intense but brief, lasting about a half hour, for the body metabolizes cocaine quickly and the user must take another dose to re-establish his high. It is this elevator effect that creates the strong psychological dependence of many users; coming down from such a high may cause a deep and profound depression for which more cocaine seems to be the only remedy. Not truly addictive in the physical sense, cocaine may create a tendency for overuse in someone with an addictive personality.

The pleasant, stimulating effects of cocaine may escalate like a speeded-up record into excitability, anxiety, talkativeness, rapid heartbeat, increased pulse rate, blood-pressure elevation, dilated pupils, headache, nausea, vomiting, increase in body temperature, and even hallucinations. These symptoms rarely occur with moderate usage, but tolerance sometimes sets in. Some users require gradually larger doses to achieve the same effect and stave off withdrawal.

A peculiar characteristic of the paranoid psychosis which can result from overuse is "formication," the hallucination that ants, insects, or snakes are crawling on or under the skin. If imaginary insect infestation doesn't concern you, how about the possibility of an unwanted nose job? Prolonged, steady use may damage nasal tissues, causing a perforated septum. The finer cocaine is chopped or ground, the less chance there is of the drug becoming lodged in the hairs of the nose and in the sinus cavities. Snorting or rinsing the nose with water after sniffing cocaine is an added precaution. The destruction of the mucous membranes lining the nose may also cause the telltale runny nose of the "horner," the regular snorter. Police often finger a user by giving his nose a playful tweak. If he screams in pain, it's a giveaway.

Repeated large doses may not only cause the nose to bleed and rot, but pallor, cold sweats, convulsions, fainting, and a halt in respiration can mean that cocaine poisoning has set in. The amount of cocaine that causes overdose varies from individual to individual. A fatal dose may range from .2 to 1.5 grams of pure cocaine, but the chance of overdosing is slim unless the coke has been taken intravenously. Overdoses can also be attributable to adulterants which have been added. Treatment for overdose is best handled under medical supervision.

All things in moderation, and this applies particularly to cocaine. Cocaine is, simply, a stimulant of the central nervous system; so is caffeine. Used in moderation, its dosage controlled, the drug produces a short-lived, pleasant high without the dangers of heroin or the other narcotics with which it has been unjustly classified. The true medical danger, aside from possible allergic reaction which may result in fatal anaphylactic shock, is cocaine's ability to produce psychological, not physical, addiction.

Moderate recreational use of cocaine is most dangerous in the legal sense. Penalties for possession can range from six months to life, with fines up to $25,000. Possession with intent to sell can result in a life sentence or up to a $50,000 fine. Missouri levies the death penalty for sale to minors under twenty-one, definitely detrimental to one's health.

Cocaine was driven underground in 1914 by the Harrison Tax Act, which mistakenly classified it as a narcotic, subject to the same penalties as opium, morphine, and heroin. Today it is under Schedule II of the Controlled Substances Act. Most laws governing cocaine are based on the largely false notion that it is physically addicting.

Myths about cocaine are perpetuated by the law itself. With little information about the drug's effects on humans, the conflict grows between those who believe it an unmitigated evil and those who believe it to be a mild euphoriant which causes ill effects only when abused.

The advent of the amphetamines, cheap and legal, caused temporary reduction in the use of cocaine. When the amphetamines were forced underground by the law, cocaine smuggling became once again widespread. Part of coke's allure may lie in its very illegality; part of the high may be the danger of arrest.

The emperor of the Incas didn't have such troubles until the sixteenth century. When the Spanish conquistadors stopped by to say hello, they knew a good thing when they saw one: an entire kingdom stoned on the leaves of a mountain shrub known as *Erythroxylon coca*. They took it away from the natives, who regarded it as divine, and brought it home to the wife and kiddies, who abused it, misused it, and gave it the bad name it carries to this day.

The Incan emperor governed the use of the coca leaf, which, when chewed, produced euphoria and the ability to work at an incredible pace. The highest privilege an Incan subject could earn was the right to chew the coca leaf. A supply was buried with each nobleman, so he would not run out in Inca heaven.

Meanwhile, up in the Andes, the Indians were chomping away at the coca leaf to survive the rigors of the harsh mountain environment. The Andean leaf chewers of today still masticate the herb to help them endure the altitude. When they descend from the heights, they find it easy to give up their high.

Sigmund Freud gave cocaine its greatest PR buildup when he chanced upon an account of the therapeutic effects of the drug and tried it for his own neuroses. So astounded was he by the results that he not only published a paper praising it, but also turned on his friends, his fiancée, and his associate, Dr. Ernst von Fleischal-

Marxow, who was addicted to morphine for a painful condition. Unfortunately, Fleischal-Marxow exchanged, not a headache for an upset stomach, but morphine addiction for cocaine dependence, and Freud disowned what he called "the magical drug."

Despite Fleischal-Marxow's metamorphosis, cocaine retained its popularity past the turn of the century. Medically, it was used as a local anesthetic in eye surgery and as a cure for alcohol and morphine addiction, and was endorsed by the Hay Fever Association for its bronchi- and sinus-clearing properties.

Recreationally, cocaine parlors were the discos of the day, and patent medicines included coca extract as a vital part of their formulae. One such concoction was Coca-Cola, made with coca leaves and sold as a "remarkable therapeutic agent" for everything from melancholy to insomnia, until Dr. Harvey Wiley used it as a target for enactment of a Pure Food and Drug Law. In 1906, Coca-Cola switched to decocainized coca leaves, still in the formula today.

Cocaine: super-high or bummer? Probably both. The consumer must decide whether an icy trip with the snow queen to the crystal heights of pleasure is worth coming down to the depths of the legal dangers, the expense, and the potential physical damage of overuse. Who nose?

CODEINE

COMMON NAME: *schoolboy*

Known to man since before recorded history, codeine is the least expensive, most effective cough suppressant and minor pain reliever available.

Although the drug is an opiate narcotic, only excessive, prolonged use can addict. Even then, withdrawal is less traumatic than that from heroin or morphine.

Chemically called methylmorphine, codeine is extracted from the milky juice of the poppy plant. Unlike its big brothers heroin and morphine, codeine is effective when ingested orally in cough syrup or tablet form. It is difficult to abuse intravenously because it is barely soluble, yet it is often used by drug addicts when other opiates are unavailable or to ease withdrawal pain.

Codeine is an ingredient in hundreds of medical compounds and depresses the central nervous system. This action not only relieves coughs and minor pains but also constricts the bowels, causing constipation. A less common effect is nausea. The drug's general effects are milder than those of morphine, but provide more pain relief than aspirin, Darvon, Demerol, Percodan, Tylenol, or Empirin. Some tendency toward psychological dependence exists, since codeine produces a sedated and euphoric "high." And because tolerance develops to its mildly pleasant dreaminess, the abuser may suffer from anxiety, depression, and irritability when use is discontinued. The nonabuser, using it up to two or three weeks for a cough or toothache, can safely use it without fear. Often combined with aspirin, antihistamines, decongestants, or antitussives in multiple painkillers, it is sold by pharmacies under such names as Actifed-C, Ambenyl, Novahistine DH, Phenergan, Benylin, Phenaphen, Codeine Sulfate, Codeine Phosphate, and Empirin Compound with Codeine Phosphate.

Although regulated under Schedule II of the federal Controlled Substances Act, when used properly codeine can be medically beneficial without the specter of addiction.

COLEUS

When psilocybin mushrooms are in short supply, and users are willing to settle for a milder but similar mind excursion, they sometimes turn to the coleus plant, particularly the species *Coleus blumei* and *Coleus pumila*. The Mazatec Indians of southern Mexico have been tripping on this psychedelic mint for years.

It takes about fifty to seventy large, colorful leaves of the coleus plant to get someone going. They can be chewed thoroughly and swallowed. If one prefers, the leaves can also be smoked and steeped in lukewarm water for about an hour, after which the liquid is strained and drunk.

No one is exactly sure what gives coleus its psychoactive kick, but we do know that only fresh leaves will work. Dried leaves have virtually no effect.

While the drug has no really unpleasant or dangerous side effects, some people do feel a degree of nausea about a half hour after getting it down. But the nausea goes away quickly and it soon replaced by a trippy, psilocybin-like state, colorful visual hallucinations and patterns, and telepathic and clairvoyant insights. The entire trip lasts for about two hours.

Coleus plants can be purchased legally at most garden centers. Those with green thumbs, who aren't too stoned to exercise them, might purchase some seeds to grow their own.

COLORINES

Next time you're in Mexico you might see some pretty little beads for sale at the marketplace in Oaxaca. If you do, heed the advice of the natives of the area and don't try to eat any, regardless of what anyone else has told you. These little beads might well be colorines, and colorines can spell big trouble.

The bright beads of these woody-plant members of the bean family come in both red and black. The red ones are usually from the *Erythrina flabelliformis* or *Rhynchosia paseloides* species, and the blacks from the *Rhynchosia pyramidalis* species.

For those who are foolish enough to eat one-quarter to one-half of one of these little beauties, a drunken feeling accompanied by hallucinations will be the reward. But in larger doses, colorines are also highly poisonous. In fact, the toxic indole in the plant that turns the brain into a spinning jumble may cause vomiting, a pounding heartbeat, convulsions, and even death.

If beads are your thing, keep them around your neck where they belong and out of your mouth.

DAMIANA

Damiana (*Turnera diffusa*) is a shrub with sweet-smelling leaves most commonly found in Africa, Mexico, Texas, and California. Some peopie consider damiana to be a mild, legal version of marijuana.

Damiana can be smoked in the same manner as grass. About a pipe bowl full of dried leaves will usually produce a mild, marijuana-like buzz for an hour or so. If the smoke seems a bit harsh, try using a waterpipe. Your throat and lungs will thank you.

If a stronger high is desired, the most effective way to use damiana is to smoke it while sipping it as a tea. To prepare damiana tea, steep about 2 tablespoons of leaves in a pint of water. Add a bit of sweetener or honey to the tea or you might find it a little too bitter for your taste. Strain, let it cool, and drink.

If you haven't been sleeping well, you might find a cup taken an hour before bedtime will produce a relaxed rest period accompanied by pleasant sexually oriented dreams.

Nobody is certain what the magic ingredient is that gives damiana its kick, but it has long been highly regarded for its aphrodisiac qualities in addition to its ability to produce a high. Drinking damiana tea about an hour before having sex generally makes people feel pleasantly relaxed, and being relaxed can easily be translated into sexy feelings for most folks.

As with other drugs, the key to successful damiana enjoyment lies in moderation. Too much, taken too often, may be harmful to your liver. But, if not overdone, damiana may act as an elixir for both the sexual organs and the nervous system. For those really interested in keeping their sexual parts in good working order, many users have found that eating a teaspoonful of dried saw-palmetto berries along with their tea each day can be particularly beneficial.

Both damiana and saw-palmetto berries can be found in many health-food shops and herb outlets at reasonable prices.

DARVON

Does it work as a minor pain reliever, or doesn't it? Not even your doctor knows for sure.

The American Medical Association considers Darvon to be about one-half to one-third as potent a painkiller as codeine. Others, including journalists, medical investigators, and Ralph Nader, to mention a few, believe Darvon is a hoax. There seems to be no consensus in the medical community about its therapeutic value, yet some eighteen million prescriptions were written in 1975, making Darvon the third most widely prescribed drug in America, right behind Valium and Librium.

Darvon has been marketed as a unique synthetic for treating common mild pains such as headache and those which accompany dental problems. Although a synthetic, it is a close cousin of codeine, morphine, heroin, and particularly methadone. Chemically referred to as propoxyphene hydrochloride, it is a soluble, white, bitter-tasting crystalline powder. The drug is profitably marketed by thirty-five companies in a dizzying array of compounds that can be bought, by prescription, in tablet, capsule, or oral liquid form. And profitable it is: Although Darvon has never been proved more effective than aspirin or codeine, it costs forty to fifty times as much. Some studies have indicated that the drug is no more than a placebo at normal dosage levels, giving the illusion of pain relief without pharmacological effect.

Since its appearance on the market in 1957, certain uncommon side effects of Darvon have become known. Dizziness, impaired mental and physical performance, sedation, sleepiness, insomnia, skin rash, nausea, vomiting, constipation, and abdominal pain have been sporadically reported. During the 1970s, massive abuse of Darvon led to an epidemic number of overdoses, causing convulsions, respiratory depression, stupor, pupil constriction, coma, and circulatory collapse. A sample survey of eighteen American cities recently indicated almost three hundred Darvon-related deaths, some resulting from multi-drug use. Darvon has been listed as the cause of death in a number of suicides. Any abuser suffering from acute Darvon reaction should be rushed to a hospital where a narcotic antagonist can be properly administered.

It now appears certain that Darvon can create tolerance. Some users unpredictably develop physical and psychological dependence.

Once such dependence develops, stopping suddenly can result in severe withdrawal symptoms. The more we learn about this medical staple, the more it resembles a narcotic, capable of causing addiction with long-term continuous use. It is now abused primarily by adolescents, a small army of undetected addicts who feed their habits by duping physicians into providing them with prescriptions. Addiction may actually result from multi-drug use, such as combining Darvon with alcohol or barbiturates, but absolute proof is still lacking.

The recent wave of Darvon addiction and suicide has prompted the United States Justice Department and the Food and Drug Administration to take a second look at the currently unregulated Darvon trade. Current recommendations tend toward placing Darvon under Schedule IV of the Controlled Substances Act, which would limit the number of refills permitted, and require pharmaceutical security and strict recordkeeping. These measures are being proposed to encourage physicians to be more cautious when prescribing Darvon, while the public is educated as to the drug's potential dangers.

Placebo or painkiller, Darvon is probably an unnecessary addition to the abuser's chemical feast. In all likelihood, its legal use will be sharply curtailed in the years ahead.

DATURA

SPECIES: *Datura meteloides, D. sanguinea, D. inoxia, D. metel, D. sauveolens, D. arborea*

As is the case with *Datura stramonium* (see Jimson weed), other members of the datura group contain significant quantities of a number of hallucinogenic alkaloids.

Tropane-bearing herbs such as datura have long been used illegally as the "Mickey Finn" of Asia. Prostitutes and thieves have used it to put clients and victims into a stupor before rolling them. It is reputed that unknowing and unwilling young virgins, male and female alike, have been seduced, raped, and otherwise lured into lives of prostitution in the Orient as a result of using this drug. Datura roots were used in witches' brews during the Middle Ages. Sometimes datura was prepared in paste form and applied to various parts of the body, including the genitals and anus. Users many times experienced the sensation of soaring flight after using datura.

Today, datura has become something of a speciality in the hallucinogenic/hypnotic spectrum of goodies. The leaves can be smoked or drunk as a tea, or the pulverized root can be eaten. Commonly used for religious purposes by Indians in the Southwestern United States and Mexico, the "devil's weed" trip for most nonreligious users can prove to be a real bummer unless one thrives on diarrhea, nausea, confusion, babbling, dryness, dizziness, agitation, and loss of motor coordination. If that's not enough to scare you away, consider the fact that datura, in overdose quantity, can cause permanent eye and heart damage, convulsions, coma, and even death.

Datura seeds are sometimes used to cut marijuana in India and other Asian countries where the latter drug may be particularly strong. Should you have occasion to get such a mixture, watch out! Recent studies have shown that prolonged use of datura can result in permanent organic brain damage.

DEMEROL

Demerol is a potent, effective painkiller for childbirth, cancer, acute injuries, and many pre- and postoperative aches; it is also useful in relieving anxiety and depression.

A synthetic opiate analgesic known by a variety of chemical names —meperidine, perthidine, dolantin, dolantol, and isonipecaine— Demerol shares with its opiate cousins the harrowing side effect of addiction. Although the drug is more habit-forming than codeine, short-term, physician-prescribed use is unlikely to result in addiction.

In pure form, Demerol is a white, crystalline powder. It is marketed as an injectible fluid, multi-colored tablet, or banana-flavored oral medicine. Most effective when injected intravenously, it can relieve excruciating pain from three to four hours. The drug should be avoided, however, by asthmatics and those suffering from pulmonary disease.

Demerol should never be taken with MAO inhibitors such as yohimbine, harmala alkaloids, tryptamines, or the drugs Marplan, Catron, Parnate, Eutonyl, Eutron, Nardil, Niamid, and Marsalid, since overdose might result in severe respiratory depression and coma.

Some users experience nausea, vomiting, dizziness, and sweating, although these side effects are relatively uncommon. Abusers seek the euphoric, lightheaded feeling the drug produces. Because Demerol impairs mental and physical functioning, activities requiring fine motor coordination and judgment, such as driving or operating complex machinery, should be restricted.

Although there is no significant underground market for Demerol, abusers do exist, managing to procure prescription refills from cooperative physicians and pharmacists. It is often used by habituated medical professions who have ready access to pharmaceutical supplies. Noted for their hazy, erratic behavior, these abusers can usually hide the true nature of their addiction from an unsuspecting world.

Demerol is regulated by federal law under Schedule II of the Controlled Substances Act.

DILAUDID

COMMON NAMES: *big D, D, dillies, junk, shit, stuff, white stuff*

Dilaudid, chemically known as hydromorphine hydrochloride, is a painkiller originally synthesized and promoted as a safe, nonaddicting substitute for morphine. Although it is a necessary and useful medicine, the drug is no less habit-forming than other opiates.

A potent semi-synthetic derivative of morphine, Dilaudid is generally effective for severe or chronic pain. It is usually prescribed for postoperative pain, heart attack, cancer, bone fractures, burns, and the acute coughs of colic, tuberculosis, bronchitis, pleurisy, and tracheitis. Processed into a fine, white, odorless, water-soluble crystalline powder, it is available as an injectible fluid, rectal suppository, cough syrup, soluble tablet, or powder for compounding. In hospitals, the drug is most often injected for optimal potency.

Dilaudid preparations are similar to those containing morphine, but are stronger and have fewer side effects. A moderate dose of Dilaudid alleviates pain in about fifteen minutes often placing the now pain-free patient in a euphoric daze for from five to six hours. Users may suffer from nausea, vomiting, constipation, dizziness, or anorexia (loss of appetite), but such reactions are rare. Generally, a medically supervised dose will relieve painful symptoms without unpleasant side effects. Although with prolonged regular use it can be addictive, the benefits derived from normal medical use far outweigh the minor risk of dependency.

A small percentage of abusers pick up their habits by swallowing tiny Dilaudid tablets and later graduate to mainlining—shooting larger and larger doses into their veins. As with any narcotic, a missed fix results in a protracted, painful period of withdrawal. Dilaudid addicts are most often limited to health professionals or their families, since there is no significant black market for the drug. Able to obtain their necessary dose, they can hide their addiction, though their minds may be clouded and dazed most of the time.

Dilaudid is regulated, as a narcotic, under Schedule II of the federal Controlled Substances Act.

DMT

More of a dropping-by-to-say-hi than a real trip to Psychedelia City, DMT provides a fast peek at the world of hallucinogens. The journey begins almost instantly, peaks within twenty or thirty minutes, and is over within the hour.

DMT, or n,n-dimethyltryptamine, is an active ingredient in several South American plants used by Indians to create hallucinogenic snuffs for their religious rituals. DMT may also be produced synthetically as a tasteless, colorless crystal powder or liquid. A close cousin, DET, or diethyltryptamine, produces a milder, longer-lasting trip than DMT, but has its roots in the same chemical family of tryptamines. A dose of 3.5–5 mg is usually combined with tobacco, parsley, or marijuana and smoked. Ground into a powder, DMT may be snorted like snuff, eaten, or prepared for injection.

The first few minutes of the trip may be intensely psychedelic, accompanied by momentary dizziness and an increase in heart and respiratory rates. Nausea will occur if DMT is taken on a full stomach. Disorientation and confusion soon give way to the LSD-like effects, as the tripper floats through a variety of sensations: perceived color and size changes, visual and time distortions, and an intoxicated, dizzy feeling combined with a sense of increased alertness and clear vision. The mini-LSD sensations are mini- in time, not effect.

Once the short journey has reached its end, no hangover or side effects remain as souvenirs, unless the user wasn't feeling well to begin with, or overdid the dosage. Moderation is the key. If the drug is taken before going to bed, sleep may be difficult.

Large doses may cause blood to rush to the head, rupturing weak capillaries in the brain. The injection of DMT may cause the usual complications associated with introducing a needle into tissue: infection, abscess, tetanus, gangrene, and malaria.

Lethal overdose is unlikely, however, and addiction is unknown.

The greatest danger of DMT is its action as an MAO inhibitor, meaning that when combined with the wrong things, it may result in dangerous changes in blood pressure, headache, heart trouble, or death. Tranquilizers, amphetamines, atropine, ritalin, insulin, antihis-

69

tamines, alcohol, avocados, broad beans (pods), excessive caffeine, canned figs, chicken liver, sedatives, mescaline, nutmeg, aged cheeses, any quantity of milk products, ripe bananas, excessive chocolate, pickled herring, yeast extract, excessive licorice, pineapple, cocoa, narcotics, sauerkraut, ephidrine, macromerine, and oils of dill, parsley, and wild fennel should be avoided. If you have combined DMT with any of the above, strong headache and vomiting will be signs that medical attention is needed.

Legal in its natural form, extracted 5-MeO-DMT falls under the Drug Abuse Control Amendment, with a fine of up to $1,000 and/or imprisonment of up to one year for a first conviction for possession.

DONA ANA

This small, spiny member of the cactus family grows primarily in southern Texas and the northern part of Mexico. Macromerine, a phenethylamine hallucinogen closely related to mescaline with about one-fifth that drug's gram potency, is its primary psychoactive chemical constituent.

To achieve an effect equal to that of mescaline in intensity requires about eight to twelve fresh Dona Ana cacti (*Coryphantha macromeris*). After the spines have been removed, the cacti should be chewed thoroughly before swallowing, or a tea may be brewed by boiling the cacti in water for about an hour and straining. Either way, do it on an empty stomach because nausea or vomiting may be experienced during the early stages of the trip. Vomiting will not in any way change the effect of the drug, however.

First Dona Ana effects begin coming on within an hour or two, and the whole hallucinogenic, mind-altering experience may last up to twelve hours.

If the user's head is screwed on reasonably well to begin with, there are no known dangerous aftereffects from this drug. In this respect it is similar to all of the LSD-like substances.

Dona Ana should not be taken in overly large doses, nor should it be combined wih MAO inhibitors such as yohimbine, harmala alkaloids, tryptamines, or the drugs Marplan, Catron, Parnate, Eutonyl, Eutron, Nardil, Niamid, and Marsalid.

EPENA

COMMON NAME: *parica, yopo*

For centuries the Indians of the Amazon have been turning on with a variety of hallucinogens that come to them through the courtesy of Mother Nature. One of the fastest-acting of all is epena.

Epena is prepared from scrapings of the red resin beneath the bark of the *Virola calophylla* tree, a member of the nutmeg family native to the rain forests of Columbia and Brazil. After the resin has been thoroughly dried, it must be crushed to a fine powder, mixed with ashes, and snorted in a manner similar to commercial snuff.

The active constituents of the plant are DMT, 5-Methoxy-DMT, and bufotenine. In all probability, DMT is the ingredient that accounts for the plant's hallucinogenic effects.

The epena trip lasts about thirty minutes. Its powerful effects are virtually instantaneous.

The half-hour excursion floats the tripper through a variety of sensations, including perceived color and size changes in objects, and an intoxicated, dizzy feeling combined with a sense of increased alertness and clear vision.

Euphoric, pleasant feelings, along with a sense of light stimulation, may continue for several hours after the more dramatic effects of the trip have subsided. Because the drug severely irritates the mucous membranes of the nose, it often causes the user to sneeze uncontrollably. To avoid that part of the experience, natives have been known to mix their snuff with water and use it as an enema to get off. A hallucinogenic cousin of epena, called cohoba, has been made from the pulverized seeds of *Anadenanthera colubrina*, also known as *Piptadenia perigrina*.

Beginners experimenting with epena usually snort small amounts for starters to avoid possible unpleasant side effects. Uncomfortable trembling for the first five minutes of the trip may be followed by headache and confusion for the next ten minutes if too much is snuffed.

Epena should be avoided by those not feeling up to par physically, since the drug exaggerates existing pain. A full stomach sometimes causes unnecessary nausea.

Epena is an MAO inhibitor, which means that if you combine it with the wrong things it can result in unpleasant consequences ranging from headache to heart trouble to death. MAO inhibitors depress the action of monoamine oxidase (MAO), a crucial enzyme in the body. They are, as a result, incompatible with substances requiring this enzyme. Keep away from tranquilizers, barbiturates, atropine, ritalin, antidepressants, insulin, amphetamines, antihistamines, alcohol, avocados, ripe bananas, broad beans (pods), excessive caffeine, canned figs, chicken liver, excessive licorice, sedatives, mescaline, nutmeg, aged cheeses, any quantity of milk products, excessive amounts of chocolate, pickled herring, yeast extract, cocoa, narcotics, sauerkraut, ephedrine, macromerine, and oils of dill, parsley, and wild fennel. If you have made the mistake of combining, potent headache and vomiting will tell you something's wrong. Get yourself to a hospital quickly!

ETHER

Discovered during the thirteenth century, diethyl ether—commonly referred to as ether—is a volatile liquid resulting from dehydration of ethyl alcohol by sulfuric acid.

Recreational use of ether was initiated by physicians and university students during the late 1700s, when it was regarded as an effective substitute for alcohol. Small doses depress the central nervous system, quickly and inexpensively producing a safe state of euphoric intoxication without causing hangover.

To become inebriated, users drank from 1 to 3 ounces of the liquid drug. Although some dangers did exist (including gastritis, overdose death, and burns from smoking while drinking the flammable drug), use of ether as an intoxicant remained popular in Britain until the late 1800s, when public concern resulted in an ether prohibition. This failed miserably; however, when alcohol became less expensive and more available in Britain during the 1920s, ether use rapidly declined.

In the United States, recreational use had a brief surge during the alcohol prohibition years, 1920–1933, when nonalcoholic beverages were often spiked with ether to provide a kick. Similarly, ether use rose in Germany during World War II in response to the shortage of alcoholic beverages.

Inhalation of ether for anesthetic purposes was introduced in 1846. Before long, recreational inhalation of the drug caught on at Harvard, and at various times since has enjoyed popularity in various parts of the United States and Europe.

Although quantities are still utilized in a wide variety of industrial processes today, medical and recreational use in America has slowed to a mere trickle.

GINSENG

Will Oriental wonders never cease? First it was the egg roll, followed by the hand laundry, then acupuncture, and now the miracle of all miracles—ginseng!

Two distinct schools of thought exist about this drug (pronounced *jin-sen* or *jin-san*) from Mother Nature's medicine chest. Orientals have extolled the virtues of ginseng for practically all of recorded time, almost seven thousand years. Many Orientals, and an increasing number of Westerners, would never think of letting a day go by without their daily ginseng fix. Yet, the ever-conservative American medical community still tends to look at ginseng with a scornful and disbelieving eye. As a result, many people in this country are still unaware of the potential benefits this plant may offer.

Consider just a few of ginseng's purported values. It prolongs life, helps prevent a wide variety of diseases and disorders including anemia, diabetes, neurasthenia, and gastritis, strengthens the heart, nerves, and glands, increases and regulates the flow of hormones, increases sexual potency, reduces susceptibility to certain poisons, helps patients to regain strength after illness, improves blood circulation, aids digestion, and provides greater powers of endurance and energy. All in all, believers—many of whom are members of the world's academic and scientific communities—agree that ginseng root, when used properly, can bring about an improvement in one's overall health.

Technically, ginseng is not a medicine for the treatment of specific diseases. It does seem to help people become more disease-resistant and to feel and function better, however.

Ginseng is made from the wrinkled, shriveled root of the *Panax schinseng* plant. It is interesting to note that the Latin name *Panax* is closely related to the word "panacea"; if you believe in literal translations, that should give you some clue as to its potential benefits.

While the American pharmacological community has refused to study the drug seriously, the Russians have been giving it a close, hard look for the past seventeen years. Because of its unique qualities, they have created a new drug classification for ginseng. They call it an "adaptogen," which, by definition, means any substance that improves the ability of the organism taking it to withstand the action of a variety of adverse environmental factors. Russian cosmonauts have used ginseng during their space missions. Specific studies done by the Russians indicate that animals and people who are fed ginseng live longer, are better able to resist leukemia and other types of cancer, are better protected from the hazards of exposure to X-ray and other radiation, and are better able to withstand and recover from the debilitating effects of heart disease.

Whether you believe in the health-giving properties of ginseng or not, don't worry about giving it a try. In virtually any quantity ginseng is harmless and nontoxic. You can take it whether you feel good or not. Either way it is safe and won't do you a bit of harm.

Many ginseng devotees talk about the plant's aphrodisiac powers. Although that is still a hotly debated topic, consider this: If you feel good, you're more likely to have a good sex life, and vice versa. Thus, if ginseng can have a tonic effect on your overall well-being . . .

The major active constituents of ginseng are panaxin, panacene, panaxic acid, phenolase, amylase, schingenin, Vitamins B_1 and B_2, and saponins. Taken separately or together, these goodies can help sharpen the medulla, stimulate the heart and arteries, relax the nervous system, and promote good metabolism.

If you're planning to try ginseng, make sure you buy an effective variety, as there are many kinds from which to choose. Short of a visit to the Orient, the best place to seek the stuff out is at health-food stores. They usually stock a wide variety of types, at a range of prices to match. The very best is Korean red ginseng, the product of a long, demanding growing process that lasts six years and results from cultivation in a climate that is ideal. Strictly controlled by that country's government, Korean red ginseng is grown in specially treated soil with no chemical fertilizers added. Next best on the quality list would be Korean white ginseng. Not as good as red, but not all that bad either. American ginseng (which actually comes from a different plant, *Panax quinquefolium*) is sold for the most part to Americans and Chinese unable to afford the better varieties. Japanese ginseng is the lowest in quality. Stick with their cameras—you'll do a lot better. No matter what kind you buy, try to get wild ginseng rather than the cultivated variety, as the former is reputed to be a lot more potent.

To ingest a dose, one of several methods can be chosen. If you don't mind the bitter taste, the most effective method is chewing. Take an inch-long piece of root, about as thick as a pencil, and chew it thoroughly every three or four hours. It may be rechewed three or four times before completely losing its potency. A teaspoon of shaved root or root filaments boiled in a pint of water for about ten minutes makes a healthful ginseng tea. Sip it slowly and try to keep it in your mouth for a while, since saliva helps activate ginseng to its highest level of performance. Though your brew is done, don't throw away the leftover pulp. It can be reused several times to make more tea before it begins to lose its potency. When you are done using and reusing the pulp as the base for your drink, you can simply chew and swallow it. Good to the last drop! Powdered root can be mixed in a cup of any beverage you like, hot or cold. Use ¼ to ½ teaspoon per cup and sip slowly so that your saliva gets a chance to activate the ginseng. If your beverage seems too bitter, feel free to add sweetener, but try to avoid refined sugar, since that won't do your health much good. Some people who have been using ginseng for a long time suggest combining it with another herb, fo-ti-tieng (gotu kola), which is available in most health-food outlets.

Don't look for any unusual feeling after downing your brew or having your chew. It won't be there. You might notice some feeling of mild stimulation, but that's about it. Those who believe in ginseng don't fool around with it on a one-shot basis. It becomes a daily part of their lives, like taking vitamins. You have nothing to lose but a few cents a day, and possibly a great deal to gain.

HASHISH

COMMON NAMES: *black Russian, hash, kif, quarter moon, soles*

Hashish, the Mercedes-Benz of cannabis preparations, is a heavyweight, double-fisted version of its weaker sister, marijuana. Usually referred to as hash, it could just as easily be called giant grass or wallop weed. Both marijuana and hashish come from the same hardy plant, *Cannabis sativa*, but hash contains about eight times the amount of THC as grass. THC, delta-9-tetrahydrocannabinol, is the psychoactive ingredient that makes marijuana and hash different from ragweed or crabgrass.

The stronger potency of hash makes it the only cannabis derivative that can produce mild hallucinogenic effects. It may well be the safest trip you can take, however, since, like grass, hash is a nontoxic, nonnarcotic, natural substance that is nonaddicting. Hash produces no permanent mental or physical damage and has never caused a single substantiated death. The usual consequence of an overdose is no more than a long, deep sleep.

Hashish is processed resin from the cannabis plant, mixed with some of the plant's fiber, water, or animal and vegetable oils to bind it together. It looks like a hard lump of rock, since the resin hardens after being extracted from the mature plant. These lumps of rock come in different shapes. Some look like pebbles, some are long and rounded like fingers, others flat and slatelike. Hash can be a light ocher brown, a deeper cocoa color, or ebony black, depending on the strength of the resin and the binder used. It can be crumbly to the touch or so hard that a knife or razor blade will be needed to cut off a smokable hunk. Usually smoked in a pipe or sprinkled into tobacco or marijuana, it has a heavy cannabis smell and taste.

Most hash is smuggled into the United States from North Africa, Pakistan, Nepal, Afghanistan, and Lebanon. These mountainous areas are the world's "Hash Basket," since their similar altitudes, temperatures, and sun conditions are ideal for resin production. Cheap labor is another necessary ingredient, as hash takes an enormous number of man-hours to process. The resin is gathered in the summer months by hand-rubbing cannabis plants and forming little beads of gooey hash. Repeated rubbing forms enough beads to make balls or fingers of the sticky, aromatic stuff. When properly rubbed, the plant lives on and continues to produce resin until the seasonal rains bring an end to harvesting. Not exactly a part-time hobby, it actually takes about two months of this painstaking process to produce a single kilo (2.2 pounds) of hash for the world's waiting pipes. This laborious process also affects the drug's market price and availability. Street prices range up to $125 an ounce, or $10 a gram ($\frac{1}{28}$ of an ounce). For this higher-than-grass price one gets extra THC, up to 14 percent of it, which can be a bargain. Most weak varieties of marijuana available in America have only 1 percent of the magic ingredient, with super-potent strains containing about 4 percent.

The only proved physical effect of hashish is a reddening of the eyes and a temporary and slightly increased heartbeat. It can be an intoxicant, relaxant, mild hallucinogen, or appetite enhancer, but is so chemically and psychologically unique that it defies categorization.

When smoked, its creeping pleasant haze can be felt almost immediately. As with marijuana, it tends to act more slowly if ingested orally as an ingredient in brownies or other foods.

Effects may not be felt for an hour or so after eating hash, but be careful! It is easy to ingest too much in food form, since there is no reliable way of knowing how much is brownie and how much is hash.

Hash is usually smoked in commercially sold "hash pipes," made of wood, metal, or stone, or in exotic-looking waterpipes and hookahs, which help regulate intake while cooling the harsh smoke.

After a dose (anywhere from a few inhalations, or "tokes," to a gram) has been smoked or eaten, a heavy-headed glee may seem to paint the world a rosy pink. Such a world is a distortion of reality, of course, and distorted perceptions are commonly experienced by the toker during his one-to-three-hour high, along with an intensification of the usual marijuana effects (see Marijuana). Sense of space and time is somewhat distorted, so that what has seemed to be hours of joy may turn out to be no more than minutes.

The body tingles, or may feel weighted with lead, as the mind races chaotically in several directions at once. Smells, tastes, colors, and sounds all merge into one field of sensitivity that blends looking, eating, touching, and listening into a symphony of sensual pleasures. Waves of relaxation course through body and mind. Everything seen and done provides added enjoyment. Friends may sit together and giggle over inane remarks that seem to be the mark of genius. These are not likely to reflect anything more profound than stoned-out smiles, but the conviviality the drug causes is real. Some people turn inward, rather than outward, with their introspective fantasies, and can be left safely in a corner to ruminate over their interior monologues.

The difference between grass and hash is in the degrees of distortion they produce. With hash, that distortion may reach mild hallucinogenic proportions, not unlike a trip on a light dose of LSD or mescaline. Some people call that an overdose, others call it nirvana. It all depends on the user and his reaction to loss of reality control. Hallucinating makes the world contort and mutate into sometimes unrecognizable forms, shapes and thoughts that can either scare or amuse, depending on who you are and where you're at. Faces may look grotesque or the mind can put on a blazing light show.

Since the tripper brings his entire being with him on his journey, latent or overt psychotics or brain-damaged or emotionally disturbed people should not experiment with such extreme states of consciousness. Enjoyable, exciting delusions that one is a powerful sensory machine, for example, can, in the imbalanced or inexperienced tripper, turn into intense anxiety or paranoia—results which are neither enjoyable nor exciting. Hash by no means always causes hallucinations, but smoking enough of it or, more likely, eating a large amount can intensify the reaction to a state of mild tripping. If intake is limited, the user ends up in a gentle but insistent state of dreamy daffiness without the disorientation of hallucination.

You'll know you have an unhappy tripper on your hands if he is in a panic of confusion and delirium, a very rare psychotic reaction that happens to about five out of every thousand users. Treat the bum tripper with comfort and understanding. As with any other bad head trip, explaining to the tripper that the cause of his panic is the drug, and not something within himself, can often help. Try to change the environment. Turn on some lights if it is dark, or turn them down if they are too bright. You may want to talk to the overdoser about the problems or visions that seem so overwhelming to him. Distract him with small talk. Do not use medication. The panic lasts only as long as the high, so in less than three hours calm should prevail. When he does calm down, he may fall into a deep, comalike sleep for up to eighteen hours. Sleep is Mother Nature's way of saying you have had too much. A groggy hangover will be the only aftereffect to deal with the morning after. Memory returns, eyes clear back to white, and the room stops spinning as soon as the high wears off. Only a slight tolerance to hash accrues with heavy use. Usually the same dose will have the same effect each time. There has been no indication that hash is addictive or causes withdrawal symptoms.

Hashish has been used medically for centuries, particularly in Africa and Asia, as an anesthetic or pain reliever for dozens of common maladies. Often sifted and granulated to produce a tincture with alcohol, it was prescribed as a medicant before marijuana fear campaigns made hash an unpopular and illegal substance throughout the world. In the late nineteenth century, particularly after police cracked down on opium dens, it became quite popular in America. The death of the opium den ushered in the birth of the hashish house, where smokers could inhale the drug in elegant surroundings that enhanced the sensuous state induced by hash through the strategic placement of light, sound, and odors. Every large city had several of these plush digs for dopers. The experimenting elite flocked to these commercial halls, many of which had thriving brothels upstairs.

Earliest known use of hashish was as a ritual intoxicant in the Muslim Kingdom around 100 A.D. Associated with religious revolutionaries, it invoked the wrath and scorn of orthodox officials, who tried to ban it. Hashish was thought of as the drug of choice of various heretics, barbarians, and murderous cults, and thus was banned because of *who* was using it, rather than for *what* it was.

Hash smoke, particularly when inhaled in conjunction with tobacco smoke, can result in severe respiratory ailments, such as bronchitis. Smoke, in any form, is not likely to increase longevity, but cooling hash smoke in a water pipe may help to reduce the damage. Evidence exists that prolonged heavy use results in psychological dependence— dependence that has led to thousands of burnt-out "hash heads" congregating in Skid Row-type byways in India and North Africa. This type of obsessive and degenerative hash use is almost nonexistent in America.

The largest single headache hash causes is the very serious migraine the user is likely to get from his possible arrest and imprisonment. It is illegal in all fifty states, although the degree of enforcement and the penalties imposed upon those prosecuted and found guilty vary from one state to another. Penalties largely coincide with those governing marijuana, with fines or imprisonment of up to one year for possession of small quantities. Some states still classify hashish with more dangerous and addictive narcotics and impose correspondingly harsher sentences—up to twenty-five years. Contrary to what returning tourists may say, it is also illegal in India, Nepal, Holland, and Denmark.

In those countries, however, limited smoking may be officially tolerated in hashish bars or certain restricted areas. Most European countries can and will impose stiff sentences on unsuspecting tourists who figure on going native. Caution and a level head are always one's best allies when using illicit drugs, so bring your brains with you if contemplating the illegal.

HASH OIL

COMMON NAMES: *Afghani, black oil, cherry leb, honey oil, Indian oil, oil, red oil, smash, son of one, the one*

If hashish is the Mercedes-Benz of the cannabis world, then hash oil has got to be a slick, high-flying Rolls-Royce. An intense high produced by two or three puffs of hash oil keeps the smoker soaring above the stratosphere for about an hour.

Hash oil is a manufactured, extracted by-product of hashish or marijuana. It is produced by boiling hash or marijuana in a solvent, usually alcohol or vodka, and then filtering out any sediment or waste. This process results in a thick, gooey liquid that can be clear, yellow, dark brown, or black in color. The most potent oil available on today's market tends to be yellowish-red to the eye.

Hash oil's incredible potency is due to its very high concentration of THC, the active ingredient in cannabis preparations that gets one stoned. Where average grass has about 1 percent of this ingredient, and potent hash maybe 8 to 14 percent, oil is loaded with 15 to 30 percent THC, and that's bound to do something serious to the smoker's equilibrium.

Predictably, it takes one fifteen times further away from reality than the usual joint. The feelings of marijuana's spacy headiness and sensual distortion are all exaggerated, with energetic mini-tripping a definite possibility (see Hashish; Marijuana). As some people find the degree of sensory input and confusion too much to take, those who find hash too heavy for them should certainly avoid oil.

Drop by drop, it can be applied to joints, cigarettes, or other smokables to enhance potency. Oil is often smeared on the inside of rolling paper, then used to roll up whatever is handy. It has no distinctive telltale odor of its own. A little bit goes a long way, so only a few drops need be applied. The most economical method of using hash oil is by smoking it in an opium pipe. A small amount is smeared on the inside of the pipe bowl. The toker holds a match about a quarter of an inch below the bowl, slowly inhaling when the smear starts to bubble and emit smoke. Evaporation of the oil will be too rapid if direct flame is applied to the pipe bowl. Hash oil's overdose potential is increased when ingested orally, so extreme caution is advised when it has been mixed with such things as coffee or wine.

The result of an overdose is a paranoid or delirious panic that will be over, fortunately, when the high wears off. The aftereffects: a deep, comalike sleep lasting up to fourteen hours. The smoker wakes up a bit groggy, but healthy, and, one hopes, wise enough not to over-indulge again.

Hash oil is a nontoxic substance that causes neither drug tolerance nor drug dependence. It has not been shown to have any deleterious physical effects, and the worst one can experience is the previously described "overdose," which will leave no permanent injury. Used medically in the United States since the early nineteenth century for treatment of a range of problems from menstrual cramps to migraines (prior to becoming illegal), it is still used therapeutically in Asia and the Middle East today.

Most domestic oil is refined from imported hashish in underground laboratories across the United States. It is usually sold in tiny glass vials containing anywhere from 1 to 5 grams of the expensive liquid. Considering that one gram can get perhaps fifty people high, its cost—about $25 to $60 for a gram at current market prices—is not considered prohibitive. Hash oil has also been refined into a white crystalline extract, sold as "THC," and packs a walloping 60 percent of the stuff in its powder. Not only is it minimally available, and often mislabeled, but its cost is as astronomical as its reputed effects—$20 to $30 per dose. Hash oils must also be kept refrigerated to avoid rapid deterioration and loss of potency. Failure to do so can result in oil that is weaker than the common joint.

Don't get so lost in oil's purported magic you forget that it is illegal in every state of the union and all foreign countries as well. The penalties in America are similar to those for simple marijuana or hashish possession—anywhere from six months to three years for a first offense.

HAWAIIAN BABY WOOD ROSE

Those too stoned or impatient to count out hundreds of morning-glory seeds may find Hawaiian baby wood rose (*Argyreia nervosa*), another legal member of the bindweed family, easier to handle.

Because these seeds are so large, it only takes from four to eight to get the tripper on his way. The immature seeds from this plant contain a healthy dose of lysergic acid amides, strychnine, and several other alkaloids. Both in terms of effect and chemistry, Hawaiian baby wood rose is almost identical to the more potent varieties of LSD-like morning-glory seeds.

Preparation of a dose requires two pods (there are four seeds in each). When removed, the seeds are found to be coated with a white fuzz containing strychnine and can be mildly sickening if eaten. Washing and scrubbing the seeds with a toothbrush or nailbrush will remove the fuzz (don't forget to wash the toothbrush before using it again). Cleaned seeds can then be chewed thoroughly and swallowed. The seeds may be ground to a powder with any appropriate kitchen appliance and put into large gelatin capsules.

A Hawaiian baby wood rose trip can last for hours or days. The tripper should be sure he's in a place that's comfortable, familiar, and peaceful. Eliminating noise and/or noisy people helps one to enjoy the trip. Too much boring chatter proves to be annoying and disconcerting.

First effects of the drug are realized in about an hour. If nausea is experienced to an uncomfortable degree, vomiting should be induced, as the cause may be strychnine ingestion. The psychoactive effect of Hawaiian baby wood rose will not be minimized in such an instance.

Once past the nausea, a feeling of peaceful bliss begins to take hold. The LSD-like trip lasts about three to four hours. A feeling of contentment and ease may linger on for days longer.

Hawaiian baby wood rose seeds are most effective when taken on an empty stomach, so users should skip the luau beforehand. High doses should be avoided unless the tripper is prepared to say aloha forever.

HELIOTROPE

COMMON NAMES: *turnsole*

Nature's garden, not to mention your own, is chock full of little goodies that can either bring people up or take them down.

Heliotrope (*Valeriana officinalis*), for example, is a common garden plant that is a moderately potent sedative and tranquilizer.

It only takes about ½ ounce of the roots or rhizomes of this plant, boiled in a covered pot for five minutes and strained, to make a tea that is drinkable. The problem with heliotrope brew is its smell. Phew! Strong enough to make even the boldest wince, the taste of the tea is tolerable, however—particularly if a bit of artificial sweetener or honey is added.

If one's nose still can't deal with the smell after straining, the brew can be boiled down to a thick gummy residue. Then a small amount of flour is added and the mixture is put into a gelatine capsule for ingestion.

The active constituents of heliotrope are chatinine, valeric, and valerine.

HENBANE

Henbane is a hairy, sticky member of the potato family. Getting involved with this stuff can be sticky business, too.

The plant can be found in sandy areas of Europe or growing wild in several parts of the United States. Seeds and dried leaves are sometimes smoked in India and Africa. The crushed roots can also be brewed into tea.

Chemically, henbane (*Hyoscyamus niger*) is very similar to datura. It has a high content of hyoscyamine, which is very much like atropine but acts twice as powerfully in its effect upon the peripheral nervous system. Henbane also contains scopolamine and several other tropanes.

In addition to producing mind-blowing visual hallucinations and a feeling of being drunk or sedated, the drug brings along a variety of dangerous and unpleasant effects: dizziness, confusion, nausea, diarrhea, pounding headache, blackout, and amnesia, to name just a few. Medieval witches, who often used henbane as a kicker in their cauldron brews, claimed the drug was capable of causing permanent insanity. Hardly worth the trip!

HEROIN

COMMON NAMES: *big H, blanks, boy, brother, brown, brown sugar, caballo, ca-ca, Chinese red, chiva, cobics, crap, doojee, dope, flea powder, goods, H, hard stuff, Harry, horse, joy powder, junk, ka-ka, Mexican mud, poison, scag, scar, schmeck, shit, skag, smack, smeck, snow, stuff, sugar, tecaba, thing, white stuff*

That pretty red poppy growing in the window box alongside the gladiolus has a not-so-pretty side to it called heroin. Actually, calling heroin not-so-pretty is like calling a nuclear explosion a nuisance. Heroin is the king of narcotics and the drug of choice of America's addict population. If the drug doesn't get you, the lifestyle will . . . ask any addict who's been using the stuff for thirty years, if you can find one that old.

Heroin is a white or brown, crystal-like, odorless, bitter-tasting soluble powder. The color depends on its origin: Mexican heroin is brown, Middle Eastern and Asian junk is white.

The drug is made by scraping the residue of poppies, boiling the gum into opium, then extracting morphine, which is ultimately converted to pure heroin. All of this can be done using nothing more than simple, inexpensive laboratory equipment.

The easily cultivated poppy grows primarily in Mexico, Turkey, China, and India, and in Burma, Laos, and Thailand, whose plentiful poppy fields have been dubbed the Golden Triangle. This name has more to do with the money to be made from heroin than with the drug's effects. It is a semi-synthetic derivative of morphine, but is up to three times as potent as morphine, and much more addictive. Heroin is a narcotic analgesic of the opiate class, which means it is a stupor-producing painkiller derived from opium. The multiple-step process of its manufacture results in a white powder combination of heroin mixed with sugar, talcum powder, Epsom salts, mannite or mannibol (a weak laxative), soap powder, quinine, or strychnine. Actually, any white powder can be mixed in, and often is, with sometimes disastrous results.

Heroin was first commercially produced in Germany around the turn of the century. Initially it was used as a substitute for the proved addictives, morphine and codeine. The drug was assumed to be so benign that it was prescribed as an alternative to liquor for chronic alcoholics. Heroin was also prescribed as a cough suppressant and sold over the counter in patent medicines for pain relief, and as a sleep-inducing tranquilizer. It suppresses coughs, all right, along with everything else controlled by the central nervous system. Intestinal muscles contract, causing severe, chronic constipation. Eye pupils constrict. Some theorize it depresses certain brain areas, reducing normal thirst and hunger desires, although this hypothesis has not been proved with certainty.

What has been proved beyond a shadow of a doubt is that heroin is highly addictive, and a habit can be picked up in as little as a week to three weeks of daily or frequent use. Physical dependence and a tolerance to the drug are the hallmarks of addiction. Such physical dependence leaves the addict with waves of withdrawal pain if he fails to get his necessary dose every four to six hours. What is considered "necessary" depends on how much heroin the addict has been using and for how long. First-time users may begin with a dose of 2–8 mg, but addicts can use as much as 450 mg each day as tolerance is acquired.

All addicts and some users inject themselves with a syringe, sometimes primitive and homemade, after diluting the heroin with a small amount of water in a teaspoon with a bent handle or a small metal bottle cap and dissolving it under the heat of a match. The drug can be injected intravenously into any vein, using a belt as a tourniquet to make a vein stand out, or subcutaneously by skin-popping just barely under the skin surface. Injection is called "mainlining" and is the preferred route, since none of the costly heroin is wasted and the initial rush of the drug is enhanced. Some addicts mix cocaine or speed (amphetamines) with their heroin; such mixtures are called speedballs or bombitas. Junk can also be sniffed or smoked. Smoking is sometimes considered too uneconomical, since much of the drug can escape into the air. All these methods can lead to addiction, though it may take the sniffers and smokers a longer time to get hooked. An incalculable number of weekend snorters, called chippers, seem to manage occasional use without getting addicted, although some do.

Why do half a million Americans risk life and limb playing Russian Roulette with these building blocks of death? Each of those thousands of users thought that he would be the one to escape the curse of addiction by using heroin indefinitely as a weekend supercocktail—and what a cocktail it is, a least at the beginning.

The first-time experimenter may feel some initial nausea or may even vomit, but when he adjusts to it, he will feel an immediate surging, pulsating euphoria and excitement as the bubbly liquid shoots through his veins. The ritual of shooting up, for most addicts, is close to an orgasmic rush, with the same postcoital feelings of peace, relief, satisfaction, and physical warmth following the initial blaze of joy. So the user tries for nirvana again, and again, and again—but once he's addicted the balloon bursts and that euphoric glaze disappears.

After the body develops a tolerance to the drug's sweetly depressant effects, a craving remains that is far from orgasmic. With prolonged use, the addict shoots up only to stave off the crushing ache and misery of withdrawal. His fix dulls all the pain and joy of reality as he becomes drowsy, lethargic, apathetic, and detached. He can ignore the world for several hours, until it is time to hustle for his next dose or fix. Things the rest of us consider vital—like food or sex or crossing the street—are of little or no importance to him. His mind is a leaded and relaxed blob. Continued use of the drug does nothing positive for him except erase pain, anxiety, fear, and depression, as it erases all human feeling. He becomes a passive junk machine, ingesting and reingesting oblivion just to keep running. The junkie knows it's time for his next fix because his skin begins to itch. He sweats profusely, his nose runs, he gets an upset stomach or cramps, hot flushes and chills, watery eyes, dilated pupils, and double vision. The only thing that will make the pain and fear of increasing pain go away is more heroin, so the junkie shoots up again.

Since dosage must increase merely to suppress pain, the addict uses more while enjoying it less. If he does not get his fix in three to eight hours he will enter the withdrawal phase, the nightmare of all addicts. For three or four days he will be caught in a maze of delirium, cold sweats, hot flashes, pain, violent yawning, nausea, diarrhea, cramps, tremors, depression, rapid breathing, fever, weakness, loss of appetite, crying, sneezing, headaches, and seizures. An almost indescribable ordeal, it is referred to as "cold turkey," because the skin feels like that of a plucked fowl and the body a frigid wasteland.

Heroin itself does not cause inevitable mental or physical deterioration or permanent brain damage. The user can retain normal coordination and judgment, but is subject to a host of maladies from the injection of the drug and its corollary effects. Use of dirty or shared needles can cause infectious or serum hepatitis, septicemia (blood poisoning that leads to abscesses in the blood vessls), and subacute bacterial endocarditis. Tetanus, gangrene, lockjaw, and cardiovascular and lung abnormalities are not uncommon occurrences. Abuse of the veins can result in their collapse or clotting and a resultant deadening of the limbs. Sleep may be fitful and a heavy dose can lead to unconsciousness. Because the addict is impervious to pain and hunger, his general physical condition is usually poor. Inadequate nutrition and the inability to cough can lead to malnutrition, pneumonia, and chronic bronchitis. The addict has frequent accidents and may meet a violent death, either in the pursuit of his supply or as a result of his detachment from reality. Heroin addiction can cause severe obstetrical complications, including giving birth to a child addicted as a fetus.

Adulterants used to cut pure heroin can cause pulmonary edema, so it is no surprise to learn that the premature death rate for addicts is twice that of the nonuser population. The abuser can suffer shock, respiratory failure, or oxygen starvation of the brain and enter a coma. Whether or not heroin itself is toxic and capable of causing death through an overdose is the subject of a current raging controversy. Little valid information exists as to the cause of death among addicts. Most medical examiners still refer to heroin overdose without any proof that such a condition exists; for many years it was assumed that a dead junkie found on the floor with a needle in his arm had merely overdosed. This assumption has been challenged recently. Tests on animals have shown that there is no such thing as a lethal heroin dose. A "lethal" dose for one addict on a certain day may not be lethal to another on a different day. Theories exist that heroin itself is not the killer. Perhaps it is the quinine adulterant, a lack of sufficient dosage, or the shocklike effect caused by the injection of crude heroin mixtures. Most theorists in this uncharted territory believe that the most likely contributor to death is the injection of heroin while the user is drunk on alcohol or sedated with barbiturates. Lives could be saved if addicts were informed of the lethal crap game they play in the form of multiple drug use.

There is an effective medical treatment for the serious overdose symptoms of abusers. The user should be taken immediately to a hospital, where Narcan or Nalline can be administered to reverse heroin's severe depressant effects. Most junkies still believe that injecting milk or saltwater fluid will stem the tide. This folk remedy is not only ineffective, but can lead to complications such as coma, brain damage, severe lung swelling, and the ultimate complication, death.

Previously described sensations and symptoms relate to the drug's actual properties. There is another whole list of likely effects caused by the lifestyle of the user, not the heroin he's injecting. These effects apply to the dog-eat-dog existence of the average street junkie, who pays inflated prices in the black market for his diluted and adulterated fix, and must run the gauntlet of ghetto crime and disease just to stay alive. There are also many middle-class, "respectable" addicts who get their legal opiate supply from the pharmacist. A high rate of such addiction exists among health professionals: doctors, their wives or husbands, nurses, and druggists, who can easily and quietly feed their habits for pennies a day. Although these users are no less addicted, society saves its scorn for the stereotypical junkie—the minority-member street runner, who steals, lies, cheats, or sells to other addicts in order to get his next fix. The street junkie's degrading and degenerative lifestyle is not caused by heroin, but by its lack of legal availability. When it is readily available as opiates can be for middle-class professionals, the drug does not have to affect the user's life, family, or job in a negative way.

Heroin tends to reduce aggression. Most crimes associated with it are crimes against property, not people. A street addict's habit can cost from $40 to over $100 a day in nickel ($5) or dime ($10) bags, or small amounts of heroin in glassine envelopes called decks. In order to keep the supply coming, the junkie must steal property worth five times the money needed, since a dealer in stolen goods is likely to pay only a small fraction of the property's actual value. That accounts for a lot of TV sets, stereos, and jewelry missing from middle- and upper-class homes across the country. To some degree, it is the unmentioned tax we pay for refusing to deal rationally with the heroin problem. We are treating a medical and sociological problem as a legal one, punishing the victim for being sick. This approach to drug control has never worked. Even law-enforcement officials admit their annual crackdowns on heroin smuggling and use have not made a dent in the number of new users or the drug's availability. The only clear effect of such action is reflected in the price of the drug, which shoots sky-high during heroin panics, requiring the street junkie to steal more and more cameras and furs to feed his never-relenting habit.

Heroin is big business, both to organized crime and to law enforcement. A $40 kilo (2.2 pounds) of Turkish opium seeds can be processed into heroin having a street value of about $45,000. The optimal drug for smuggling, its white powder is both highly potent and low in bulk. Cost of government control is astronomical. Government spends about $1 billion a year to play cat and mouse with the addict population. Society pays for the illegality of heroin to the tune of some $4 billion a year in stolen property. The addict pays for it by his physical deterioration and his obsessive focus on a route to his next fix. The only thing the street addict can think about is planning the next burglary or conning his fellow junkies into parting with their life-sustaining elixir. Nobody wins in the current system of heroin distribution except the top-level producers and sellers, who rake in billions a year as a result of heroin's illegal status.

The American heroin story was not always rooted in a punitive and puritanical legal approach. During the late nineteenth century there were more opiate addicts in this country than there are today. Since morphine, opium, and heroin were routinely prescribed for coughs, headaches, and menstrual cramps, it should come as no surprise to learn that the overwhelming majority of users were women and children. Addiction was not seen as a scourge on society, since users continued their daily routines and the legal cost of such drugs was affordable. Though not exactly viewed as a social plus, addiction was tolerated somewhat as closet alcoholism is today.

In 1914, Congress passed the Harrison Narcotics Act, which required opiate producers and sellers to apply for a license and register for a newly imposed tax on the drugs. Cumbersome licensing, tax, and recordkeeping regulations discouraged doctors from prescribing the drugs. By 1924, federal law prohibited all domestic manufacture of heroin, and the black market swelled. The government set up legal narcotics-dispensing clinics for existing addicts, but unfortunately, poor diagnosis, distribution, and administration led to their demise before the effect of free heroin could be accurately measured. The junkie population did not just fade away, however; rather, it entered the netherworld of crime and addiction.

After World War II, the number of addicts grew as morphine and other opiates (see Morphine; Opium), prescribed for the pain of battlefield injuries, became a necessity for the Stateside veteran. Alarming numbers of Vietnam veterans returned as casualties of heroin addiction. Their battlefield days and nights were so full of dread and fear that locally produced, high-grade heroin, available for a few cents a dose, seemed the likely cure.

Affluent, cynical, suburban flower children of the sixties and seventies accounted for the next wave of addicts, in large part because of the official misinformation being spread about *all* drugs. When Uncle Sam continued to rail about the dangers of marijuana and hallucinogens, long after youthful users had tried these drugs themselves and repudiated such scare stories, information about the dangers of heroin also came to be questioned. The logical conclusion reached was that "official" drug information was not to be trusted, and so heroin was thought to be far safer than touted.

The law today includes stiff penalties for heroin use and sale, and coordinating statutes for civil commitment to rehabilitation centers in lieu of imprisonment. The federal law provides for one year in jail or a $5,000 fine for first-offender users, and two years or $10,000 for subsequent heroin infractions. Under Schedule I of the Federal Controlled Substances Act, manufacture or sale of heroin the first time out brings a maximum of fifteen years in jail or a $25,000 fine, and the second time can lead to thirty years or a $50,000 fine. State laws vary, but most of them subscribe to the Uniform Narcotics Act, making heroin convictions a felony. New York, with the largest number of addicts (some estimates place as many as half the nation's addicts there), has recently tried draconian measures that can get even a small-time dealer or possessor a mandatory one-year-to-life sentence. To the surprise of no one except the legislators, such penalties have not deterred continued heroin use. The misleadingly simple explanation for the failure of law in this area is the absolute fact that heroin is *addicting*. Society is misled into believing that heroin addiction is curable and within the control of a user who sincerely wants to change. Experts have documented a universal reaction to addiction, even after many years of abstinence, that goes a long way toward proving that personal willpower is not a rational or even possible solution. The addict can withdraw and detoxify with any number of medical aids, or even by using the cold-turkey approach, but almost always he will be subject to the postaddiction syndrome. Although research in this area is spotty, we do know that even after withdrawal the craving for heroin can and usually does recur, particularly during times of anxiety or when an "ex-addict" is confronted with former junkie friends and neighborhoods. Scientists speculate that a potential physical craving, as well as a strong psychological desire, may be caused by permanent biochemical changes in the abstinent "ex-addict." The almost nonexistent success rate of the various treatments should lead us to reconsider the nature, cause, and effect of addiction. Unfortunately, it may be true that once an addict, always an addict, and that the best possible treatment is the substitution of one drug for another. No emancipation proclamation has yet been devised that will successfully free the junkie from the slavery of addiction and relapse and lead him to a normal, drug-free state.

One course of treatment has been by detoxification, through the facilities of a number of centers now available for addicts for this purpose. The detoxification phase can be eased, and the pain of withdrawal reduced, by the injection or ingestion of methadone, LAAM (see LAAM; Methadone), or Darvon-N, each of which acts to reverse heroin's effects and to block the usual insatiable craving. However, these antagonists are themselves addictive and subject to abuse through overdosage and street resale. The use of megavitamins also seems to alleviate the physical shock of withdrawal. Unfortunately, after detoxification, the "ex-addict" is still plagued by that gnawing craving. Without constant crisis intervention and supervision, he is likely to return to heroin. In order to keep expenses down, many addicts detoxify regularly and then, just as regularly, return to their miserable treadmills.

Another "answer" has been incarceration, on the theory that punishment and enforced abstinence will work some miracle on the addict. Such deterrence treatment has not worked, however, because many prisons have a thriving drug trade among guards, visitors, and inmates. More important, when the "ex-addict" is released he invariably returns to his old haunts and his old friend, heroin, in response to that postaddiction syndrome of anxiety, discomfort and depression.

Then there is the growing number of therapeutic communities, known as TCs, which create a rigid but protective environment for addicts, who often enter into such programs under the threat of incarceration. These communities, such as Phoenix House, Daytop, and Synanon, strive for total drug-free behavior modification by teaching nutritional habits and vocational skills and encourage searing personal revelations through encounter therapy, peer-group pressure, and rap sessions. Infractions of the rules lead to expulsion for those who have not dropped out during the first week. The therapeutic communities are generally run by "ex-addicts" who, it is felt, have the only nitty-gritty experience the addict-initiate respects. These "ex-addicts" often lecture to schools or church groups citing their own recoveries to validate the success of such communities. As their own records disclose, however, the problem is that the only addicts who seem to be cured are those who still reside within the community, subject to constant pressure. Relapse figures of those who "graduate" are as dismal as for any other course of treatment. Once again, the simple fact that heroin is *addicting*, and likely to remain so even after withdrawal, is forgotten in the rush to find a "cure." It is particularly dangerous to preach the gospel of cures to schoolchildren and other potential users, since there is no evidence that a drug-free solution exists. They may foolishly experiment with heroin under the mistaken belief that even if they become hooked, they will be able ultimately to leave their addictions by the wayside.

Methadone maintenance is the latest miracle to come down the heroin-cure pike. While, in fact, it may be the most effective treatment available today, it is by no means without its pitfalls. Methadone is a synthetic chemical mixture that not only lessens the torturous craving for heroin, but actually blocks heroin's dizzying rushes and pleasures, just in case the addict tries to mix his old friend with his new medicine. Originally, it was thought that large amounts of methadone could be administered by tablet or liquid to the detoxifying addict and then continued in ever-decreasing amounts until it could be totally eliminated. The addict, it was assumed, could then walk out the clinic door drug-free with a good chance for long-term recovery if he just exercised willpower over his nasty habit. Again, the realities of the nature of addiction were dismissed. "Ex-addicts" who walked out the door with all good intentions quickly succumbed to that inner voice screaming for heroin. Methadone treatment is now generally considered to be a lifelong maintenance plan, and its problems do not stop there. Methadone is itself addictive, and the addict is justifiably wary of trading his existing problem for an unknown bag full of authorized junk. Although one taking methadone can perform all normal functions without having to direct his life toward his next burglary or mugging, he must report to a clinic on a daily basis to receive his dose of methadone or face a milder form of withdrawal. Many areas of the United States have yet to open full-service methadone clinics, and others have long waiting lists of the walking dead. The returns on methadone (and the even newer LAAM) are not yet in, and no accurate information as to "success rate" will be available for many years.

There is one "solution" that has not been tried for fifty years, although it is recommended by such groups as the American Medical Association, the American Bar Association, the National Council of Churches, and *The Wall Street Journal*, and was backed by President Kennedy's Advisory Commission on Narcotic and Drug Abuse. The idea of legalizing or decriminalizing heroin in some manner, either by establishing special dispensaries or permitting it to be prescribed, has been floating around ever since the American heroin clinics were abandoned as unworkable in the 1920s. The British system of heroin maintenance is often cited as a model of sane drug policy. Since 1924,

England has had an addict-registration program, under which any registered opiate addict can receive a prescription for his drug of choice. Dosage cost per day is thus reduced to pennies, virtually putting the black market out of business. Drug-related crime is substantially reduced as well, since there is no longer any need to steal. The incidence of new addicts decreased once heroin lost some of its non-existent "glamour" and no longer had to be "pushed" for profit. Having only a handful of nonregistered addicts to police, law-enforcement personnel have been able to spend their time on the lookout for diverted prescriptions, ensuring a minimal number of newcomers to the addict ranks.

By American standards, the British had only a handful of addicts and a small black market to begin with. By the mid-1960s, as alarmist anti-drug propaganda rose to a crescendo of worldwide hysteria, Britain began to believe that a heroin epidemic was imminent, and adjusted its heroin maintenance program. In addition to allowing heroin to be dispensed by certified and specially trained doctors or drug clinics, Britain also encourages methadone treatment and drug-free goals.

Although much controversy surrounds the effectiveness of the British system, it has never made the mistake of trying to keep the addict population from its opiate supply, and so has never denied a true realization of the nature of addiction.

The U.S. government has tried paying Turkish poppy growers to abolish their crops. Rehabilitation has been offered to Vietnam vets, methadone and drug-free programs to convicted felons. Uncle Sam has proselytized against heroin in schools, the armed forces, and at the United Nations. At the same time, the government has prosecuted violators of the laws it created and has crowded the prisons with thousands of sick addicts. All these "solutions" have failed.

Should the United States try a free-heroin system? If the experts are right, it appears that the psychological and physiological imperatives of addiction make it impossible to dream of a world of drug-free ex-addicts. Certainly dispensing heroin through regulated distribution would reduce organized crime's bloated treasury and the disgraceful exploitation of the addict. In the end, the tax we all pay in stolen peace of mind and property would be lowered, and addicts might return to the taxpayer rolls as productive members of society.

HOPS

Long used as a flavoring in the beer-brewing process, hops are now becoming well known among druggies. The plant (*Humulus lupulus*) contains lupuline, a yellow resinous powder that is the closest chemical relative to THC, the psychoactive ingredient in marijuana.

Not only is the hop plant a legal relative of cannabis, but it will get users reasonably stoned. If smoked in the form of a joint, the sweet-sour, flaky fruiting parts of the plant will produce a mild, grasslike high accompanied by a feeling of peace and serenity.

If you'd like to try hops for their sedative qualities, bring out the old teapot. Simply steep an ounce of dried hops flakes in a pint of water, let the brew stand for about two hours, strain out the excess flakes, and drink a tablespoonful before each meal and before hitting the hay at night. Just like counting sheep . . . zzz-zzz!

Hops should not be abused, especially if you're the sensitive type. Too much taken over too long a period of time might begin to produce some side effects such as dizziness, an intoxicated feeling, and symptoms of jaundice.

Those with a green thumb might be interested in the fact that the hop vine can be successfully grafted to marijuana root stock. What the grower ends up with is a hop vine loaded with marijuana's active resins. The crushed, dried leaves work as potently as grass when smoked. However, the plant looks just like a legal hop vine, keeping the curious from knowing what is being raised in the grower's garden of delights.

Hop cuttings are now difficult to obtain, since the government has asked growers not to sell them to the general public. But there's no law against trying, and the effort might well be worth the home cultivator's legal while.

HYDRANGEA

COMMON NAME: *seven barks*

Hydrangea (*Hydrangea paniculata grandiflora*), one of the favorite shrubs of American gardeners, has leaves that can be rolled into joints that will either get one very stoned or very sick. And that's where the problem lies.

The stuff that gives hydrangea its kick is a chemical member of the cyanide family (remember those little pills spies always carried to take in case they got caught?). Cyanide can be very toxic.

If intake is limited to one joint, the smoker will probably achieve a pleasant, marijuana-like high along with a slightly drunken feeling. Smoking hydrangea leaves too often or in excessive quantities, however, may produce more cyanide than the body can comfortably handle, and the dividing line between enough and too much is a fine one, indeed.

If the poison build up is too great, big trouble can develop. Let a word to the wise be sufficient: Keep away from this one. If your curiosity does get the better of you, know your limit or you may end up as dead as the proverbial cat.

IBOGA

The iboga (*Tabernanthe iboga*), an equatorial African forest shrub found in both the Congo and Gabon, has been popular for hundreds of years among the natives, who have used it as a divinatory agent, stimulant, and aphrodisiac.

Iboga belongs to a group of substances known as indole alkaloids and, while different, is a cousin of the better-known indoles LSD, yohimbine, and psilocybin. The bark of the shrub and its roots contain 6 percent mixed indole alkaloids, of which the main active constituent is ibogaine, a stimulant and hallucinogen. Ibogaine is illegal in the United States, although the reason for this has never been clear.

Effects of iboga vary greatly depending upon dosage. A low dose of about one gram of bark or roots can act as an aphrodisiac, or even as a cure for impotency. Users claim that iboga gives them strength enough to engage in nonstop sexual activity for anywhere from six to seventeen hours. The drug also acts as a stimulant that increases muscle strength and endurance. Tribesmen find this most helpful when they are out hunting, for it enables them to remain awake, mentally alert, and able to stand in a motionless state for up to forty-eight hours at a time—bad news for any lion that might happen by.

The psychedelic effects of iboga, comparable to a heavy mescaline trip, become evident at a dosage level of 300 mg. Users experience the unique state of dreaming without any loss of consciousness. For this reason, many feel iboga could be a boon to the psychiatric community if the ban on the drug is ever lifted.

In order for one actually to hallucinate, a very high dose is required, and that can cause definite problems. In addition to his hallucinations, the user may shriek in a maniacal fashion (thought to be a form of prophecy by the natives) and end up in a taut, unpleasant, epileptic-like state. When dosage is overdone to a toxic level, iboga may bring on convulsions, paralysis, and even death from respiratory failure. Because of these dangerous side effects, natives rarely use iboga for the express purpose of hallucinating except as a part of rare religious rites. More often, they stick to low doses to experience the drug's aphrodisiac and stimulant effects only.

Iboga can be ingested by thoroughly chewing and swallowing about a gram of the shrub's roots, stripped from the bark, or by boiling with water into a tea.

INHALANTS: GLUE, SOLVENTS, AEROSOLS

COMMON NAME: *gunk*

Sniffing glue as an intoxicant was a phenomenon virtually unknown in the United States until 1959, when stories published in the Denver *Post* served as an unintended introduction and lure. Most of these stories concerned toluene, the active ingredient in model-airplane glue commonly used by youngsters. Newspaper accounts informed readers that sniffing could get them high, and pictures were provided demonstrating how to inhale glue. Toluene was purported to cause severe brain damage and death. In reality, such damage is generally found only in extreme industrial situations where workers are exposed to fumes on an all-day basis for extended periods of time, or where substantial quantities of the chemical are swallowed.

Soon after journalistic accounts first appeared, glue sniffing rose to epidemic proportions in Denver. As newspapers across the nation jumped on the bandwagon by further publicizing sniffing, similar epidemics broke out in other urban areas. By 1966, thousands of arrests had resulted.

Medical authorities were claiming that toluene would not only permanently dull the brain and possibly kill the inhaler but also that it could cause murderous impulses, burned-out nose membranes, gallbladder perforations, bone-marrow destruction, kidney damage, sexual promiscuity, homosexuality, damage to the respiratory organs and liver, blindness, robbery, and rape.

Interest in glue sniffing prompted many youngsters to experiment with inhalation of a variety of petroleum-based products as well. By 1971, newspaper stories had also aroused curiosity toward aerosol propellants, sprayed into paper bags or balloons, then inhaled to yield a floating high comparable to that produced by nitrous oxide.

A broad range of inhalants, each capable of producing a deliriant high, are used by a small, devoted following of young people across the nation—primarily male minority-group members between the ages of eight and sixteen. These vapors are found in common products such as airplane glue, model cement, varnish, varnish remover, cigarette lighter fluid, charcoal lighter, transmission fluid, gasoline, paint, enamel, lacquer, paint thinner, hair spray, deodorant, window cleaner,

101

spot remover, dry-cleaning agents, glass chillers, fingernail polish and remover, and spray-on cooking lubricants.

Sniffing, or "huffing," fumes from these or related substances produces effects similar to those caused by alcohol, as well as hallucinations when ingested in high doses. Effects can include euphoria, numbness, restlessness, confusion, excitement, disorientation, and loss of coordination. Repeated inhalation may cause giddiness, dizziness, distortion of space and time, alterations in color perception, and feelings of omnipotence or great strength. If overdone, nausea, vomiting, unconsciousness, fatigue, muscular weakness, stomach pain, weight loss, tremor, ataxia, itching, fear, loneliness, guilt, neuritis, peripheral and cranial nerve paralysis, delirium, and coma may follow.

With all the scare stories in print, one might wonder why children use such substances. First and foremost, because they create a "high" —a pleasing, euphoric, inebriated feeling—by depressing the central nervous system. Second, they are easy to obtain, while other intoxicants such as alcohol and marijuana are difficult for young children to get. Finally, many children do not believe the information about sniffing which emanates from establishment sources.

As far as the purported dangers of inhalants are concerned— particularly those attributed to the use of toluene—most stories have been gross exaggerations and distortions. Reported deaths have almost always proved to be indirectly related to use of toluene, and generally have resulted from causes such as asphyxiation in plastic bags during inhalation. While no one is presently endorsing glue sniffing as safe, serious damage does not seem to occur until relatively high doses are taken over a prolonged period of time. Even then, most adverse effects may be reversed by discontinuing use.

Normal glue-sniffing dosage is one or two tubes per several-hour session, producing a high for fifteen minutes to a few hours. Inhalation of vapors from a bag or balloon is the most common method, although users may also sniff solvent-soaked rags or handkerchiefs to produce the desired result.

Tolerance can develop with weekly use over a period of about three months, requiring increasingly higher doses to produce the same effect. In rare instances, huffers have been known to use as many as twenty to forty tubes per session. Physical addiction is unknown, although psychological dependence can possibly develop in extremely frequent users.

While stories about glue sniffing have been based, for the most part, upon false or exaggerated information, some other inhalants can cause real problems. Lead poisoning may result from inhaling vapors found in paint, transmission fluid, and other lead-based petroleum products. Some believe that freon, a common aerosol propellant, may freeze the lungs and larynx when inhaled, causing respiratory arrest. Oily sprays, such as Pam, can coat the inside of the lungs and result in asphyxiation. Inhalants sometimes speed the heart to a point where it cannot handle extreme physical stress. Running, playing, and engaging in other strenuous activities after deeply inhaling solvents or aerosols have resulted in heart failure and death.

Breathing sufficient amounts of oxygen along with an inhalant generally minimizes the possibility of death. Even when too little oxygen is provided, the user normally becomes unconscious long before a lethal level can be reached. Unconsciousness prevents the huffer from inhaling more vapor and thus acts as a natural barrier to overdose. If loss of consciousness results, fresh air should be provided. When the overdoser awakens he should be calmly "talked down" in a well-ventilated, relaxed environment, free of bright lights and loud noise, until he has fully recovered.

Contrary to popular belief, permanent brain damage resulting from glue sniffing has not been proved, although some authorities contend this danger may exist for those who are heavy or regular indulgers.

At present, there are no federal laws pertaining to sale or possession of glue, aerosols, solvents, and related substances. Some states and municipalities have statutes prohibiting sale to minors.

Is sniffing a real problem or a manufactured one? Only additional research will answer the question. It does appear, however, that dangers related to it have been largely exaggerated over the years. When used excessively, some inhalants do present the potential for real danger. As with all drugs, only when we present our young people with a truthful, accurate picture of inhalants can we expect them to adopt a sensible, rational attitude toward their use.

(For additional inhalant information, see Chloroform; Ether; Nitrous Oxide.)

JIMSON WEED

COMMON NAMES: *devil's apple, devil's trumpet, devil's weed, loco-weed, stinkweed, thorn apple, white man's plant, yerba del diablo*

Datura stramonium, Jimson weed, is the best-known species of datura found in the United States. Growing profusely in fields, vacant lots, and along the nation's roadsides, it can also be found in the wilds of Mexico and parts of India.

With its large, thin, dark-green leaves and bell-shaped white or light purple flowers, this rank-smelling plant is a member of the potato family and a close relative of belladonna, mandrake, and henbane. It is loaded with several alkaloids: atropine, hyoscyamine, mandragorine, and scopolamine, and when smoked or eaten, can produce a truly hallucinogenic experience. For most people, however, the trip will prove to be a bummer.

First effects begin in about twenty minutes. Along with some periods of euphoria, chills and fever accompanied by a bit of nausea and diarrhea may be experienced. Soon, if the user is not too confused to tell what is happening, he will note some loss of coordination, a dry burning sensation in the mouth, difficulty talking or swallowing, dry hot skin, rash, scaling, vomiting, and loss of memory, along with dizziness, pressure in the head, agitation, and severe visual blurring and distortion. If a high enough dose is taken, hallucinations will follow. These hallucinations can often be more intense than those experienced while on LSD, lasting up to several days, and, in rare cases, followed by convulsions or coma. Other side effects include mental disorientation and feelings of extreme panic. The whole business is pretty much a downer.

Jimson weed, legal in the United States, is not physically addictive, although it can make the user psychologically dependent. After prolonged regular use, larger and larger doses become necessary to achieve the same desired effects. While the body builds a tolerance to the drug the heart does not, and will ultimately suffer severe damage. The alkaloids in Jimson weed are extremely potent and dangerous, easily capable of causing death from respiratory failure.

KAVA KAVA

COMMON NAMES: *ava, awa, kava, kawa, kawa kawa, wati, yagona*

For centuries kava kava has been the favorite social drug of natives throughout the South Pacific. Kava kava is actually a drink made from the root pulp and lower stems of a tall shrub, *Piper methysticum*, which has the odor of lilac and is a member of the pepper family native to Hawaii, New Guinea, and the South Pacific Islands. It has been used over the years for a variety of purposes: as a ceremonial brew, medicine, and just something to make one feel good. While kava kava is powerful, strangely enough it is generally acknowledged by scientists to be harmless.

Before missionaries came to the South Pacific, kava kava enjoyed widespread popularity. The missionaries convinced the natives that the pleasure-giving drink should be forbidden, however, and for a while, it was replaced, by and large, by alcohol, a far more dangerous drug. Nowadays, kava kava seems to be making a well-received comeback. In many Pacific areas it is actually being used to wean the fallen from their Western-inspired habit of alcoholism.

The ingredients that give kava kava its kick are kawain, dihydro-kawain, methysticin, dihydromethysticin, yangonin, and dihydroyangonin.

In the islands, natives have several methods of preparing kava kava. One of the most common ways is to shave away the outer bark from the plant root until the pale-pink or yellow inner rhizome is all that remains. Two mouthfuls are then cut into small pieces, chewed thoroughly, and swallowed.

A mild version of kava kava can be enjoyed at teatime by boiling the bark in water. The tea serves as a kind of elixir, and the result of sipping is a light "up."

For those who prefer a sedated feeling, kava kava may also do the trick. The roots must be chewed until finely pulverized, then soaked in water for a while before drinking.

For a stronger brew, take about 3 tablespoons of fresh rhizome or 6 tablespoons of dried bark, boil for five minutes in a pint of water, and cover. Strain the mix, refrigerate it, and twenty-four to thirty-six hours later, sip slowly.

These days, fewer and fewer people bother with complex kava-kava recipes. More often, they simply take about ⅓ ounce of dried kava root ground into a fine powder and mix it with any liquid they enjoy drinking.

Depending upon how much has been consumed and whether the bark is fresh or dried, a kava-kava trip should last anywhere from two to six hours. Small doses will provide a mild up—a happy, light kind of feeling. Larger doses, still safe, will take one through a range of experiences. First feelings, which come on after about thirty minutes, are ones of pleasant stimulation, peace, euphoria, and talkativeness. In another half-hour a much higher, more sleepy and lethargic state will be experienced. Yet because the drug only affects spinal, rather than mental, activity, the user remains very alert at the same time. If a lot has been consumed, the imbiber ends up in a very pleasant, dream-filled sleep. When he awakes, he still enjoys a relaxed feeling with no signs of hangover (unless he has consumed alcohol somewhere along the way).

Generally, islanders limit themselves to using kava kava once or twice a week. This level of consumption is not only safe but appears to have some beneficial effects, including appetite stimulation for those skinnies who need it.

If kava kava is overdone for a period of months, some problems may arise. When used excessively, the drink can become habit-forming. In addition, the skin may develop rashes and ulcers and may even turn yellow. Loss of appetite and weight, diarrhea, and weakening of vision can also result. Should any of these problems be experienced, consumption of kava kava should be stopped completely. After the abuser has abstained for a week or two, however, all symptoms of overuse will disappear.

All in all, this is one bark whose bite doesn't seem too bad.

KETAMINE HYDROCHLORIDE

COMMON NAME: *green*

In response to the never-ending demand by trippers for alternative drugs, a new thriller is now making the psychedelic rounds. Its name is ketamine hydrochloride, but if you get an offer it's likely to be called "green."

Ketamine hydrochloride, marketed for medical use under the names Ketalar and Ketaject, is a disassociative anesthetic discovered in the United States in 1961. Green first became known to the general public as a result of the Vietnam War, where it served as the most widely used battlefield anesthetic.

For medical purposes, the drug is sold as a liquid to be injected in normal surgical anesthesia doses ranging from 400 to 700 mg. On the street, the drug appears in a variety of forms: pills (poppable), powder (snortable), and even in cigarette form (smokable). Most often the color of the drug is green, hence its nickname. Normal abuser's dose is 50 mg.

What one gets for his 50 mg is an intense forty-five-minute trip not unlike that produced by LSD. The tripper feels as if he is floating in a dreamlike state while experiencing vivid visual images.

Danger associated with ketamine hydrochloride lies in one's taking too heavy a dose. An excessive quantity will anesthetize the breathing apparatus, causing a halt in respiration, and will bring the party to an abrupt end. Keep that in mind if this new "find" makes its way to your neighborhood.

KHAT

To Yemenites and some East Africans, khat seems to be nature's answer to amphetamines. Want to stay awake? Take a bit of khat. Want to lose weight? Take a bit of khat. Just want to feel a speedlike up? Take some khat.

Khat (*Catha edulis*) is a large shrub member of the burning-bush family native to the woods of Ethiopia and its neighbors. While it is not a drug that causes physical dependence, regular users do find that over a period of time a strong level of psychic dependence can develop. Natives chew the young buds, fresh leaves, and stems of the plant, or brew them into a tea which they drink on an everyday basis not unlike the pattern developed by coffee drinkers in the Western World. Any similarity to coffee stops there. Khat can be a lot more dangerous.

Khat is a mild central-nervous-system stimulant containing cathine, cathidine, cathinine, and a high concentration of vitamin C. The vitamin C helps to minimize some of the adverse effects of the drug.

A dose of khat can produce anything from a mildly happy high to a state of hilarity. The user may be talkative and stimulated (due to an increased pulse and respiratory rate), and sense a strong feeling of increased mental clarity. He may also experience some hallucinations as part of the trip.

But it doesn't always happen that way. For some unexplained reason, sometimes the feelings experienced range from dizziness to stomach pain to weariness to depression, or any combination of these. Not a very good trip at all. And, if overdone, the drug can cause a heavy case of tremors, serious loss of appetite, and heart trouble.

Sex goes out the window with this one. Use of khat often severely reduces sexual drive. And don't forget, the drug can be habit-forming. All in all, this is one khat that appears to be something of a dog.

KIF

We've included mention of kif only because it is discussed and used so often by druggies who are into the mystique of the world of cannabis.

Kif is a name used by the "heads" of Morocco to describe a mixture they smoke made up of strong tobacco and marijuana. Sometimes the name is used to describe the marijuana plants Moroccans grow for their smoking mix.

And that's the story of kif. While we're on the subject of Morocco, we might also mention that while dope is easily available to tourists visiting that country, buyers should be very cautious in their dealings there. Both police and customs officials have been known to hassle tourists caught with illegal dope. If you want to keep out of a Moroccan jail and save yourself lots of money for lawyers and bribes, keep away from drugs while visiting that area of the world.

KOLA NUTS

Among sophisticates in Los Angeles, New York, and Miami, cocaine is now used as a form of currency, since it has great monetary value and can be traded for goods and services without having to report anything to the IRS. The fact is, you don't have to be a sophisticated urbanite to use drugs in place of dollars. For many years natives of certain parts of Africa—people who can barely write their names in the dirt with sticks—have been trading kola nuts for everything from slaves to wives. About the only disadvantage we can see to this economic practice is the need for a very fat wallet.

Kola nuts come from the African *Cola nitida* tree. Tribesmen use kola nuts for a variety of purposes. Some believe them to be an effective aphrodisiac for men. Others feel they help women to conceive easily. Many find they reduce fatigue, sharpen the mind, and add to physical strength. Much of this latter feeling can be attributed to the 2 percent caffeine content of kola nuts, almost the same as that found in coffee. There is, however, a little extra kick in the essential kola oil found in the nuts, which acts as a stimulant when ingested.

Those interested can take their kola nuts in one of two ways: chewed or brewed. Chewers should start with about two nuts. Brewers should use about one tablespoon of ground nuts per cup; add a couple of teaspoons of honey and you'll really have a delicious-tasting concoction.

Use a little caution when dealing with kola nuts, just as you should with coffee (see Caffeine). Excessive use can cause such troubles as insomnia and nervousness, and in some cases, too much consumption will reduce sexual drive. You might want to limit your intake to one or two cups daily, for just as coffee can be habit-forming if you use too much too often, so can kola nuts.

LAAM

The National Institute of Drug Abuse is currently testing LAAM, levo-alpha-acetylmethadol-hydrochloride, a synthetic new opiate sub-stitute, for use in heroin-addiction treatment.

LAAM is a white, crystalline, soluble, morphine-like compound, a central-nervous-system depressant being investigated as a longer-lasting alternative to methadone—currently the most widespread treatment for addiction. The drug is as highly addictive as methadone, but experts are generally in agreement that opiate addiction can be stemmed only by the substitution of another addiction.

At present, a reformed junkie undergoing treatment must report to a methadone clinic once a day to receive his "medicine," while a LAAM patient's dose can last up to seventy-two hours. This time factor is the big advantage of LAAM. The drug produces a cross-tolerance to other opiates. Shooting up while taking LAAM will be a waste of the addict's time and money, since all of heroin's euphoric effect will be blocked. As it is taken orally, LAAM eliminates the dangerous side effects of needle use. Another important factor is that the drug suppresses the user's uncontrollable desire for heroin and other opiates both during the time he is addicted and after he has been detoxified. LAAM takes effect about two to six hours after ingestion, blocking potential withdrawal symptoms. In about two weeks the patient is effectively weaned from heroin to LAAM, without dis-comfort.

Scientists believe infrequent cases of LAAM overdose may actually be due to multi-drug use. Alcohol and LAAM are like oil and water, not to be mixed under any circumstances. People with low narcotics tolerance are also potential LAAM overdose cases. No illicit street sale of the drug has yet been reported. Indeed, there may never be a thriving black market in LAAM, even if it does become widely dis-pensed, since it lacks the one ingredient the drug user seeks—it won't get him high. The drug's sustained, level effect makes the addict sim-ply feel "normal." Patients do not feel sedated or euphoric, and preliminary findings indicate they seem to be more alert than those taking methadone.

Since the addict has to visit his drug clinic for LAAM only three times a week, psychological dependency on daily heroin or methadone use is reduced, allowing for alteration of previously established nega-tive drug behavior patterns. He begins to feel like a member of the drug-free world, although present indications are that he will have to be maintained on LAAM indefinitely. He does not have to take the drug home on weekends, since the effect of a dose lasts from Friday to Monday. This factor may minimize potential abuse and diversion of LAAM to the illicit market.

Side effects vary from person to person. Mild sweating, constipation, anxiety, insomnia, and nausea have been reported sporadically. Since LAAM's effect on pregnancy and childbearing is unknown, all six thousand test subjects thus far have been male.

If LAAM's viability as a long-lasting, effective narcotic alternative is ultimately proved, treatment of addiction may become more economical and efficient. Three times the number of addicts could be treated in existing drug centers at one-third the expense of methadone therapy.

LAAM's main advantage over heroin is its legal, although restricted, status. LAAM's primary advantage over methadone is the necessity for less frequent administration. The junkie can trade the expensive and socially disruptive monkey on his back for the apparently safe, convenient, and free drug LAAM.

LETTUCE OPIUM

Next time you see someone staring lovingly at a salad, don't be so amazed: Perhaps it's the lettuce that is turning him on.

Yes, it's true. Wild lettuce (*Lactuca virosa*) and most other varieties, including common head lettuce (*Sativa capita*), contain lactucarium, a bitter alkaloid similar in physical properties to opium. In fact, lactucarium has even been used by physicians as a substitute for opium when that drug was not readily available. Before running for the French dressing, however, read on. A bit of preparatory work will be necessary before lettuce will do its thing.

To extract lettuce opium (lactucarium), liquefy the wild lettuce plant, or the hearts and roots of supermarket lettuce, in an electric juicer. At least a pint of liquid is needed to produce a useful quantity.

Let the resulting liquid stand in a bowl under heat lamps or hot sunlight until it has evaporated, leaving a brownish-green sticky substance. Scrape this residue from the bowl and put a small piece into an opium pipe. Pointing the pipe downward, so the lactucarium will not go into the stem, heat the bowl over a match or flame until the residue begins to bubble. It will give off a white smoke which should be inhaled and held in the lungs for about thirty seconds.

Real opium produces a sleepy, dreamy, intense, spaced-out high. Lettuce opium, less potent than the real thing, will produce a milder, sedated high.

Addiction is no problem; an enormous amount of this legal drug would have to be ingested over a long period of time to get one hooked. However, large quantities can be toxic.

Several American manufacturers currently market ready-to-use lettuce-opium brands as legal substitutes for hashish and cocaine. These products are reputed to contain resin extracted from South American wild lettuce, somewhat more potent and lower in pesticides than our supermarket variety. Experimenters claim that, aside from looking like the real things, both types can bring on a high. As is the case with homemade lettuce opium, excessive smoking should be avoided.

LOBELIA

COMMON NAMES: *asthma weed, gag root, Indian tobacco, pukeweed*

For hundreds of years lobelia has been a staple item in the herbal medicine cabinet of North American Indians. More recently, the leaves, seeds, and stems of the *Lobelia inflata* plant have been used by American druggies to produce a legal, mild, marijuana-like high.

Lobelia can be taken in any one of several forms. If you don't mind its acrid taste, you can smoke lobelia in the form of a joint. Inhale deeply as one would with grass. The result will be a feeling of mental clarity combined with a general sense of happiness and well-being. Brewing it as a tea produces even stronger results. The mix required for an individual dose is about 2 tablespoons of crushed leaves and stems to a pint of water. Simmer, strain and drink—you'll be on your way to a state of mental stimulation combined with tingly body sensations.

Imbibing lobelia may cause a prickly feeling in your mouth and throat. If you find this unpleasant or unappealing, brew a double-strength tea, strain it, and boil it down to a sticky residue. Mix that with some dried lobelia leaves and pack the whole business into a large gelatin capsule suitable for ingestion.

However lobelia is prepared, it should be taken on an empty stomach; occasionally users may experience nausea and vomiting. Over 15 grams will almost always bring on immediate vomiting. People who suffer from migraines may get a slight headache from smoking lobelia. Heavy doses may cause circulatory problems or may even be toxic.

LSD

COMMON NAMES: *acid, barrels, beast, big D, blotter, blue acid, blue cheer, blue heaven, blue mist, brown dots, California sunshine, cherry top, chocolate chips, clear light, coffee, contact lens, cubes, cupcakes, domes, dots, 50, flats, haze, heavenly blue, instant zen, Lucy in the sky with diamonds, mellow yellows, microdots, orange mushrooms, orange sunshine, orange wedges, owsley, paper acid, pearly gates, purple haze, purple microdot, royal blue, strawberry fields, sugar, sugar lump, sunshine, the chief, the hawk, 25, wedding bells acid, wedges, wedgies, white lightning, window pane, yellows, zen*

The 1960s dropped into eternity as a technicolored tumble of aphrodesia, Beatlemania, and psychedelia. LSD (lysergic acid diethylamide) was the plumb line, and all its abstractions and distractions distorted the decade and made a straight world look cock-eyed.

Fables and myths have sprung up about the drug, endowing it with properties unfamiliar to modern science, but cherished by followers of druids and gnomes. Magical ingredient of witches' brew, third eye to the universe, LSD has been praised and cursed without mercy—and without justification.

Odorless, colorless, and tasteless, LSD is ounce for ounce the most powerful drug known. A crystalline solid in pure form, it can also be produced as a liquid. One ounce is enough to provide 300,000 average doses. Five thousand times as potent as mescaline and two hundred times as potent as psilocybin, the drug is easily transformed into ingestible tablets, capsules, sugar cubes, dots, pieces of blotter paper, or gelatin squares, and may even be impregnated onto stamps, chewing gum, hard candy, or soda crackers.

Dosage is so small that LSD is measured in micrograms, or "mikes." One microgram equals one millionth of a gram. One hundred micrograms will produce a full-blown trip. Street doses usually range from 50 to 400 micrograms—capable of producing trips of eight to twelve hours. Dosage is a problem with LSD because measurement is difficult in such minuscule amounts. Overdosage is less evident than with other drugs such as mescaline. Too much mescaline and it is promptly vomited up; too much LSD and it stays with you, so it is easy to ingest far more than a usual dose by accident. Overdose in the case of LSD is

115

usually related more to set and setting than drug toxicity. Some claim that true LSD overdose only occurs at astronomical ingestion levels of about seven million micrograms.

LSD is a semi-synthetic derivative of lysergic acid, an alkaloid found in ergot, and also in morning-glory seeds. Ergot is a fungus that grows as a rust on rye; medieval tales of madness and entire villages running amok have been attributed to the townies eating infested bread.

LSD research has been retarded because of public and governmental fear and repression. There is growing proof, however, that expanded therapeutic and research use of LSD is not only warranted but necessary if we are to progress and expand our knowledge of the human mind. Successes have been documented in the fields of psychiatric experimentation, and in dealing with alcoholism, opiate addiction, criminal rehabilitation, mental retardation, and childhood schizophrenia. The drug has also been used to alleviate anxiety and pain in cancer patients, as well as to help the dying adjust to their fates. However, because the government sees LSD as a useless drug, research projects have dropped dramatically, with the National Institute of Mental Health conducting what little research remains.

LSD is considered a psychomimetic drug: It induces symptoms which mimic some psychoses, such as schizophrenia. Why this occurs is not really known, since LSD remains in the brain only about twenty minutes.

The largest percentage of the drug goes to the liver and kidneys. LSD can be detected in the bloodstream up to two hours after taken. Its effects are achieved either by releasing or inhibiting substances naturally occurring in the brain, causing chemical imbalances.

Medically, but incorrectly, classified as a hallucinogen, LSD is neither toxic, addicting, nor hallucinogenic. The user does not hallucinate. He either sees what is there in a distorted kaleidoscopic manner, or misinterprets what he is seeing. If he does witness a mental light show or panorama of improbable visions, he is usually aware that it is drug-induced and does not accept it as reality. While physical dependence does not occur, there is a very rapid buildup of tolerance, if several doses are taken in succession. Tolerance abates rapidly, though, usually within three days after use is discontinued. There are no withdrawal symptoms, and the intensity of the mind-boggling experience causes trippers to be hesitant about frequent use.

More so than with any other drug, the success of an LSD voyage into the far reaches of consciousness is determined by two things: set and setting. "Set" refers to the frame of mind in which one finds himself when beginning a trip and determines whether the drug's effects will be pleasant or disturbing. Those who are fearful may well have a fear-filled trip; a repressive personality who has bottled up desires, fears, or emotions may find himself confronted with those bugaboos. Mental blocks may be necessary defenses for some people; breaking them down via an LSD trip may unleash a backlash of problems that may or may not be solved as the trip progresses.

"Setting" includes the physical place, the people and objects present, and the reassurance given to the tripper as his journey progresses. All these factors are as important in molding his experience as the drug itself, since the tripper is particularly sensitive to his environment.

The first effects of LSD are physical. About one hour after ingestion, initial reaction may be vague anxiety and nausea, followed by amphetamine-like rapid pulse, dilated pupils, flushed face, elevations in temperature, heartbeat, and blood pressure, appetite depression, exhilaration and restlessness, and a metallic taste in the mouth.

The next step on the journey is subjective, since the tripper is now in a state where suggestibility and expectations will largely determine what happens. Reason and rationality take a back seat to the undifferentiated stimuli and subconscious material that come bubbling to the surface. He loses the ability to perceive and to analyze data in a structured manner.

The subjective experience is what is often referred to as psychedelic or mind-expanding. The senses are jangled and bombarded, with a "cross-over," called synesthesia, occurring: Music may be seen and color heard; one kind of sensation is converted to another. Depth perception is altered, colors vibrate in their beauty and intensity, objects and patterns become to some three-dimensional and alive; the visual trip alone is worth the price of admission.

Every sense is tickled awake by LSD's illusionary fingers: Smell, taste, hearing, and touch are more acute. Hearing music can be a totally encompassing activity, involving all the senses, not just the auditory. Eidetic images—vivid images seen with the eyes closed—may present themselves as a movie, often starring the tripper, projected within his head. The body image may change, fragment, and redefine itself. "Tracking" may occur—the visual effect of a series of afterimpressions left once an object has moved across the field of vision.

With the loss of the sensation of boundaries between body and space comes a loss of the sense of time. As the mental processes accelerate, time becomes distorted and hours of subjective experience seem to occur within a few minutes of objective (or clock-measured) time. Past, present, and future tangle, becoming timeless, simultaneous occurrences.

The LSD trip may progress from a purely sensory experience to an awareness of self, inwardly, in a soul-searching sense, and outwardly, where the ego detaches and observes itself as a link in the infinite hierarchy of life. Used to develop such awareness, LSD might be a valuable tool in several fields, including psychotherapy and sociology. Some say that in the LSD state, we become conscious not only of our physical reality but of an infinite number of other realities as well. The drug releases only what is already in the mind, opening the door to the subconscious. It brings in nothing new; it only opens the windows— or, some feel, Pandora's box.

Claims about the therapeutic effects of LSD have been documented: self-improvement; magnification of concern for philosophical, theological, and cosmological questions; and spiritual enlightenment. Learned patterns of behavior and emotional responses may be altered, resulting in an eventual change of lifestyle, with the user behaving in a more fundamental manner. Empathy and communication may accelerate to the point of telepathy. Then again, all this may be the result of "portentousness," the sense, while tripping, that even a trivial platitude is rife with cosmic significance.

Most of the major life changes often attributed to LSD experiences can be explained sociologically, rather than chemically. While a few users become more passive, introspective, euphoric, and benign, preferring the dream world of LSD to reality, this may happen because the drug is commonly taken in group situations where a feeling of belonging develops among members. Major behavioral changes rarely occur without strong positive emotional attachments, and sharing LSD may create the aura allowing for such changes.

The hazards of LSD, though well publicized, are not all based on fact. Dangers do exist, but because of the muddle of information, scare stories, and lack of research, people tend either to consider LSD the horror drug of the sixties, or totally dismiss any warnings as fairy tales. One of these horror stories was the Great Chromosome Scare of 1967. Fantasy based on fact, it turned many users off LSD and onto other drugs—quite often amphetamines.

LSD *can* damage chromosomes. Aspirin can damage chromosomes. X-rays, virus infections, and orange juice can damage chromosomes, as can caffeine, suntans, and a fever. White-blood-cell chromosomes in test tubes, animals, and humans have been done in by all of these. LSD damage was the major one publicized. The publicity failed to mention that damage to white-blood-cell chromosomes is not a reliable index of genetic damage. If chromosomes in white blood cells are damaged, they will not affect other cells, reproduce strangely, or permanently alter the chromosomes in the body. Whether LSD is capable of causing alterations in the chromosome pattern itself can only be determined by further research.

"Flashbacks" are temporary recurrences of the LSD experience which happen days or months after the initial dose. This "here-we-go-again" aspect of the drug may be triggered spontaneously by psychological stress, medications such as antihistamines, or stimuli reminiscent of the tripper's initial experience, such as music or neon lights. While no one really knows what causes flashbacks, it is thought they are psychological rather than chemical in nature. All intense experience is stored in the memory, perhaps to be jolted into the present by an emotional or perceptual response. True LSD-triggered flashbacks are rare, almost never occurring among infrequent users. Indeed, everyone flashes back occasionally to some moment in his past, only we call it remembering.

Long-term effects of LSD use have not been determined, but if basic precautions are taken, the chance of psychotic reaction is minimal. Taken by psychologically healthy individuals, briefed in advance as to what will happen, LSD under supervision in controlled dosage has not been shown to be harmful. Unsupervised use may result in a temporary state of panic, paranoia, depression, or psychosis, since acid can uncover suppressed inner conflicts. Rarely, "unmasking" occurs, in which a true psychotic personality emerges. The principal sign of unmasking is a prolonged state of altered consciousness lasting for two or more days. Such cases require psychiatric help.

During LSD's heyday from 1962 to 1969, an increase in hospitalizations and accidents caused by acid was reported. Several factors contributed to this increase: bad trips caused by initial apprehension of the drug, unknown dosage, contamination and adulteration, lack of information, availability to everyone (including psychotics and schizophrenics), and unwitting use. Trippers were incarcerated. LSD was blamed for everything, from reactions to other drugs to crime to suicides. Once the paranoia abated, the acute "adverse" effects followed suit.

"Thou shalt not commit adulteration" should be a drug commandment. LSD is the least often adulterated of the street drugs because it is cheap and comparatively easy to produce, particularly in the small dosages required. The formula may be obtained from the U.S. Patent Office for 50 cents. However, contaminated street LSD exists. Syndicate-produced acid may cause speedlike reactions. Adulterated LSD is cut with "garbage psychedelics"—lysergic waste materials left over from synthesis, or belladonna, speed, or PCP. Acid may be improperly synthesized. It may not be LSD at all, but rather amphetamine, phencyclidine, atropine, or, as some claim, strychnine. The only way to be sure that acid is pure is to have it chemically analyzed by a drug expert.

A bummer, or bad trip, can sometimes be aborted or minimized with the right technique. Everything is intensified, so panic reactions, disorientation, hyperventilation, and physical discomfort may seem overwhelming to the tripper. Stay calm, stay reassuring, and, above all, stay *with* him: The comfort of human contact balances his disturbing LSD illusion with reality. Direct the tripper's mind back to reality by putting him in touch with himself and his surroundings. Since LSD is a directional drug which focuses on one thing at a time, breath control or yoga breathing may be good distractions. Reassure him that it is the drug that is causing the effects. Encourage him to ride with the flow of sensory images, rather than to fight them. Be warm, distracting, and keep exterior noise and light to a minimum. Don't moralize; this is no time to play psychiatrist. If hyperventilation occurs—total terror with rapid shallow breathing and very active reflexes—have him breathe into a paper bag to increase the CO_2 level in his blood.

Antagonist drugs such as Valium, Librium, or niacinamide may possibly help to bring the tripper down. Thorazine is used, but not recommended, because it brings the tripper down with a crash and may produce other bad reactions if the LSD has been adulterated. Drugs should be used only as an emergency measure; a bummer is best treated by friendship and understanding.

Paradoxically, the popularization of LSD coincided with the creation of stronger laws and stricter penalties. Now legally classified as an illicit drug under Schedule I of the Federal Controlled Substances Act, LSD was subject to no legal restrictions until 1963, when the AMA asked Harvard campus physician Dana L. Farnsworth for an opinion on acid. His reply was a statement urging the imposition of controls on LSD. By 1968, half the states had enacted legislation against possession. Penalties range from fines of $1,000 to $10,000 and/or imprisonment of up to five years for possession, and ten to fifteen years with fines to $20,000 for selling.

Anti-LSD campaigns, repressive legislation, tough penalties, and propaganda scares all resulted in an increased demand for and supply of LSD. The warnings served as lures, and new distributors were attracted by the higher prices caused by strict law enforcement.

The first official LSD trip was logged in 1943 by Dr. Albert Hoffman, a chemist working at Sandoz Laboratories. While working with derivatives of ergot, he somehow ingested a minute quantity of d-lysergic acid diethylamide, the twenty-fifth compound in the test series. So long, Albert—he went on a mini-trip of two hours, accompanied by his own inflight movies. Not sure whether it was the LSD that caused his voyage, he decided to try again, this time with ¼ mg. Six hours later he returned, replete with Alice-in-Wonderland tales of fantasy. His published account is especially significant because his experience was uncontaminated by hopes, fears, or preconceptions. Hoffman's vision of an altered reality was pure.

The sixties brought the psychedelics to Everyman, illuminated by the bright lights of the media. Presenting . . . Cosmic Consciousness, starring Allen Ginsberg, Aldous Huxley, Richard Alpert, and . . . Timothy Leary! "Tune in, turn on, drop out," said Leary, and the Age of Aquarius began.

Is LSD the key to man's mind, or is it the lock on his sanity? A barrier exists between the chemical nature of the brain and its spiritual relation to the infinite. LSD may someday open the door.

MANDRAKE

COMMON NAMES: *devil's testicle, mandragora, Satan's apple*

When witches brewed their evilest concoctions during the Middle Ages, they rarely left out mandrake, another member of the potato family similar in chemistry to datura, Jimson weed, henbane, and belladonna.

Found primarily in the stony fields of southern Europe, mandrake (*Mandragora officinarum*) has a particularly high quantity of mandragorine (a potent hypnotic and narcotic), as well as atropine, scopolamine, hyoscyamine, and other tropanes in its leaves and parsnip-shaped root.

Smoke enough of the dried leaves of this one, or drink enough of the extract made from boiling the crushed root, and you're in big trouble. Your hallucinations will be accompanied by dizziness, pounding headache, nausea, diarrhea, cramps, and confusion. If you really overdo it, you'll fall into a deep trance which may later result in insanity or death. Even if you turn on with mandrake and do survive, you may be doing some pretty serious damage to your heart.

Our advice to the curious: Seek your kicks elsewhere.

MARIJUANA

Marijuana is the least debilitating of all common intoxicants and has never accounted for a substantiated drug death. It does not cause brain damage, sterility, impotence, insanity, or drug addiction. Pharmacologically, aspirin causes more problems. Socially and medically, alcohol is more deadly.

Reliable scientific evidence and the experience of 250 million users worldwide, including over forty-five million Americans, leads to the conclusion that the single greatest danger of marijuana use is possible arrest and imprisonment.

Marijuana comes from the Indian hemp plant, *Cannabis sativa*, a hardy weed that grows all over the world. Often uncultivated, it can be extremely difficult to eradicate. Street buyers generally see it as a prepared mixture of chopped dried leaves, stems, flowers, and seeds. Ranging in color from gray to green to brown to red to blond, in texture it resembles the small granules of oregano or the larger leaves of tea. When smoked, it smells like sweet, burned rope or dried grasses.

The active ingredient of the plant, found in the gooey, yellow, fragrant resin of the upper leaves and flowers, is the tongue-twisting delta-9-tetrahydrocannabinol, more familiarly known as THC.

Marijuana gives rise to unique chemical and psychological effects. Different things to different people, it can be a light hallucinogen, relaxant, tranquilizer, appetite stimulant, or intoxicant. Effects de-

123

pend on the amount smoked and the potency of the grass, as well as on the expectations and perceptions of the user.

Marijuana is usually smoked in pipes or homemade cigarettes called joints. Depending on the quality of the grass, joints average about 4 to 40 mg of THC each.

A joint can produce a luminous haze for one to three hours. First feelings occur a couple of minutes after smoking. If marijuana is eaten alone, or as an ingredient in food dishes, the high can last from four to ten hours. First effects from eating take at least an hour before most people begin to feel them.

When smoked, marijuana comes on like a soft blanket. Don't expect a sunburst in your head. Most first-time and beginning users swear they don't feel a thing after their big experiment, and, in some ways, they may be right. With a small or moderate dose the high is so gentle, subtle, and understated that many triers don't think anything is happening at all. In time, however, they learn to relax, letting the drug's warm glow suffuse the environment.

The only physical changes that occur are a temporarily increased heartbeat with a rise in blood pressure, slight lowering of body temperature, and, for some, a telltale reddening of the eyes.

Mind changes range from the uncomfortable to the glorious, depending upon who is using it, where it is being used, and what the user's expectations are. You may feel alive all over, as if the hairs on your skin were dancing to a beat. Your head swims a gentle backstroke and feels empty and heavy at the same time. For some, the body may calm down to a purr, entering a quiet, introspective euphoria. Others may find themselves in a gregarious mood, engaging in ridiculous, giggly conversation with friends and loved ones.

Marijuana has a habit of intensifying concentration on the minute core of the moment—whether that be staring at snow falling from the sky or playing the same game of solitaire over and over again. Whatever activity is chosen, it seems perfect, and the smoker is unlikely to give it up until forced or cajoled into the next activity, which, lo and behold, is also perfect.

Awareness of self and the outside world is distorted, yet heightened. Distortion may make problems seem more intense, but it also adds an extra fillip to pleasures. When stoned, you can quickly change your thoughts, like flipping over a record, by focusing on a painting, repotting the begonias, or just directing your feet to the sunny side of the street.

Profound revelations can be experienced when stoned. At least they seem profound at the time. The likelihood, however, is that when morning comes you will see how inane that great discovery was. That brilliant flash wasn't meant to make the afternoon papers or win a Nobel prize.

The stoned mind operates on many levels at once. One level may play with another until, sometimes, confusion sets in. Again, you can control your high and take it elsewhere if confusion is not your thing. For some, the confused state is what they look forward to as they smoke themselves into a stupor. Part of this confusion is simple forgetfulness—the kind that makes you search for your glasses when they are sitting on your nose. You go to the closet, but by the time you get there you have forgotten why. Keys have a way of disappearing; so do conversations. There usually comes a moment when everyone has forgotten the point. The usual remedy: Start another point, and the conversation returns to its circular path. It doesn't seem to matter very much, though, since everything seems silly and funny. You can always flip the record and go back to staring at that crack in the wall or to endlessly peeling that orange. You stare and stare, maybe for hours, maybe for minutes. Time and space can be misjudged during your high. You can't be trusted to take the casserole out of the oven in fifteen minutes or to hang that picture over the bed. Just remember to use clocks and rulers when attempting any time or space computation.

While under the influence, certain compulsions are difficult to deny. Most grass users experience an obsession for food when they are smoking—any food, since it all looks juicy and tastes great. There are cookie freaks who don't consider it a night out without their favorite brand. "Meaningful" debates about the virtues of Oreos over Hydrox can ensue. Hamburger fans have been known to trek out in a blinding snowstorm to get their double-beef patties with onions, pickle, and special sauce on a sesame-seed bun. People will eat almost anything when high, devouring any table set before them, especially if it includes sweets. Much of the craving for food has to do with an unending desire to chew. The throat, mouth, and lips will feel dry and parched, so soft drinks, beer, wine, and juices will be equally appreciated.

Another common obsession for many smokers when stoned is music. The industry has long been aware of the connection between grass and its products. Their cash registers rang up astronomical sales as the flower children of the sixties bloomed into the affluent, potsmoking middle class of the seventies. Music became the magic carpet to stoned-out bliss. A good band may sound great when the toker has begun to move his shoulders more freely. Live rock music theatrics play to heightened sensibilities by overstimulating with flashing lights, mirrors, and glittering, sequined costumes. Close your eyes and you are lost in a trance where you can hear sights and see sounds. That unmistakable sweet odor at any rock concert is only the sign of people having a good time as they absorb driving rhythms pounding away at ear-splitting decibel levels.

For many, the doors of sensual delight are opened by a few pulls or tokes on a joint. Although grass is not a clinically proved aphrodisiac, it tends to produce a happy, relaxed mood, setting a comfortable stage for sexual enjoyment. Inhibitions can be washed away by a dreamy wave of joyous freedom. Sensations swirl; everything feels smooth and glorious—the perfect condition for pleasurable sex.

Psychotics, or users beset with serious problems and anxieties, can experience what is called a "bummer," or bad grass trip—a spiraling web of depression or paranoia that may seem overwhelming. In such instances, the help of a friend may be needed to move the tripper's mind away from its fixation on misery, fear, and panic. Talk softly about his bum trip, reminding him it is grass-induced. A change of scene might also be a good idea, but the most important relief will ultimately come from the passage of time. Problems will lessen as the high wears off—a matter of an hour or two at most—so hang in there, giving your friend as much support and comfort as you can in the meantime.

Except for such rare bum trips, the physiological and psychological effects of marijuana are considered minor in the world of psychoactive drugs. Most experienced users are capable of performing almost any task, responding to any stimuli, or coping with any emergency as if they were not high. Scientists call this the compensation factor. Laboratory tests have shown that many marijuana users can compensate 100 percent when stoned.

It seems safe to recommend that an inexperienced pot user should not drive, or at least should abstain from driving until he gets used to the drug's effects. There is no doubt that marijuana alters perceptions and reflexes, and both are needed to drive safely. Some claim that experienced drivers can, however, call upon their compensation factor and drive confidently, without noticeable impairment. But, your best bet is to avoid all intoxicants, if possible, when getting behind the wheel. If the thought of driving stoned makes you feel uncomfortable, listen to your head and give the car keys to a friend.

Grass is usually marketed by a loose network of informal entrepreneurs known as "connections." These dealers usually turn out to be friends, co-workers, and students, rather than the sinister types who sell "hard" drugs. They usually deal only in cannabis products and buy their metric kilos (2.2 pounds) or pounds in tightly compressed bricks from wholesalers who bring it into the country by small aircraft or boats at border locations, usually around Mexico or Florida. Local dealers generally sell grass to the consumer in ounces (an ounce will make thirty to forty joints), lids (usually a little less than an ounce), dime bags (about ¼ to ½ ounce), nickel bags (enough to get one high for a night or two), or individual joints. Prices currently range from a low of about $15 per ounce to a high of $90 per ounce for premium quality. Individual joints can bring about $1 each.

Some legendary, potent strains of grass such as Acapulco Gold, Columbian, Jamaican, Lebanon Red, and Panama Red are named for the regions where they grow. Except for a small number of experienced connoisseurs, most people can't tell the difference, by sight or smell, between these exotic species. One can easily be fooled into paying a premium price for not-so-premium marijuana. The common way for the consumer to rate his purchase is by "tasting" (smoking) the offered grass before buying.

After one purchases his baggie full of marijuana leaves, buds, stems, twigs, and seeds, he goes about cleaning it, removing everything but the leaves and buds by pushing them through a strainer or any of the many commercial grass cleaners sold in head shops (marijuana paraphernalia stores) or through counterculture magazines. Those with a green thumb or limited budget save their seeds for future home-growing, and stems and twigs for brewing tea. If grass is not cleaned, when smoked the seeds have a tendency to burst like firecrackers, causing mini-fires or little holes in your clothes, furniture, and bedding.

Grass destined for cooking should be strained to a fine powder so it won't taste like chalky talc or a dusty road in the spice cake. Use it in highly flavored foods to avoid its unappetizing, gritty taste. Marijuana must be cooked before it is eaten or used as a recipe ingredient. Raw grass is abrasive to the stomach and can cause nausea and/or painful ulcers.

If you are not eating it, you are smoking it, and that can be done in many ways, too. Joints can be made by rolling grass by hand or in commercially available rolling machines. Rolling papers are available in a variety of colors and flavors, with a gummed edge for easy licking and sealing. They can be found at your local supermarket, general store, drugstore, or head shop. They are the same papers used legally by cowboys and money-savers to roll tobacco cigarettes from bulk. In an effort to reduce throat irritation, some smoke grass in waterpipes, filled with wine or water. Many other types of pipes are available, some made of metal, wood, or stone. One current favorite is a glass air-pressure contraption called a carburetor, or bhong. These come in a dizzying variety of shapes and sizes, many of which resemble museum sculpture pieces.

Most "heads" (frequent grass users) smoke communally, passing a joint or pipe from mouth to mouth in a ritual manner. As the joint burns down to a very short length it becomes hard to handle, unless one likes the feeling of singed fingertips. You are then left with the "roach." Roach clips of different sizes and shapes are sold in head shops. Homemade versions can be fashioned from tweezers, a hemostat, or even a used paper match, split open to hold the roach (called a Jefferson Airplane).

Producing home-grown grass has become a widespread cottage industry, with the amateur gardener becoming his own supplier. A wide selection of grower's guides is available in bookstores and head shops across the country.

Marijuana has a long and colorful history. As far back as the year 2737 B.C., the then-reigning Chinese emperor taught his subjects to use cannabis variants as medicinal preparations. Since ancient records are very rare, it is difficult to accurately follow the trail of grass across the continents, but it seems to have traveled through many countries and was used both medically and for religious purposes. There are even references to cannabis in the Old Testament. The writings of Marco Polo and others all demonstrate that marijuana was grown in Asia and the Near East not only for use of the plant's hemp fibers, but also because of its psychoactive properties.

Marijuana was introduced to the New World by the Spaniards, who planted it in Chile in the late sixteenth century. Later, King James I of England commanded the first American settlers to grow the hemp plant to provide the British fleet with fiber needed for making rope. After 1860, marijuana's value as a basic cash crop diminished when hemp was no longer in such demand. Much later, the Department of Agriculture encouraged increased growing in an effort to supply our troops with fiber for rope during the shortage of imported hemp caused by World War II.

Recreational use of marijuana got a shot in the arm from rhapsodic descriptions of grass provided by European writers and intellectuals in the nineteenth century. All the rage among the smart set in Paris, it was reputed to be a creative stimulus. Prior to alcohol prohibition in the 1920s, recreational use of pot in the United States was limited and temporary. Smokers were mainly Mexican immigrants, black cavalry soldiers, and the social elite. Hashish houses existed, much like bars, for an evening's pleasure. At one time, New York City alone was estimated to have over five hundred of these late-night smokeries.

Ten years later the lid clamped down and the weed was outlawed. Pot use was continued by small groups such as the black jazz musicians of the thirties who wrote and sang many a song about the pleasures of pot in a colloquial code that left the straight world wondering what their smiles were all about.

Nationwide, popular use of grass in America accelerated during the 1960s when beatniks passed on what they had learned from their black musician friends to their white, middle-class cousins. It didn't take long for this educational effort to reach epidemic proportions. The generation raised on Timothy Leary, communes, Vietnam, and rock 'n' roll was, by no coincidence, also raised on grass. Marijuana was a major cultural influence during the sixties as thousands of stoned flower children poured into San Francisco, or fought in far-away Asian trenches with heads buzzing from strong native weed. The drug revolution went hand in hand with the political and social revolutions of the sixties, as marijuana became the symbol of youth in revolt.

In the seventies, marijuana use has spread from the young collegians and soldiers of the sixties to a broad range of otherwise respectable, law-abiding, middle-class users of all ages.

While the world turns on to relax or giggle, medicine men and scientists throughout history have been prescribing marijuana for a host of ailments. It was used as an anesthetic in China almost four thousand years ago and there is evidence Egyptians recommended soothing sore eyes with cannabis fluids thousands of years ago. Modern scientists today are experimenting along similar lines for the treatment of glaucoma. Asian and African cultures used cannabis as a medication as well as an intoxicant. A common folk medicine, it has been used to treat coughs, headaches, and menstrual cramps. Queen Victoria's personal physician, after thirty years of research, concluded that marijuana was useful for the treatment of migraines, cramps, senile insomnia, epileptoid states, depressions, and asthma attacks.

During the mid-1800s it was recommended in medical texts for everything from gout to insanity to impotence. In 1860 the Ohio

Medical Society found hemp to be useful for tetanus, rheumatic pain, asthma, post-partum psychoses, convulsions, gonorrhea, and chronic bronchitis. They found it produced a more natural sleep, without interfering with the action of internal organs, and was therefore preferable to the stronger opium compounds then available for such purposes. Hundreds of scholarly articles were written on cannabis' medical properties between 1839 and 1900, and various cannabis preparations were available in the United States, without prescription. Listed in the official U.S. Pharmacopoeia from 1850 until 1942, it was sold in fluid extracts by such reputable companies as Parke-Davis, Squibb, and Lilly. One drug company marketed ready-made marijuana cigarettes as an asthma remedy.

The Western medical establishment lost enthusiasm for medical use of cannabis around 1900 when research produced synthesized morphine and barbiturates, which were much easier to administer and permitted closer dosage control.

The Marijuana Tax Act of 1937, while not prohibiting its use as a medicant or denying its value as such, made it difficult and unpopular to prescribe. Removed from the lexicon of American pharmacology in 1942, the drug can now be legally obtained only by a limited number of closely supervised researchers. These scientists have found that marijuana may have potential use as a treatment for glaucoma, loss of appetite, anorexia nervosa, heart attack, migraine headache, hypertension, epileptic seizure, and insomnia. Medically, marijuana appears to be remarkably safe, with addiction and toxicity potential well below that of aspirin.

One might logically ask, if grass is so helpful and harmless, why is it still illegal and, in many corners, despised? This question can be answered only by looking at the history of misinformation and hysteria that has always surrounded cannabis.

American repression of marijuana gained momentum in the 1920s when sensational, exaggerated reports about its effects appeared in the New Orleans daily newspapers. Screaming headlines proclaimed that schoolchildren were buying joints, marauding about the city, shooting and maiming anything that moved. By 1927, Louisiana had made grass illegal. Many other newspapers then took up the battle against this purported danger to society. They were joined in this war against the weed by Harry J. Anslinger, commissioner of the newly formed Bureau of Narcotics. In an apparent effort to justify its existence, this spanking-new segment of the bureaucracy led the holy crusade through the various state legislatures.

By 1946, almost every state in the union had restrained the "creeping menace" of marijuana, either by adopting the Uniform Anti-Narcotics Act or by passing its own ill-informed laws. Hundreds of anti-grass articles were fed to the public, with the covert or overt assistance of Mr. Anslinger. The Federal Marijuana Tax Act of 1937 totally outlawed nonmedical, untaxed possession or sale. Anslinger tried to drive marijuana out of legitimate medical practice and, sure enough, its listing was ultimately dropped from the U.S. Pharmacopoeia. There was no proof to support Mr. Anslinger's charges about the drug, but the public had been so assaulted with tales of addiction and violent crime that the facts no longer seemed to matter. In 1938, New York Mayor Fiorello LaGuardia financed a marijuana study that found no proof of addiction, no link to aggressive or anti-social behavior, and no sign of tolerance or withdrawal symptoms. Its findings were ignored, however, and marijuana retained its unjust association with hard drugs and hardened criminals.

Although scare stories about deranged potheads no longer make the rounds, new ones about purported medical dangers are now circulating. The only significant verified danger related to grass smoking is the smoke itself. As with any other smokable substance, marijuana has a high carbon-monoxide yield, comparable to that of stale nonfiltered cigarettes. Those with pre-existing bronchitis or respiratory problems may suffer acutely from marijuana-smoke inhalation, just as they would from tobacco.

One of the scarier allegations is that marijuana causes permanent brain damage, premature aging of the brain, and a type of mental lethargy scientists refer to as the antimotivational syndrome. This charge emanated from a highly questionable, biased study of only ten participants, all of whom were multiple drug users or had prior brain damage! Other similar reports have resulted from tests done on rhesus monkeys given the equivalent of thirty joints, three times a day, for six months. If you are not a monkey smoking every minute every day, you need not worry.

A major study funded by the National Institute of Mental Health was conducted in 1972 using a group of Jamaicans who had smoked an average of seven joints a day for more than seventeen years. Much of today's reliable information about marijuana comes from this study, since extensive medical and psychiatric tests were administered to this carefully controlled group. Findings showed no difference in brain dysfunction between chronic users and nonusers.

There is some evidence that chronic users of extremely high daily doses are more likely to exhibit abnormal behavior or suffer greater mental deterioration than the general population. This finding has not been confirmed, though, since it is difficult to ascertain whether constant high-dosage pot use is the cause or the symptom of mental and emotional disturbance. Among the Jamaicans studied, there was no difference in rate of employment, job stability, or academic achievement between smokers and nonsmokers. Apparently, marijuana will not turn you into a vegetable, unless you planted those seeds yourself many years before your first high.

Another "fact" often quoted about marijuana is that it lowers the body's resistance to infectious disease and cancer. The unconfirmed test from which this supposed result came has been contradicted by the Jamaican study, which showed disease and mortality rates of users to be no different from those of nonusers.

Some claim frequent marijuana use increases the likelihood of birth defects and other genetic diseases. This chromosome-damage charge has been hurled at every pleasure-giving substance since manna. One study indicated such a possibility, but its findings must be seriously questioned because participants were all multi-drug users. Five other studies have subsequently failed to sustain that finding. One even found a higher rate of chromosome damage in nonsmokers.

Marijuana has also been accused of causing precancerous responses in the lung cells, as well as other lung ailments. As previously noted, there is no doubt that any type of inhaled smoke is bad for the lungs, but with the limited number of joints smoked, even by heavy users, damage is imperceptible. Comparisons of lung X-rays between users and nonusers have shown no difference.

It has been suggested that marijuana use may lead to sterility or impotence in men. Again, no determinative causal link has been documented. In fact, the Jamaican study and other major research efforts found that after two weeks of grass abstinence the subjects' hormonal levels were in the upper range of normal. When the users returned to heavy smoking these levels did not diminish.

With regard to pregnancy, research has indicated that even at quantities ten to a hundred times the effective human dose, marijuana appears to cause no damaging effects to the fetus, the mother, or the newborn child. However, all non-prescribed drugs should be avoided during pregnancy.

Marijuana is easy and inexpensive to grow, doesn't hurt you, won't kill you, and may even help you. But it is illegal, and that is its primary danger at the moment. Since 1970, nearly two million people have been arrested for offenses related to marijuana. This accounts for almost 70 percent of all drug arrests and costs the taxpayer over $600 million annually. This figure alone should be decisive in the continuing push for decriminalization of grass.

Some states, including Oregon, Maine, South Dakota, New York, Mississippi, Colorado, California, Ohio, Minnesota, and Alaska, now have arrest-free procedures that require payment of a fine upon the issuance of a citation for minor marijuana offenses. This procedure applies to possession of small amounts of grass and does not include sale or importation. Every state has reduced the seriousness of the offense from a felony to a misdemeanor, with the exception of Nevada. The maximum federal penalty for simple possession is presently one year in jail and/or a $5,000 fine. Increasingly, people are questioning the morality of condemning marijuana users to lives burdened by the stigma of a criminal record, as evidenced by the push for some form of decriminalization or legalization in every state.

Several groups have organized to promote the legalization effort. The foremost lobby for repeal of our antiquated marijuana laws is NORML, the National Organization for the Reform of Marijuana Laws. Members of NORML's advisory board include such prominent Americans as Ramsey Clark, Senator Jacob Javits, Dr. Benjamin Spock, and the Reverend Canon Walter D. Denis.

Legalization would result in governmentally controlled use, sale, and distribution of marijuana, like alcohol. No state has yet proceeded on this course.

Decriminalization would eliminate all criminal penalties for minor marijuana offenses, using the citation/fine method instead. Decriminalization has been recommended by, among others, the American Bar Association, Consumers Union, the American Public Health Association, B'nai B'rith, the National Council of Churches, the Governing Board of the American Medical Association, the American Academy of Pediatrics, William F. Buckley, Jr., Art Linkletter, Ann Landers, the National Education Association, and the National Commission on Marijuana and Drug Abuse.

In fact, the National Commission on Marijuana and Drug Abuse issued a report at the President's request which verified the safety of marijuana and urged repeal of our unrealistic laws. This report was soundly rejected by then-President Nixon prior to publication.

No effort to suppress the use of marijuana—and there have been many—has been successful. True eradication of the marijuana "problem" lies in decriminalization or legalization.

MDA

COMMON NAMES: *love drug, mellow drug of America*

One of the most popular of the alphabet-soup drugs—the amphetamine-related psychedelics which include STP, MMDA, MDM, DOEM, and the more dangerous PMA, TMA, and DOB—MDA is similar both chemically and in effect to mescaline and the amphetamines.

Easily synthesized, MDA, or 3,4-methylenedioxyamphetamine, is a white powder usually made into capsules or tablets, although it may also be sniffed or dissolved for injection. Average dosage is 50–150 mg, which takes effect within an hour after ingestion, peaks within two hours, and lasts up to eight hours.

MDA combines aspects of both the amphetamines and the hallucinogens. Amphetamine-like increased pulse and blood pressure, dilation of pupils, insomnia, and loss of appetite occur without the accompanying tension associated with speed. Low doses result in a peaceful euphoria, while higher doses create an LSD-like effect without hallucinations. Communication and interpersonal relationships become important. A warmth and tenderness envelop the tripper, creating a tranquil feeling of joy and peace. The mystical insights, perceptual distortions, and illusions of LSD are replaced by a gentle sensuousness.

Despite the ease with which it is synthesized, street MDA is real only about 50 percent of the time. LSD or LSD/PCP is often substituted. Overdose potential is unknown, and physical addiction does not occur.

MDA was first synthesized in the 1930s, about the same time as amphetamines. Originally devised as an appetite depressant, it was later considered for use as a weapon to tranquilize the enemy into submission.

In the 1960s, it was rediscovered as a recreational drug. It was once considered as a possible aid in psychotherapy, but that notion was dismissed when MDA was placed under Schedule I of the Federal Controlled Substances Act on the specious but commonly held theory that if it's fun, it must be bad. Unfortunately, because of this premature ban, little information about the drug's dangers, if any, is presently available.

134

MESCAL BEANS

Don't let the name of this potential killer fool you. The mescal bean is not mescaline, nor is it the alcoholic beverage mescal. Rather than make you high, it can put you 6 feet under.

These dark-red beans come from the *Sophora secundiflora* shrub, or Texas mountain laurel, which grows wild on the limestone hills of northern Mexico and in the southwestern United States. Once used for ritual purposes by Indians, mescal beans have since been replaced by peyote. Nowadays, even the Indians won't touch this drug with a 10-foot peace pipe.

The kicker in mescal beans is a toxic pyridine called cytisine, a pharmacological cousin of the deadly poison nicotine.

A ritual dose used to be a quarter of a bean or less, first roasted, then crushed, chewed, and swallowed. The drug is so toxic, however, that even a fraction of a bean too much can throw the user into convulsions and cause death from respiratory failure.

This is one hallucinogen that is just not worth the chance. Even if it doesn't kill you, the trip won't be much fun—unless your idea of fun includes unpleasant effects such as a disturbing level of excitement, nausea, vomiting, a heavy drunk feeling, damaging heart palpitations, and unconsciousness. Effects can last up to three days following ingestion, during which the user may experience long periods of deep sleep.

Do yourself a favor. Unless you're looking to take a trip to the happy hunting ground, keep away from this psychedelic.

MESCALINE

COMMON NAMES: *anhalonium, beans, buttons, cactus, hikori, huatari, mesc, mescal, mescal buttons, moon, plants, seni, wakowi*

Mescaline is the hallucinatory heart of peyote. Excised from the scrubby peyote cactus, *Lophorophora williamsii,* by the scalpel of chemistry and transplanted into the mind of man, mescaline beats its LSD-like rhythm with only a slight change of tempo.

Just one of several alkaloids in peyote (see Peyote), mescaline is the main psychoactive chemical, triggering the senses into creating an illusion-filled world. It is available in its natural state as peyote buttons, or it may be extracted as organic mescaline, which looks and tastes like brown dirt. Synthetic mescaline sulfate comes in white needlepoint crystals, without much improvement in flavor. Since dosage ranges from 300 to 800 mg, a capsule of mescaline sulfate would have to be either a No. 1 or No. 0 size, or as large as a horse capsule. True synthetic mescaline is rarely, if ever, sold on the street. What is usually passed off as mescaline is either PCP, LSD, a combination of LSD/PCP, amphetamines, STP, belladonna alkaloids, or improperly synthesized contaminants.

A member of the amine group of chemicals, which includes speed, STP, and adrenalin, mescaline differs structurally from other hallucinogenic drugs such as LSD and psilocybin. Its chemical name is 3,4,5-trimethoxyphenylethylamine and it is related to the hormone epinephrine and the neurohormone norepinephrine.

Rarely injected, mescaline can be made into capsules, tablets, or a liquid, but cannot be compressed into little pills. It is most commonly ingested in capsule form, one way to disguise its unpalatability, or chewed as peyote buttons. One to six buttons are held in the mouth until soft, then swallowed, either chewed or unchewed. Some prefer macerating the buttons in a coffee grinder first, but either way, there's no avoiding the inevitable bitter, soapy taste and probable subsequent vomiting. Throwing up, if necessary, is recommended. It does not alter the drug's effects, and the relief it provides is immense.

Stomach disruption is common. Peyote fibers are emetic, and though they may be cleaned off, nausea-producing elements of the mescaline itself will remain. Synthetic mescaline sulfate is preferred over natural peyote because its side effects, including nausea, are less intense.

Medically classified as a hallucinogen, mescaline has been used in psychotherapy and as a treatment for opiate dependency and alcoholism. The drug acts as a heart and respiratory stimulant, though pulse may decrease slightly.

Once absorbed by the intestinal tract, mescaline heads immediately for the kidneys, liver, pancreas, and spleen. Within twenty-four hours, 60 to 90 percent of the drug has been excreted unchanged in the urine. Effects appear within one to two hours after ingestion, peak after two hours, and may continue up to twelve hours.

Mescaline's action stimulates the visual and visuo-psychic areas of the brain. Blocking effects have been noted on muscles and neuromuscular complexes, and an increase in deep tendon reflexes, systolic blood pressure, and temperature, as well as pupil dilation, may occur.

All of this body action is preparation for a trip to what has been called an "optical fairyland." Visual perception is altered to such a degree that even the mundane becomes miraculous. Colors gain a stained-glass depth and richness, concentrating on central, bright color rather than peripheral, dim color. Everyday objects undergo a phantasmagorical transformation, shifting and slipping in color and form, creating their own reality. Synesthesia, a crossover of the senses where color is heard and music is seen, is common.

True hallucinations do not occur. The tripper is aware that the illusions and fantasies which dance through his head are a vaudeville show he entered with a mescaline ticket. Aldous Huxley and Carlos Castaneda saw mescaline as not merely the source of a show, but as an entrée into a mystical world as well. While sensual perception—sight, sound, taste, touch, and smell—is in delightful turmoil, intellect and judgment remain clear and functional. Past experiences may not only be recalled, but re-experienced, as well, in the mind.

As with LSD, set and setting are vital in determining the direction of a mescaline trip. Set (the mood, expectations and personality of the tripper) and setting (physical surroundings and emotional environment) psychologically affect the tripper and may tip him to either side of the illusionary tightrope. One way, and he's off on a mystical sensory trip; the other, and he may exhibit schizophrenic tendencies—extreme moodiness, unprovoked blasts of emotion, anxiety, confusion, depression, and tremors. Nausea, anorexia, and insomnia may occur, regardless of the direction the trip is taking. Ambivalent feelings are not uncommon; feeling happy and sad, giddy and mad, the tripper may be bewildered by the haphazard rain of emotions he experiences.

While tolerance develops rapidly—within three to six days—mescaline is not considered either physiologically or psychologically addicting, since withdrawal symptoms do not occur. A cross-tolerance to LSD and psilocybin exists. Overdose is unlikely unless mescaline is combined with other drugs such as barbiturates, physostigmine, and insulin. Hyperinsulinism may result from the combination of mescaline and insulin.

A bad trip should be treated psychologically rather than chemically. Reassurance, comfort, and support can transform a frightening experience into a learning experience. Introduction of other drugs may magnify the bad trip, causing possible shock or death.

Other hazards include the drug's potential for pushing borderline schizophrenics over the edge, and, in the case of needle freaks, exposing trippers to the problems of injection: hepatitis, tetanus, gas gangrene, local abscesses, and other infections. Lung disease, heart disease, and diseases of the blood vessels have been known to occur. Like most other drugs, mescaline should be avoided during pregnancy.

Listed along with LSD, STP, marijuana, and psilocybin as a Schedule I drug under the Controlled Substances Act, mescaline is legal only for members of the Native American Church (see Peyote). Manufacture, production, and distribution of mescaline is punishable by a maximum prison sentence and fine of five years and/or $15,000. Possession is punished by imprisonment of not more than one year and/or a fine of not more than $5,000.

The name "mescaline" comes from the Mescalero Apaches, a tribe that adopted the peyote ritual of the Mexican Indians and helped spread the mystical religion northward to other American Indian tribes.

A German chemist first isolated mescaline from the peyote plant in 1896, long after the Indians had discovered its effects. The drug was synthesized twenty-three years later.

Mescaline made its street debut in the form of peyote buttons in the 1950s, then graduated in the late 1960s to popular use in both organic and synthetic states. Former LSD users, frightened by the Great Chromosome Scare, turned to mescaline and other chemicals to achieve an altered state of consciousness. Difficult to obtain, surrounded by myth, mescaline remains an elusive guide to our inner visions.

METHADONE

Some narcotics, such as heroin, are cloaked in a shroud of crime, degradation, and death, while others, such as opium, evoke images of strange places and exotic rituals. Then there are narcotics, such as methadone, that sound like medicine. Actually, methadone is no less a narcotic than the others, but it is considered the "cure" for opiate addicts, their passport to a taxpaying, middle-class way of life.

Methadone is a synthetic opiate analgesic currently used in America as the leading treatment for narcotics addiction. A soluble white crystalline powder, usually ingested by tablet or mixed in a liquid such as orange juice, it is rarely injected, unless the addict has found some illicit source offering it as an injectable fluid.

First synthesized by the Germans during World War II to substitute for scarce morphine, methadone is only slightly more potent than morphine as a painkiller. Methadone has the distinct advantage over other narcotics of being nearly as effective orally as by injection. In addition, while most opiates must be administered every four to six hours to stave off withdrawal pains and anxieties, an adequate methadone dose lasts a full twenty-four-hour day, and can supplant narcotic cravings for up to forty-eight hours. The drug is manufactured by Eli Lilly & Company, and its legal use is totally restricted to licensed, regulated methadone clinics and hospitals; it cannot be purchased by prescription. As a result of illegal diversion of legally obtained doses, however, it can often be purchased on the street by addicts.

Methadone, a central-nervous-system depressant, is an effective painkiller and cough suppressant. However, the Federal Drug Administration has not approved its medical use. The drug can only be legally dispensed for treatment of addiction.

The history of addiction treatment is a curious one. At one time cocaine and heroin were thought to be harmless, nonaddicting alternatives to opium addiction, and opium was used for the treatment of alcoholics. Methadone is now prescribed for heroin addiction. A highly addictive substance that chemically blocks the craving for heroin, it does not provide heroin's warm, euphoric rush. Nor is it a drug that creates tolerance in the user. The methadone addict does not

139

need increasingly larger doses to remain comfortably "normal." In fact, dosage can usually be reduced after the addict has been detoxified from heroin. The drug produces a cross-tolerance to heroin. This means that if an addict tries heroin while on methadone, the heroin will have no effect.

There are some scattered reports of bone-muscle pain, hallucinations, constipation, nausea, mental lethargy, and impotence from methadone use, but the majority of evidence supports the view that it causes no permanent physiological damage and leaves the addict clear-headed and healthy. Heroin's illegality and high price often cause a disruptive, criminal lifestyle that becomes unnecessary when the addict can get free methadone at the local clinic. Methadone patients commonly lead normal, productive lives, taking care of their families and showing up regularly for work.

If the addict does not get his adequate daily methadone dose, he is subject to withdrawal trauma—diarrhea, hot and cold flashes, sweating, insomnia, and stomach pain. The withdrawal phase may be less intense than heroin's three days of horror, but it can last as long as two weeks.

Methadone obliterates what is known as post-abstinence syndrome —that intermittent, gnawing desire for heroin that lingers on after withdrawal. The drug decreases anxiety, although it is not a potent mood elevator. Methadone creates psychological and physical dependence, which may help explain its success in addiction treatment. In all cases, prescribing proper dosage should be left to professionals. Addicts with low tolerance levels may require special dosage to avoid potentially lethal results. Nonaddicts can easily die from using methadone.

Of the approximately 500,000 American opiate addicts, 75,000 to 100,000 are currently undergoing methadone treatment. Large doses of the drug are administered for about two weeks to detoxify heroin addicts and ease withdrawal pain. A few heroin addicts detoxify regularly, later returning to the use of illicit heroin at a lower dosage level and cost. Methadone maintenance clinics have been in operation for over ten years. Their "success rate" is quite impressive, judging by the percentage of patients who do not revert to heroin use. Clinic sources claim that 80 percent of their patients stay in the program, and, of those, 90 percent remain heroin-free.

Initially, methadone treatment was envisioned as a temporary therapy that could be discontinued after a patient had received decreasing doses for several months. Methadone maintenance is now believed to be a permanent treatment. The patient must regularly visit a clinic and receive his daily medication or he will revert to his previous opiate addiction. For reasons that may have more to do with human nature than with pharmacology, most heroin-free methadone patients dabble in other drugs, including barbiturates, cocaine, and alcohol; 20 percent become alcoholics. Only 2 percent of methadone patients stay free of other drugs, so methadone's "success rate" must be carefully considered.

Why not legalize and dispense heroin itself if the addict must stay on methadone, another opiate, the rest of his life? Certain advantages to methadone use lead most health professionals to prefer it in the treatment of opiate addiction. Since the drug is fully effective when taken orally, the need for injection is eliminated, along with debilitative diseases such as hepatitis, caused by the use of needles. Methadone is also longer-acting than heroin. The addict need report for a methadone dose only once a day. A new, experimental opiate substitute, LAAM, has the advantage of lasting up to seventy-two hours (see LAAM).

Although the medical benefits of methadone are real, the primary advantage to the addict is that the drug is free, or available for a small fee. He no longer has to hustle in heroin's gutter underworld. Without the addict's constant pressure to feed his expensive $50-to-$100-a-day habit, society benefits from a reduced crime rate.

The "best" treatment for opiate addiction would be an absolute cure, or at least addiction prevention through effective education. Until this happens, methadone seems to provide a relatively safe and economical alternative to the ravages of heroin.

The drug is currently listed and regulated under Schedule II of the Federal Controlled Substances Act.

METHAQUALONE

COMMON NAMES: *French Quaalude, ludes, mandrakes, quas, quacks, quads, 714s, soaps, soapers, sopes, super Quaaludes, super soper*

Pop a lude and you're off on a boozeless drunk, flying high with the Quaalude Culture of the seventies. "Safe and nonaddictive!" proclaimed the manufacturers of the magic little tablets. "Let's have a party!" cheered fun-seekers everywhere. So they partied and popped till they couldn't stop; they were addicted.

For those who succeed in defying the "Betcha can't eat just one" dare, an occasional lude trip can be as harmless as an occasional alcoholic drunk. The trick is to keep it occasional. Called a "Jekyll and Hyde drug" by Senator Birch Bayh, methaqualone's effects can insidiously creep up until you discover you are another soaper statistic.

A nonbarbiturate sedative-hypnotic, unrelated chemically to other sedatives, methaqualone is classified as a central-nervous-system depressant. Quaaludes and Sopors are pure methaqualone, while Parest, Optimil, and Somnafac are methaqualone hydrochloride. Biphetamine T and Biphetamine T 20 add amphetamine and dextroamphetamine to the methaqualone.

Tasteless and odorless, methaqualone comes in either tablets or capsules selling legally for about 10 to 30 cents each, or illicitly from $2 to $5 each. The standard hypnotic dose to induce sleep is 150–300 mg, with 75 mg for daytime sedation. A dose of 2.4 grams may produce coma, and 8–20 grams can cause severe toxicosis or death.

A few needle freaks have attempted to shoot Quaalude intravenously, which can lead to abscesses and cellulitis. Alkaline, it is soluble in alcohol and ether, but only slightly soluble in water.

Touted medically and pharmaceutically as a sleep inducer and sedative, methaqualone acts on a different central-nervous-system site than other hypnotic drugs, such as barbiturates. Once absorbed from the gastrointestinal tract, it is distributed in body fat, brain tissue, and the liver—the primary site of metabolism—then excreted through the bile and kidneys. It reduces the intensity of transmissions along the neural pathways in the brain and suppresses REM (rapid eye movement) during dreams.

Methaqualone's soporific, or sleep-inducing, effects are resisted by abusers who prefer staying awake to enjoy its mellow, euphoric high. Drowsiness occurs within ten to twenty minutes, but if sleep is avoided, the body relaxes to the point of noncoordination. Walking and talking become difficult. The user tends to bump into things; hence the term "wallbanger."

Confident, relaxed, and loose, the tripper drops his inhibitions, becoming warm and friendly, witty and wise. His head and body feel light, his pain threshold is high. Slurred speech, similar to that of a drunk, interferes with his desire to communicate intimately with those around him. Light doses can produce aphrodisiac effects for some, but as is the case with alcohol, heavy doses may have the opposite effect, particularly in males. The user's sensual, euphoric state may degenerate into simple nodding out, and hangovers are not uncommon.

Physical and psychological dependence can occur within two weeks at a daily dosage of 300–600 mg, with overdose occurring at eight 300-mg tablets. Tolerance can develop after four days, requiring more and more of the drug to achieve the same results. At this point, overdose becomes a real possibility. Physical tolerance rises more slowly than psychological tolerance; while the abuser's head is calling for more ludes, his body is crying, "Enough already!"

Dependence is indicated when withdrawal symptoms begin: headache, fatigue, dizziness, "pins and needles" in limbs, nausea, gastric problems, restlessness, anxiety, anorexia, dry mouth, and allergic skin problems. Anemia and foul perspiration occasionally occur. As withdrawal continues in the heavy user, insomnia, cramps, tremors, seizures, vomiting, and depression are added to the symptoms, making it similar to "cold-turkey" withdrawal from heroin or barbiturates.

The head-rolling, incoherent, unmotivated heavy luder may magnify his problems tenfold if he combines methaqualone, a respiratory depressant, with alcohol or barbiturates. Each potentiates the effects of the other. The combination can lead to delirium, coma, convulsions, liver and kidney damage, pulmonary edema, respiratory arrest, and death. Indeed, most methaqualone deaths are caused by combining the drug with alcohol.

In addition to the synergistic effect of methaqualone and alcohol, overdose potential is increased because the user may misjudge the potency of these innocent-looking pills. Since his memory is now blown, the user may forget how many pills he has taken, or worse, he may not even care about the risk of taking more pills than he needs.

Overdose is indicated by grand mal convulsions, delirium, mania, delirium tremens, and stomach hemorrhaging. Professional medical aid is a must. Treatment requires close supervision. Voluntary vomiting can be induced within twenty minutes of ingestion by drinking soapy water or using the time-honored finger-down-the-throat technique. If the abuser is already hovering on the brink of unconsciousness, this is not advised. His respiratory center is already depressed and reflexes in the back of the throat are slowed, so he may aspirate his own vomit, as did rock star Jimi Hendrix. Keep the victim awake, as coma may occur rapidly if he falls asleep. Don't be fooled by normal pulse and respiratory rates. Sudden respiratory failure can occur.

Hospitalization is a necessity for detoxification. Methaqualone addiction is more difficult to cure than barbiturate addiction. Total abstinence is attained by first substituting barbiturates for methaqualone, and then treating the abuser for barbiturate addiction and withdrawal.

Controversy exists as to whether stricter controls should be applied to methaqualone. Presently, sale or possession without a prescription is punishable by a fine not exceeding $5,000 and/or imprisonment from one to ten years.

Methaqualone, first synthesized in 1950, was initially introduced to India and Africa as an antimalarial drug. By 1972, the drug industry had Madison-Avenued it into the sixth most popular prescription drug in the United States, claiming it to be a safe and nonaddictive sedative-downer.

After 274 poisonings, overdoses, and attempted suicides (not to mention sixteen deaths), doubts about its safety were raised. Abuse became rampant in the United States. During the 1972 Democratic Convention, Miami's Flamingo Park was known as "Quaalude Alley." Other countries experienced similar problems. Methaqualone accounted for half of Japan's total drug addiction, and Britain became alarmed enough to put it under strict control in 1971.

The world was getting Quaalude-quazy. High school and college kids were "luding out"—taking 300–450 mg of methaqualone with wine. "Juice bars" became the new speakeasies, dispensing fruit juice to luders instead of bathtub gin, plus disco music for dancing. When legal prescriptions became difficult to get, ludes went underground, obtainable from cooperative doctors and, on the street, from diverted legal shipments.

With methaqualone the drug industry has once again discovered a way to keep us sleepy, stoned, and smiling. They merely forget to tell

144

us that the lude laugh may be a death's-head laugh—a not-so-jolly roger.

Quaalude (Rorer): 150 mg (white), "Rorer 712" on pills; 300 mg (white), "Rorer 714" on pills

Sopor (Anar-Stone): 75 mg (green), 150 mg (yellow), 300 mg (orange); "A/S" on pills

Optimil (Wallace): 200 mg, 400 mg, in pink or blue capsules

Somnafac (Smith, Miller and Patch): 200 mg (two-tone blue capsules), 400 mg—SomnaFac Fourte—(dark-blue capsules)

Parest (Parke-Davis): 200 mg and 400 mg, in pink or blue capsules

Biphetamine-T (Strasenburgh): "12½," 6.25 mg amphetamine, 6.25 mg dextroamphetamine, 40 mg methaqualone; "20," 10 mg amphetamine, 10 mg dextroamphetamine, 40 mg methaqualone

Mandrax (English)

Tuazole (Strasenburgh)

MORNING-GLORY SEEDS

COMMON NAMES: *badoh negro, blue star, flying saucers, glory seeds, heavenly blues, pearly gates, pearly whites, seeds, summer skies, Tlitiltzen, wedding bells*

Those seeking hallucinogenic experiences need go no farther than the local flower shop or garden center to find a cheap, legal cousin of LSD, morning-glory seeds.

Discovered by South American Aztec Indians, they have been used in sacred rituals for hundreds of years. Morning-glory seeds, *Rivea corymbosa*, made their initial inroads with American drug users a decade ago when scientific journals published a number of articles relating them to LSD. The black or brown seeds contain d-lysergic acid amide, an alkaloid derivative with one-tenth the potency of LSD. While this alkaloid is present in the entire plant, the seeds themselves carry the greatest concentrations.

About fifteen varieties of morning-glory seeds are available to the potential user. Because of their high lysergic content, the two most popular types have been dubbed heavenly blues and pearly gates. Dosage needed for a trip of four to fourteen hours ranges from a minimum of 100 triangular-shaped seeds to a maximum of 300, or 5 to 10 grams, depending on seed size. This quantity will produce about the same effects as 200 to 300 micrograms of LSD-25.

While morning-glory seeds may be ground and brewed into tea or taken intravenously, the most common method of ingestion is by thorough chewing. This action, before swallowing, permits the seeds' psychoactive chemicals to be easily absorbed by the body.

In an effort to discourage use of morning-glory seeds as a recreational drug, most commercial seed producers treat their products with a poisonous coating. The poison is not easily removed by washing and can make one quite sick if a quantity of seeds great enough to induce a high is ingested. Thus, even if a somewhat stimulating hallucinogenic effect is experienced, the high may be accompanied by unpleasant side effects such as diarrhea, nausea, vomiting, chills, and dizziness, as well as a good deal of abdominal pain. Although overdose potential is low, high doses can be toxic and may result in psychotic reaction, shock, or heart failure.

Bearing this in mind, unless uncoated seeds are available—either homegrown or from a bulk distributor—morning-glory seeds should be considered only for garden use.

MORPHINE

Morphine (morphine sulphate), one of the most effective pain-killers ever discovered, is the ingredient responsible for opium's psychological bliss. Like every opiate narcotic, morphine is powerful and addictive. Once he is hooked, the addict's road back to normalcy is a difficult one. Only frequent and prolonged use, however, guarantees a habit. When it is prescribed for short-term, sporadic medical use, the likelihood of addiction is almost nil, unless the patient decides illicitly to self-prescribe the drug when he leaves the hospital.

Morphine is derived from crude opium grown in Mexico and the Middle, Near, and Far East, and reaches the pharmacy as tablets, capsules, or an injectible solution that is usually shot into a muscle or popped under the skin. In pure white crystal or odorless light-brown or white powder form the drug can also be smoked, although morphine smokers are a rarity since the drug is most effective when injected in solution.

The drug depresses the central nervous system. The first-time user may experience fright, nausea, or vomiting, but after adjusting to morphine's potent effects his mind eases into a state of contentment. Life becomes a golden cloud of detachment, minus pain, anxiety, or reality. No wonder the German scientist who first discovered the drug named it after Morpheus, the Greek god of dreams. Moderate doses can constrict the bowels and depress normal drives, such as those for food and sex. The mind is sedated and unshakably tranquil. Limbs feel heavy as the drug warms the body and mind into a pleasurable haze.

When prescribed medically, morphine reduces severe pain as well as its associated anxiety and sends the patient into blissful sleep where discomfort becomes a distant blur. Although he, too, feels an initial surging rush, the addict does not enjoy the euphoria of the infrequent or medical user. Shortly after taking his dose he merely feels "normal" until three or four hours pass, when he becomes sweaty and irritable and his body begins to demand its next fix. Denied morphine, the body experiences withdrawal, with chills, hot and cold flashes, nausea, cramps, profuse sweating, fever, tremors, restlessness, and anxiety. High doses or toxic reactions can constrict the pupils of the eye and cause low blood pressure, cold, moist, bluish skin, shock, unconsciousness, coma, respiratory failure, and even death.

Scientists now theorize that traumatic reactions to morphine are not caused by the drug itself, but rather by a mixture of the narcotic with alcohol, barbiturates, or the adulterant quinine. Even an ordinary medical dose of morphine taken with alcohol can prove deadly for certain individuals. An overdosed morphine abuser should be rushed to a hospital where an opiate antagonist, such as Nalline, can be administered, permitting medically supervised withdrawal to begin.

First synthesized about 1805, morphine was at one time prescribed widely for a host of pains and illnesses. The 1800s were the salad days of morphine use, when it was commonly sold as an over-the-counter patent medicine in pharmacies and grocery stores to control diarrhea, coughs, and many other disorders. Morphine came to be preferred medically as a painkiller with the invention of the syringe in 1850, permitting the drug's use as a standardized, controllable solution. Heavily prescribed for the searing pain of battlefield injuries, the drug first hooked Civil War combatants. Not until the end of the century, however, did doctors become aware that it was highly addictive. Ironically, heroin was invented and initially promoted as a "harmless" morphine substitute before its own addictive properties were recognized.

In 1914, the Harrison Act began regulating the huge legal morphine trade through licensing and taxation. Tight restrictions have continued. Today, morphine is listed under Schedule II of the Federal Controlled Substances Act. Only available now for specific medical use, the drug is rarely sold in the street. Morphine is not the drug of choice of modern-day American opiate addicts. Heroin has that distinction because addicts buy what is available, and what is available is heroin.

NIANDO

Niando (*Alchornea floribunda*) is a shrub member of the spurge family common to Uganda, Liberia, and Nigeria.

When used as an aphrodisiac by African natives, sometimes in combination with other drugs such as iboga, niando is generally prepared by steeping the root bark in palm or banana wine. This method of preparation is part of the drug's problem.

Since yohimbine may be the main active ingredient in niando, combining it with alcohol can be deadly. These two chemicals potentiate each other and can be highly toxic when used together. Never use the drug with antihistamines, amphetamines, or other narcotics, either. If you suffer from hepatitis, hypoglycemia, or blood-pressure disorders, or from kidney, heart, or liver trouble, forget it.

Niando can stimulate sex drive, but as the drug wears off deep depression can set in. Sometimes death follows . . . hardly worth the trouble.

Our advice: If you need sexual stimulation, see an X-rated movie and forget niando.

NITROUS OXIDE

COMMON NAMES: *gas, laughing gas, nitrous*

"It's a gas!" it is said, referring to anything in the way of fun, hilarity, and general giddiness. Nitrous oxide (nitrogen monoxide) may well be the source of that expression, for it is relatively harmless, relatively legal, and superlatively mind-blowing.

A colorless gas with a sweet taste and odor, nitrous oxide is an artificial compound of nitrogen and oxygen. Tanks are available to the medical profession, although fun-seekers everywhere have managed to obtain their own supplies. Once a tank of the stuff is obtained, it can be taken back for refills time and again with no problem. A large tank costs about $60, the gas for it another $60, and refills still another $60. Small quantities of whipped-cream propellant can be sniffed from upright aerosol containers, and pressurized pellets, similar to CO_2 cartridges, are also available.

Inhalation, which affects the brain most rapidly, is the only route for nitrous: Nitrous freaks find it much more efficient to fill large party or weather balloons with the gas, passing these ritually like joints, rather than battling each other for a turn at an unwieldy tank. Some sharers find that surgical tubing and clips attached to a tank enable everyone to sniff from the same source, but this is more involved and less efficient than the balloon method. Sniffing from aerosol cans is chancy and can result in complications such as death.

More and more dentists are discovering that nitrous makes patients not only willing, but enthusiastic. A gaseous tranquilizer, it sedates and creates an analgesic effect by changing the patient's mood and interpretation of pain. Sedated, the patient feels something he may or may not interpret as pain; but either way, he doesn't care. Some dentists don't use it because the equipment, incorporating a device that mixes oxygen with nitrogen, is expensive. Although a few patients may experience anxiety or nausea, and painkillers such as Novocain still have to be administered, the placid feeling produced by the gas for most has generally desirable effects.

Nitrous has other medical uses beyond dentistry. In a Russian hospital, a Harvard cardiologist found tanks of nitrous next to each coronary patient's bed. A study published in the *Journal of the American Medical Association* confirmed the superiority of nitrous over the more traditional oxygen and morphine, now used for heart-attack pain. Used during childbirth, it is safe for both mother and baby.

Correctly used, it is always administered with 20 to 35 percent oxygen, necessary to prevent anoxia, or oxygen deprivation. Effects are almost immediate, beginning within fifteen to thirty seconds, remaining about one to three minutes, and totally out of the system within five to ten minutes. Repeated inhalation creates a continuous high. It is nonaddictive and nonallergenic, with very slight tolerance development after repeated or prolonged administration. No withdrawal symptoms occur, and nitrous may be used safely in conjunction with other narcotic agents, or local anesthetic injections.

Inhalation at moderate doses produces euphoria with a numbing of the body, dizziness, tingling in the fingers and toes, and buzzing or humming in the head. Warm sensations wash over the body and a crossover of the senses, such as hearing sights and seeing sounds, may occur. Sensations gradually diminish, with hearing dissolving to a constant, electronic-like throbbing. Nitrous can release subconscious material. Thus, revelations and insights may occur in a magnified or distorted fashion, similar to LSD visions. Transitory, they are soon erased until the next inhalation.

Depending on dosage, nitrous may have a short-term effect on memory, concentration, and sensory function. Feelings of floating, driving, or flying have been noted, and there is a general sense of detachment from the body. Properly used, it is one of the safest of all drugs.

Anesthetic in action, the gas affects the central nervous system, obliterating one's perception of pain. Rather than depressing the central nervous system, nitrous stimulates it, although no one is quite sure how. Scientists say the gas stimulates the brain electrically in a manner similar to LSD, affecting the metabolism of the brain cells. It does not break down chemically in the body; it enters and exits the lungs in an unchanged state.

Oxygen deprivation is the chief danger of nitrous use. Sustained inhalation, unaccompanied by adequate oxygen, may be rapidly followed by severe decerebration (brain death), heart failure, pulmonary edema, or organic brain damage. Cyanosis, indicated by slow pulse, rise in blood pressure, twitching of the muscles, violent respiration which becomes increasingly shallow and irregular, and delirium, may accompany oxygen shortage. White-blood-cell count may drop and tissues may dry out, resulting in bronchial irritation.

Nitrous oxide's side effects and dangers can be eliminated by taking simple safety precautions. Nausea may be avoided by refraining from eating large meals before a nitrous trip. Keep the tank vertical and don't breathe straight from it, or you may freeze your lips and larynx. Don't attach the source of the gas to the nose or mouth, or undue pressure may be exerted on the lungs by the force of the rushing gas. Since it is important to breathe deeply between hits to balance the oxygen level, not attaching the gas also ensures that you won't become unconscious from lack of oxygen. Don't fill up a small enclosed area, like a car or closet, with the gas, and don't stuff your head into a plastic bag full of gas unless you want to suffocate.

Nitrous is one of those quasi-legal drugs whose medical use and distribution are monitored by federal regulations applied to prescription drugs. Penalty for unapproved possession is imprisonment for not more than one year and/or a fine of up to $5,000. If you're into concocting your own illicit supply, nitrous may be made by applying heat to ammonium nitrate crystals. This is not recommended unless you are a chemistry whiz.

Joseph Priestley, the discoverer of oxygen, also identified nitrous oxide in 1776, but never used it. Sir Humphrey Davy, in the same year, synthesized nitrous by exposing nitrous peroxide to iron, removing three of the four oxygen atoms, and all his inhibitions. A deep whiff of N_2O, Davy discovered, resulted in a riotous state of excitement and glee. Naturally, he wanted to share this pleasure with his good friends, so the nitrous party was born. Prominent among the inhalers were Samuel Taylor Coleridge, Robert Southey, Josiah Wedgwood, and Peter Mark Roget (of thesaurus fame). This jolly group favored the effects of N_2O over those of alcohol. Davy noted that one of these effects was the alleviation of pain. In 1799 he proposed that nitrous be used during surgery, but no one took him seriously for another forty-five years.

At its inception, nitrous was a mere entertainment. Demonstrations of "laughing gas" and another amusement, electricity, toured the country. Horace Wells, a dentist, attended one of these carnival acts put on by Gardner Quincy Colton in 1844, and had a flash: painless dentistry! His first demonstration in 1845 at Massachusetts General

NITROUS OXIDE

Hospital was a disaster. The patient came out of the gas too soon and screamed in pain—definitely a downer for Wells. However, use of nitrous spread, and today it enjoys a dual reputation as pain repressant and pleasure producer—nothing to sniff at.

NUTMEG

Those looking to add a bit of spice to their lives sometimes become curious about nutmeg.

This well-known commercial spice is made from ground, dried seeds of the tropical evergreen tree, *Myristica fragrans*, first brought to Europe in the seventeenth century by the Dutch.

When ingested, nutmeg powder acts as a mind-altering drug, sedative and aphrodisiac. On the potency scale, it ranks somewhere below LSD and above mescaline when taken in quantity. The substances in nutmeg believed to be responsible for its effects are myristicin, elemecin, and safrole.

Popular for centuries in India, nutmeg's use in the Western World has been most common among drug-starved prisoners and teen-agers when other pleasure-givers were unavailable.

The intensity of a nutmeg trip depends upon the quantity taken. General dosage ranges from 5 to 20 grams (⅓ ounce equals approximately 10 grams); a level teaspoon is usually enough. For some the trip can be fun, for others a bummer. A 10-gram dose can produce effects similar to those from one marijuana cigarette, but not before forty-five minutes of severe nausea and diarrhea may be experienced. Once this has passed, a heavy, leaden feeling settles into the limbs. The user falls out in a drunken, lethargic manner. If not too much has been taken, after two hours the user may alternate between lightheaded giggles and a dreamy, detached state of mind. Time and space seem distorted. More than 10 grams can produce some unpleasant feelings: dizziness, flushes, parched mouth and throat, rapid heartbeat, bloodshot eyes, constipation, urinary difficulty, and a high level of panic and agitation.

Those aiming to hallucinate can be in for trouble. The dose of nutmeg required to reach that state is dangerously close to overdose level. Overdose deaths have been attributed to liver failure, as nutmeg oils can cause tumors and may be toxic to the liver. Anyone with a personal or family history of liver problems should avoid nutmeg. Even without a history to serve as a reason, excessive use should be avoided.

The total nutmeg trip lasts from four to twelve hours, depending on how much you have managed to get down. It will be followed by a hangover and aching muscles. All in all, the user feels washed out for a day or so afterward.

Virola, another member of the nutmeg family, is used as a snuff by Amazon Indians. To prepare it, resin is scraped off fresh bark from the *Virola colophylla* or *V. calophylloidea* tree before daybreak. It is then boiled down to a gummy paste, mixed with the ashes of coca stems, dried, crushed into a fine powder, and snorted. To avoid overdose, amateurs are cautioned not to ingest more than $\frac{1}{3}$ teaspoon of this powder.

Another closely related drug is the common spice mace, which comes from the fibrous seed covering of the nutmeg plant, *Myristica fragrans*. Mace can be brewed into a tea that will produce much the same kind of trip as nutmeg when used in similar quantity.

OLOLUIQUI

Ololuiqui is the Aztec Indian psychedelic big brother to morning-glory seeds. The two have similar mind-altering properties.

Produced from the seeds of the *Rivea corymbosa* vine, a member of the bindweed family found in the mountains of southern Mexico, ololuiqui can transport the user on a legal LSD-like trip for about six hours. To prepare a dose, users soak about fifteen crushed seeds in ½ cup of water and drink the resulting mixture.

The first feeling is a pleasant intoxication lasting about three hours. Following that, the tripper hallucinates and has other LSD-like experiences—which is not surprising considering the fact that the active chemical in ololuiqui is d-lysergic acid amide (see LSD). Following the trip, the only aftereffect is a deep sense of relaxation.

This drug should be ingested on an empty stomach, since nausea may occur during early stages of the experience. As is the case with LSD, people with liver problems should stay away.

OPIUM

Opium. Fortunes have been won and lost for it. Dynasties have come and gone in its wake, and a three-year war was waged in its name, leaving thousands of casualties and half of China's adult male population addicted by 1900.

The opium poppy is the source of the various opiates traded by pharmacists and "French connections" alike—heroin, morphine, opium, codeine, Demerol, Percodan, and laudanum, the elixir of many a nineteenth-century proper Bostonian matron. These poppy derivatives share a common black thread; all can be addictive. This is the chief drawback of the opiates, but the word "drawback" hardly describes what addiction is like.

Addiction is anything but pleasant. In time, the addict builds up a tolerance to his opiate. No longer getting high or euphoric, he needs larger and larger doses just to feel "normal." If the addict does not get his dose he feels abnormal in the extreme, faced with a withdrawal period of one to ten days that can include such horrors as chills, tremors, diarrhea, weeping, heavy sweating, nausea, vomiting, muscular and abdominal cramps, uncontrollable yawning, runny nose, goose flesh, appetite loss, and insomnia. Some of these symptoms may continue for months, and even then the addict is not off the hook. Researchers now believe that opiates cause permament biochemical molecular changes, leaving the addict prone to readdiction years after withdrawal. This phenomenon, known as the post-abstinence syndrome, may account for the overwhelming recidivism rate among "ex-addicts." It also explodes the myth that moral guidance and personal willpower can "cure" an addict forever. This is one monkey that keeps crawling on the victim's back and hanging on with claws of steel.

Opium, the granddaddy of opiates, is just as addicting as heroin, its sinister sister. The drug is made by opening the opium poppy's unripe seed pods or capsules and drying the milky white juice until it turns brown. The resulting brown goo is then scraped, boiled, collected into balls or bricks, wrapped, and sold as opium, or sent to processors who convert it to morphine, heroin, codeine, or other opiates. Grown in Southeast Asia, Turkey, China, Mexico, Lebanon, Greece, Iran, Yugoslavia, and Bulgaria, its potency depends upon freshness, country of origin, processing, and adulteration.

Opium's painkilling properties come from its many alkaloids; the alkaloid morphine provides its pleasurable punch. For thousands of years, the drug has been used as a painkilling sedative or tranquilizer-type remedy for ailments such as dysentery, diarrhea, gout, diabetes, tetanus, insanity, and even nymphomania. During the nineteenth century, the Age of Opium, it was proposed as a cure for alcoholism. Chronic tipplers were weaned from alcohol to opium, unaware of the dangers of the "cure."

Opium usually comes in a bitter-tasting brown or black gummy bar. It can also be reduced to an opiate powder, sold in capsule or tablet form. A user does not really smoke opium, but rather heats it indirectly, inhaling its white or yellow vapors. Most neophytes make the mistake of directly lighting the drug in a pipe, mixed with marijuana or hashish. Direct flame destroys opium's magical properties and its pleasurable effect. Inhaled properly, its creeping suffusion of peace begins immediately. It can also be dissolved under the tongue or brewed as a tea. Using these methods, its effects will not be felt for thirty minutes to an hour. Eating opium may cause nausea or irritate the stomach lining. Nonaddicts sometimes apply liquid paregoric, a combination of opium and camphor, to cigarettes. Heroin addicts may use paregoric or laudanum, an opium tincture with alcohol, in times of heroin shortage. A less popular method of ingestion is the use of opium as a rectal suppository. Injection is risky, since opium is rarely free of impurities. The use of homemade or shared syringes further subjects the needle freak to possible hepatitis, abscess, infection, tetanus, and gangrene.

Opium is not the American addict's drug of choice, since it does not provide the warm, orgasmic rush of an injectable narcotic—but don't count it out in the pleasure department. A moderate dose eases one into the tranquil joy of sensuous fantasy and intoxicating dreams. Detached and apathetic to life's stress and anxiety for three to four hours, the user's judgment and coordination are not impaired. The novice often suffers from nausea, vomiting, anxiety, dizziness, or shortness of breath, while the regular user ignores these symptoms, getting lost in a serenely pleasurable haze. The user is passive and nonviolent. His limbs become heavy, his mind lethargic, and aggression and hunger drives are reduced. These effects are considered medically innocuous, and opium causes no long-term organic damage.

Large doses induce nothing more serious than slow breathing, low blood pressure, and sleep. But opium is addicting, and the horrors of addiction cannot be overemphasized. Inhaling moderate amounts of opium on a sporadic basis is unlikely to cause addiction, but every individual has a different "break point," where blissful dreaminess turns into painful disaster. Once the user is addicted, those days of sweet stupor are replaced by a feeling of nothingness. The addict no longer gets high, but simply feeds his habit to keep away the crushing pain of withdrawal.

Needing larger and larger doses just to feel normal, an addict can die from the effects of withdrawal if opium use is discontinued. Accidental overdose can occur when dosage reaches soaring heights, or if the drug is mixed with alcohol or barbiturates. Overdose symptoms may include slow breathing, nausea, vomiting, constricted pupils, moist, cold bluish skin, and uncontrollable drowsiness. Drowsiness can turn into coma and respiratory failure, resulting in death. The overdosed addict should be forced to stay awake and rushed to a hospital, where narcotics antagonists such as Nalline (nalorphine) can reverse opium's depressant effects and bring on withdrawal. Until professional help arrives, mix 2 tablespoons of Epsom salts in two glasses of water and feed to the victim. As an alternative, 2 tablespoons of powdered charcoal or powdered burnt toast may be mixed with 1 tablespoon of milk of magnesia in 4 tablespoons of strong tea. Do not rely on the curative powers of these potions, since complications may set in. Hospital facilities are definitely preferred.

Unlicensed possession, manufacture, and sale of opium are illegal under Schedule II of the Controlled Substances Act. Until 1914, the drug was not only unrestricted, but was actually dispensed in thousands of over-the-counter patent medicines, distributed by mail order, and sold in grocery stores and pharmacies. It was particularly promoted to ease infants' teething, suppress coughs (see Codeine), alleviate menstrual cramps, and eliminate all manner of aches and pains. Opiate cough syrups and laudanum, originally sold for medicinal purposes, became pain relievers of another sort. What started by prescription was continued for pleasure, with the excuse of rheumatism or headache providing the proper nineteenth-century "cover" for getting high. Many addicts were women and children whose maladies had been treated with opium.

Opium's previous widespread medicinal application and promotion are easily understood. In fact, the drug is an effective painkiller, allaying fear and anxiety. In India and Iran, opium was a standard folk remedy for stomach and respiratory ailments, while in Great Britain, laudanum was given to children to keep them quiet. From Homer to Sherlock Holmes, opium use has spanned the ages.

Chinese immigrants, brought to America to build railroads, brought Asian-produced opium with them. Before long, the medical community recognized its value. Opium, and its hundreds of derivatives and preparations, became staples in everyone's medicine chest. Those who used it for pleasure frequented opium dens in major cities. Addicts and fun seekers were often admired citizens, maintaining their families, jobs, and self-respect. Although addiction was not considered moral or respectable, it was accepted, much like gambling or dancing. Addicts were not seen as weak-willed parasites until opiate importation was made illegal around the turn of the century, forcing them to prey on society to meet the inflated cost of illicit drugs. Initially, opium was taxed, then licensed, then discouraged, and ultimately made illegal for most uses under the Harrison Narcotics Act of 1914.

Opium laws, invention of the syringe in 1850, and the discovery of synthetic heroin in 1897 caused heroin and morphine to become overwhelming drug favorites for both medical and recreational use. Doctors administered heroin and morphine because dosage was more predictable and injection more controllable. Pleasure seekers discovered the orgasmic rush that only an injectable narcotic can provide. The syringe became the trademark of heroin and morphine addiction.

Recreationally, opium has now been relegated to the back drawer of soft-drug dealers, who sometimes sell it to marijuana and hashish users as a special "treat." The varieties of opium available in the United States are generally not of sufficient potency to addict anyone. On today's American drug-abuse scene, it is considered no more than an exotic curiosity to be tried and forgotten.

As with any other narcotic, its seductive pleasures should be carefully and seriously weighed against its potential for addiction.

PAREGORIC

COMMON NAME: goric

In the world of narcotics, paregoric is merely kids' stuff. The drug is so mild it can be safely recommended as an effective remedy not only for adults but for infant and childhood diarrhea as well. In primitive and less than hygienic lands, it is often the traveler's best friend in times of distress on the Montezuma Trail.

Paregoric is an opiate narcotic made from opium, camphor, benzoic acid, and anise oil. Opium causes a constriction of the bowels that relieves diarrhea, while anise is responsible for its strong licorice-like taste.

The drug is usually taken by mouth, swallowed straight, or diluted with water. Recommended dose is usually 1 teaspoon every four to six hours. When taken as prescribed, for short periods, there is no danger of addiction. The average dose contains 4 percent tincture of opium, or ¼ grain morphine—not enough to get you hooked.

Because it has been abused, paregoric is regulated under federal narcotics laws. Although clearly not favored by opiate addicts, in times of narcotics scarcity they used it to stave off withdrawal until more potent drugs could be obtained. Addicts drink it by the bottle to simulate a mildly narcotic, sedative state. Less frequently, abusers inject residue scrapings from paregoric bottles. Injection is a dangerous procedure, however, since paregoric residue can cause abscesses and blood diseases. Pleasure seekers have been known to dip a cigarette or marijuana joint in paregoric liquid before smoking to provide an extra lift.

PASSIONFLOWER

Next time you smell the heady aroma of marijuana in the air, don't be so sure it is the real thing. It might just be passionflower.

The passionflower vine (*Passiflora incarnata*) not only smells like grass when burned but its dried, strained leaves produce a legal, mild marijuana-like high for a short time when smoked.

This yellow-flowering perennial, originally found in the West Indies and the southern United States, now grows throughout the world. In some areas it is smoked for pleasure, while in others it has been used as a tobacco substitute by people trying to kick nicotine addiction.

Passionflower can also be brewed as a tea. The recipe calls for ½ ounce of leaves per pint of boiled water. Rather than producing a high, the tea causes the user to feel tranquil and sedated. Some women find the tea gives them relief from tension produced by the menstrual cycle.

The active ingredients of the passionflower vine are harmine and a group of related alkaloids. Since these alkaloids are MAO inhibitors, users should not combine passionflower with tranquilizers, amphetamines, antihistamines, alcohol, avocados, ripe bananas, broad beans (pods), excessive caffeine, canned figs, chicken liver, sedatives, mescaline, nutmeg, aged cheeses, any quantity of milk products, cocoa, excessive amounts of chocolate, pickled herring, yeast extract, narcotics, sauerkraut, ephedrine, macromerine, and oils of dill, parsley, or wild fennel. If you have made the mistake of combining any of these with passionflower, powerful headache and/or vomiting will indicate that something is wrong. In such instances, hospital treatment should be sought promptly.

PCP

COMMON NAMES: *amoeba, angel dust, angel hair, animal tranquilizer, CJ, Cadillac, crystal, crystal joints, cyclones, DOA (dead on arrival), dust, elephant tranquilizer, goon, hog, horse tranquilizer, KJ, killer weed (when combined with cannabis), mist, peace pill, pig tranquilizer, rocket fuel, scuffle, sheets, snorts, soma, supergrass, superweed, surfer, synthetic marijuana, weed*

Phencyclidine, commonly known as PCP, is one of the most unpredictable of all street drugs. It is unpredictable because it is often falsely represented on the street as THC, mescaline, psilocybin, or LSD. Even more chancy is the drug's effect, ranging from an exhilarating, tingly high to an unpleasant, disconcerting bout with delirium.

PCP may now represent up to 25 percent of all "psychedelic" drug abuse, although technically it is not a psychedelic at all. Since PCP causes dizzyingly different effects at varying dosages, it cannot be placed with accuracy in any standard drug category. Most experts call it a tranquilizer-anesthetic with hallucinogenic properties, although it is chemically unrelated to LSD or mescaline. To most people it is simply a dangerous substance, with high bummer and overdose potential, even when used by knowledgeable druggies.

PCP comes in many forms, but is impossible to identify with the human eye. Produced as a white, crystalline powder, it can be combined with other drugs, often LSD, in gelatin capsules, or sprinkled on any smokable substance, such as tobacco, marijuana, parsley, or mint leaves, to create a powerful high.

One gram of PCP can "doctor" four to twenty-four joints, depending on the degree of potency desired. PCP emits a distinctly chemical odor when smoked.

Bio-Ceutic Laboratories, sole legal distributor of the drug, markets it for use as a veterinary anesthetic, under the name Sernylan. Parke, Davis & Co., the original manufacturer, first synthesized it in 1957. Although it was tested on humans for several years, its side effects made it unsuitable for therapeutic purposes. Mass marketing as a recreational mind expander has been left to street merchants, who sell it as "pure THC" to unsuspecting buyers, taking in a whopping $12,000 to $14,000 per pound.

What PCP does depends on several variables, some which the user can control, others no more controllable or predictable than a roulette wheel. Although the drug's method of action is still unclear, we do know that it acts on the sensory cortex, thalamus, and midbrain in such a manner as to "scramble" internal stimuli, thereby impairing perceptual functions. Effects on the body and mind depend upon the user's psychopathology, dosage, and method of ingestion and the circumstances under which the drug is taken, including physical setting, immediate feelings, and the presence of other people. Dosage is the most important and least controllable factor in determining PCP's effect, particularly since most users take it under the mistaken belief they are ingesting some other substance.

PCP can produce a one- to six-hour trip. Low dosage (5 mg or less), ingested orally by tablet, capsule, or smoking, results in a state of physical sedation, characterized by general numbness of the face, arms, hands, legs, and feet. The cardiovascular system shows a rise in blood pressure and heart rate. Users may experience euphoria, alcohol-like intoxication with loss of muscular coordination, double or blurred vision, blank staring, dizziness, nausea, or vomiting. While breathing rate increases, respiration remains shallow. The user feels flushed, sweats profusely, and undergoes mild arterial relaxation. Hallucinations can occur.

Subjective psychological effects progress through three stages. First, the user experiences a reaction to changes in body image, or the sense of getting smaller and smaller, accompanied by feelings of depersonalization, weightlessness, and out-of-body experiences. He may alternate delight with panic while in a noncommunicative state of oblivion and fantasy.

The next stage is one of perceptual distortion, including possible visual or auditory hallucinations and an inability to judge space and time accurately. Feelings such as gravitational pulls and levitation may be experienced. At this point, the user often becomes excessively talkative.

The third stage may be evidenced by varying levels of apathy, indifference, alienation, estrangement, and emotional or social isolation. As the high diminishes, the user can suffer depression and paranoia. During this final stage, feelings of emptiness and despair often develop into a preoccupation with imminent death.

The experience, not unlike the effects of sensory deprivation, may cause difficulties in thinking and concentration and impairment of sensory input organization. Learning and memory functions can be disturbed, and the user often feels drowsy. Even low doses of PCP can cause intensification and aggravation of pre-existing overt or latent psychotic tendencies. This effect has been so pronounced that medical researchers have concluded that exaggeration of present psychoses is more intense under PCP than under any other tested drug, including LSD and mescaline. Therefore, psychotics should definitely avoid use of PCP.

It takes PCP users about twenty-four hours to return to a normal state after tripping. Although the drug's effects are difficult to describe, users claim that these are quite different from those produced by other drugs. For first-time or unaware users, the PCP experience can be somewhat scary and unpleasant.

Moderate doses (5–10 mg) cause decreased blood pressure, respiration, and heart rate. Physical disturbances may include nausea, vomiting, blurred vision, rolling eye movements, shivering, increased salivation, repetitive movements, watering of the eyes, loss of balance, dizziness, and muscular rigidity.

Low doses cause the arms and legs to become numb. With larger doses, limbs may not budge at all. Moderate doses of PCP will produce analgesic (painkilling) and anesthetic (sleep-inducing) results. Psychological effects are the same as those caused by low doses, but misperceptions and negative feelings are magnified. The user may experience some loss of contact with his environment.

When high doses (over 10 mg) of PCP are ingested, the drug ceases to resemble any other medically used anesthetic. A state of agitation can occur, sometimes accompanied by convulsions or seizures resulting in coma for as long as twelve hours. Symptoms of schizophrenia, such as delusions and mental confusion, may surface, requiring prompt, professional medical attention. Attempted suicides have been attributed to use of this drug.

Long-term PCP effects are not entirely certain, but present indications are not reassuring. Researchers have documented flashbacks, prolonged anxiety, and severe depression. Extended use may result in physical addiction. Chronic heavy users, even while temporarily drug-free, complain of feeling crazy and disoriented, and have difficulty coping with normal life stresses.

PCP has a bad-trip rate five times greater than any other psychedelic. This high proportion of bummers may, however, result because the uninformed user, having experienced no stronger psychedelics, expects no more than a pleasant, mellow, but enhanced marijuana-like high. Instead, he finds his body deadened and his mind becomes a maze of fear and pain.

Those on a bum trip should be placed in a cozy, safe environment, protected from self-harm. An attempt should be made to explain, as quietly, calmly, and simply as possible, the cause of the problem. Reduce verbal and visual stimulation to relieve anxiety, which is often death-related and can be very frightening. Extreme states of excitation, caused by high doses, can be medically controlled by chlorpromazine and phenobarbital. Administration of such drugs should be handled only by professionals, however, as they can result in extreme depression and possible respiratory arrest.

If respiration becomes labored, or heavy vomiting occurs, rush the user to a hospital, where respiratory-support equipment and necessary medical care are available. Watch for preconvulsant signs, such as jerking movements. Generally, the user will show wildly delusional behavior before convulsing. This is no time to go rummaging through the medicine cabinet for common tranquilizers or sedatives. The comatose or convulsive person should be taken to a hospital for treatment immediately. Effective anti-overdose medication and dosage require skilled, professional knowledge, and their effects on the user must be closely monitored.

To minimize the possibility of overdose, large amounts of PCP should be avoided. It should never be used in combination with other drugs, particularly alcohol, barbiturates, heroin, or other depressants. Since the drug is mentally and physically incapacitating, driving a car or operating dangerous machinery should be ruled out.

In the United States, PCP is considered a controlled dangerous substance under the Comprehensive Drug Abuse Prevention and Control Act of 1970. Possession is punishable by imprisonment for up to one year, or a maximum $5,000 fine. Illicit manufacture and sale can bring first offenders a five-year term and a fine as high as $15,000. Subsequent convictions may result in even greater penalties.

There are many similar chemical analogs of PCP that can be easily synthesized. It seems inevitable that some will appear on the street market. Effects of these new compounds cannot be predicted, but caution should be exercised.

With all the dangers of PCP catalogued and documented, why do people still use it for "fun"? Some just know nothing about it, some do not believe it to be dangerous in small quantities, and others mistakenly believe their PCP to be another mind-altering drug, usually LSD, mescaline, psilocybin, or, most commonly, THC. Since "pure" THC is about as rare as snow in the Sahara, hungry druggies leap at the chance to plunk down their cash for the "golden" powder. Unfortunately, the gold sometimes turns out to be tarnished metal, since the user has often purchased a potentially unpleasant or dangerous dose of PCP. Buyer beware!

PEMOLINE

COMMON NAME: *MBD*

During World War II, while the Red Baron was flying high on amphetamines provided by his Nazi superiors, British and American pilots were downing a mind-sharpener called pemoline, a drug that kept them alert during long missions.

Pemoline is a synthetic chemical that can provide mental stimulation without getting the central nervous system overly excited, as is the case with amphetamines. A dose of 20–50 mg, taken orally, gives the user a pleasant feeling of physical relaxation combined with a high degree of mental alertness and recall for six to twelve hours.

The drug is not addictive and produces no dangerous or annoying side effects, short of a possible case of insomnia if taken too close to bedtime.

Pemoline magnesium, harder to come by in the street market, is a mixture of pemoline and magnesium hydroxide. This drug has the same basic effect as pemoline but more acutely sharpens the memory of the user. Although Abbott Laboratories, manufacturer of the drug (sold under the name Cylert), steadfastly claims it has only one medical application, as an adjunct in managing children with hyperkinesis due to minimal brain dysfunction, current research indicates it may ultimately be used to increase memory efficiency in both young people and the senile by as much as 60 percent.

PERCODAN

Percodan is another derivative of nature's dubious gift, the opium poppy. A narcotic, prescription drug, it is often dispensed for pain caused by cancer, fractured bones, surgery, and other ailments. Percodan can be both psychologically and physically habit-forming.

Chemically known as oxycodone terephthalate, Percodan is a codeine derivative sold in yellow or pink pills usually containing aspirin, phenacetin, and caffeine. Percobarb, a mixture of Percodan and a barbiturate, is marketed in blue-and-white or blue-and-yellow capsules.

Though similar to codeine and morphine, Percodan is generally addictive only when abused. A normal dose, taken orally every six hours, will relieve pain without causing addiction, unless the drug is used frequently over a long period of time for its euphoric, narcotic effect. Possibility of addiction to Percodan increases when it is combined with other central-nervous-system depressants such as tranquilizers, sedatives, and alcohol. The drug's potency makes its use inadvisable for children. Adults often feel lightheaded, experiencing both physical and mental impairment. Driving, operating machinery, and other activities requiring good motor coordination and judgment may have to be curtailed.

Percodan is regulated under the federal Controlled Substances Act and remains one of the most popular and effective pain relievers in use today.

PEYOTE

COMMON NAMES: *anhalonium, hikori, huatari, mescal, mescal buttons, peyotyl, seni, wakowi*

Spanning centuries of oppression and controversy, the homely peyote button has been dropped like a token in the turnstile on the path to what Carlos Castaneda has termed "a separate reality."

The small, mouse-colored cactus *Lophophora williamsii* is native to Mexico and the southwestern United States. The unassuming source of the peyote button, it appears in its growing state as a fleshy green tip, tufted with white hair and barely protruding from the earth like the fingertips of a leprechaun. When dried for consumption, the buttons turn brown and ugly, unappetizing in appearance even when sliced for serving. Bitter in taste, somewhat like dried orange rind, the furry foulness of the button seems to foreshadow its physical effects on the consumer. Vomiting is almost inevitable; in fact, it is suggested. Rather than diminish peyote's effects, vomiting permits the user to enjoy his trip without the distraction of overwhelming nausea.

Some prefer their peyote straight, popping three to six buttons in the mouth and leaving them there to soften, even chewing the nasty-tasting little devils, before swallowing them whole. Lesser stoics may brew them as a tea and wash them down with a strong citrus juice, or grind them up and disguise them in capsules. It doesn't matter—nausea and vomiting are almost unavoidable preliminaries to peyote paradise.

Peyote is composed of an array of active alkaloids which include a reflex excitant, a convulsant, and a respiratory stimulant. The psychoactive star of this chemical show is mescaline, responsible for the hallucinatory effects that have elevated peyote to food-of-the-gods status (see Mescaline). Mescaline may be isolated or synthesized as 3,4,5-trimethoxy-phenethylamine. Because of its additional alkaloids, however, peyote's effects are more intense than those of mescaline alone.

After one to two hours, and the inevitable barf, peyote's effects begin. Increased perspiration and dilated pupils, accompanied by a feeling of weightlessness and depersonalization, precede the LSD-like sensory shower which follows. A visual storm erupts; colors intensify.

Senses cross over; music may be experienced as visual or tactile. This synesthesia ushers the tripper into a world within his world—a mystical creation that became a religion for Mexican Indians, then spread northward to American Indians and more recently to the Native American Church.

Pre-Columbian Mexican Indians, including the Aztecs, communed with their gods via peyote, an integral part of their ritual and ceremony. The Spanish conquistadors could not convince the Indians that peyote was an evil substance, rather than a shortcut to heaven. The Inquisition ended use of the drug by the conquering Spaniards and their slaves, but the Indians' mystical belief in the power of peyote survived the steamrolling religious hysteria of the invaders. Peyote eaters multiplied, spreading their religion among the tribes of Mexico. It was later introduced to the United States by the Mescalero Apaches. By the late 1800s, peyote had begun to play an important role in the religions of the Comanche, Kiowas, Shawnees, Pawnees, Delawares, Cheyennes, Arapahoes, and others, easing the mental pain of subjugation by the white man and unifying the tribes. Peyote was an effective weapon against alcohol. Indians willingly gave up their firewater for the peaceful love button.

The 1906 confederation of peyote-taking tribes known as the "Mescal Bean Eaters" has evolved into the Native American Church, which today claims 250,000 members throughout the United States and Canada. Peyote, the communion of the church, is legal to its members, although for the general populace it falls under Schedule I of the Controlled Substances Act. Several states have attempted to enact legislation forbidding the church's use of peyote as a sacrament, but have failed because such a law would be an unconstitutional violation of the Bill of Rights' guarantee of freedom of religion.

Peyote is neither physically nor psychologically addictive, producing no withdrawal symptoms upon discontinuance of use. Native American Church members are privy to an experience allowing them a relatively harmless exploration of inner space, a world we deny ourselves out of ignorance and fear.

PIPIZINTZINTLI

Chemically similar to the coleus plant, this broadleaf sage member of the mint family is often used for tripping by Mexican Indians when magic mushrooms (see Psilocybin) are in short supply.

About fifty to seventy fresh pipizintzintli (*Salvia divinorum*) leaves are needed to prepare a dose. Leaves can be chewed and swallowed. If preferred, they may be soaked in lukewarm water for about an hour. The resulting brew is strained before drinking.

Pipizintzintli may produce some nausea after about a half-hour, followed by a trippy, psilocybin-like state, colorful hallucinations and visual patterns, along with a possible increase in ESP abilities. The total trip lasts about two hours.

This legal drug has no known dangerous side effects and is slightly more potent than the coleus species (see Coleus).

While in rare instances pipizintzintli can be found in the United States, it is most common to regions of southern Mexico.

PSILOCYBIN

COMMON NAMES: *hombrecitos ("little men"), las mujercitas ("the little women"), los ninos ("the children"), magic mushroom, mushroom, noble princess of the waters*

The mushroom: Thirty-eight thousand varieties exist, hidden in dark, musty corners of the world like the gold of Midas.

Outstanding among this panoply of edible and poisonous stalks is the mystical magic mushroom. Not until recently was it discovered that the magic mushroom is not one specie, but many—all containing the hallucinogen psilocybin.

At least twenty mushrooms contain the psychoactive ingredients psilocybin and psilocin, including *Psilocybe cubensis* and *Psilocybe mexicana*. Native to Mexico and parts of the southern United States, psilocybin mushrooms are often confused with several poisonous species, resulting in about one hundred deaths a year. The *Amanita* group—including *Amanita virosa, A. verna,* and *A. phalloides*—is particularly dangerous. A close cousin, *Amanita muscaria*, contains the hallucinogen muscarin, rather than psilocybin (see *Amanita muscaria*).

Before stalking the wild mushroom, certain precautions are essential. A method of botanical identification, as well as a procedure for testing before ingestion, are necessities. One common method is to break off a piece of fresh mushroom. If the broken area turns bluish within an hour, it *may* be a psilocybin mushroom, although some poisonous species have been known to react in a similar manner. Analyses made with chemical reagents are more reliable and advisable.

Some mushrooms sold on the street as psilocybin may actually be the innocuous grocery-store variety spiked with LSD. To test, mash a mushroom and soak it overnight in methanol. The following day, hold it up to a black light. If it gives off a blue glow, you have an LSD-doctored mushroom.

The psilocybin mushroom grows in the temperature range between 65 and 85 degrees, and only on the manure of farm animals such as cows, pigs, and goats. The need for such selective growing conditions means that the fresh psilocybin mushroom is not often available; however, psilocybin can be manufactured as well. It is difficult and expensive to produce synthetically and store properly, and only one in a thousand street samples is genuine. The rest are either acid or an LSD/PCP combination. True synthetic psilocybin is a crystalline white powder, sold in the form of tablets, capsules, or liquid.

Organic psilocybin can be obtained in capsules containing powdered spores or dried, ground mushrooms. The mushroom itself may be ingested fresh or dried at room temperature. Dried mushrooms remain potent for years. Psilocybin can be extracted by drying and grinding the mushroom to a powder, soaking it in methyl alcohol for several days, and permitting the resulting clear liquid to evaporate in a flat dish until a residue remains. Resoaking and re-evaporating the residue will increase its potency.

Some prefer boiling the mushroom, skimming the residue from the water's surface, and combining with Kool-Aid or orange juice to create a Fungus Delight. Psilocybin may be sniffed or smoked, if you like the taste and smell of burning plastic. Injection is possible in liquid form.

Psilocybin dosage is from 1 to 5 grams dry weight, 10 to 50 grams fresh, or five to fifteen of the rancid-tasting whole mushrooms, depending on size and species. Effects appear within fifteen to forty-five minutes and last three to six hours, the length of time increasing with dosage. If the drug is injected, tripping begins more rapidly, within five to ten minutes.

Albert Hofmann, the father of LSD, was the first to extract psilocybin and psilocin from the magic mushroom. Relatively unstable, psilocybin is converted to psilocin by the body. The LSD-like effects attributed to psilocybin are actually the work of psilocin. Known formally as ortho-phosphoryl-4-hydroxy-N-di-methyltryptamine, psilocybin chemically resembles LSD and produces a similar but less intense trip.

Experimental medical use of psilocybin has been conducted in the fields of psychotherapy, criminal rehabilitation, and chronic alcoholism. Some feel psilocybin opens a door to the subconscious, permitting a view of the conscious world from a different perspective. Although it is scientifically classified as a hallucinogen, its effects are more illusionary than hallucinatory, since the tripper is aware that the sensations he is experiencing are drug-induced.

Like those of other hallucinogens, psilocybin's effects are determined by set (emotional and psychological makeup) and setting (surroundings and environment). Initial reaction is mainly physical:

nausea, pupil dilation, and increases in deep tendon reflexes, pulse, blood pressure, and temperature. Shivering, anxiety, facial numbness, and dizziness are not uncommon. Within an hour, these discomforts are replaced by heightened sensory awareness. Colors take on lives of their own, objects are perceivable in minute detail, patterns and designs kaleidoscope rainbow colors across the field of vision. Sound becomes sight; time and space are suspended as the tripper soars beyond reality. Unable to concentrate or communicate, he slurs his speech and giggles excessively. Some claim objects take on a purple aura; others claim a new spirituality.

Disorientation, paranoid reactions, inability to distinguish between fantasy and reality, intense anxiety and panic, or depression are symptomatic of a bad trip. "Talking down" is the preferred method of coping with a psilocybin bummer. Comfort, assurance, and a soothing environment, free of bright lights and loud noises, are more successful than tranquilizers, which may potentiate, rather than alleviate, bad effects.

While tolerance develops with psilocybin, there is no physical or psychological dependence, overdose potential, or possibility of addiction. Psilocybin has a cross-tolerance to LSD and mescaline, meaning the use of one will add to the cumulative tolerance of the other.

Legally classified under Schedule I of the Controlled Substances Act of 1970, possession carries a sentence of imprisonment for not more than one year and/or a fine of not more than $5,000. Manufacture or sale could mean a maximum sentence of five years and/or a fine of not more than $15,000.

The road to mushroom heaven was paved by the Indian cultures of Mexico and Central America centuries ago. "Teonanacatl," or "food of the gods," was consumed by Mayans in Guatemala over 3,500 years ago. Magic mushrooms were the basis for cults of worship which flourished in secret for centuries.

The Aztec, Mazatec, and Oaxacan Indians denied the existence of the mushroom until 1953, when R. Gordon Wasson and his wife, Valentina Pavlovna, rediscovered the ancient Oaxacan mushroom ritual. They promptly smuggled some of the mushrooms to Roger Heim, a French expert, who identified them as members of the genus *Psilocybe*.

The first recorded use of psilocybin mushrooms was at Montezuma's coronation in 1502. Unprepared for and frightened by the drug's effects, the Spanish conquerors experienced a wave of mycophobia—fear of mushrooms. As a result, they attempted to demolish the Indians' religion and drove the mushroom underground until it had achieved the status of a myth.

Until recently, hallucinogenic mushrooms were virtually unknown in North America. During the late sixties and early seventies, the younger generation discovered psilocybin and used it as a "safe" substitute for LSD. Popular, exotic, and difficult to obtain, psilocybin became a new hallucinogenic object to worship.

SAN PEDRO

San Pedro (*Trichocereus pachanoi*) is a tall, branching cactus that has been an Indian turn-on in Peru and Ecuador for almost three thousand years. Today, the plant is not only found in South America, but can be legally purchased or grown in the United States as well.

The ingredient that gives San Pedro its hallucinogenic kick is mescaline. Although peyote has the same active ingredient in about the same concentration, San Pedro has several advantages. For one, it does not necessarily produce a strong feeling of nausea, as peyote will. For another, since the drug is less of a stimulant, it produces more tranquil feelings in the user.

To prepare a dose, a 3-by-3-inch cut is made in the cactus. The cactus skin is then peeled away from this area. Peeling must be done carefully, since it is the lining of the inside skin wall that contains the plant's hallucinogenic ingredient. After peeling, pieces can be chewed until soft enough to swallow. Cactus slices can also be cut into small pieces, crushed, and boiled in a quart of water for about two hours. The resulting mixture should be strained before drinking. In either case, San Pedro should be ingested over a leisurely forty-five minutes or so to avoid causing too much of a shock to one's system.

The trip lasts up to six hours. First feelings begin in about an hour. While the experience may include increased mental clarity, heightened sound and color perception, and brilliantly hued visions, the user should be prepared for some potential negative feelings as well. Some people do not react well to drugs containing mescaline. Nausea may be experienced, along with a degree of chills, anxiety, and even a feeling of terror.

Physically, San Pedro is not addictive. In rare instances, some Indians have developed a degree of psychic dependence on the drug, but that does not occur with infrequent use.

SLEEPING PILLS, NON-BARBITURATE

COMMON NAMES: *goofers, sleepers*

If money spent is any indication, insomnia is one of the most widespread problems affecting our population. More than 25 million Americans spend in excess of $100 million annually on a variety of medications promising safe and restful sleep, sleep, sleep. Of those suffering from this malady, one in six resorts to some form of sleeping pill either occasionally or on a regular basis.

Although the most potent and frightening sleep medications are barbiturates (see Barbiturates), many nonbarbiturates also promise relief to the sleepless. In some cases, these promises are worth no more than those made by the proverbial traveling salesman to the unwary farmer's daughter. Whether prescribed by a physician or self-prescribed, many of these sleeping pills are relatively ineffective and potentially dangerous.

Using sleepers may backfire by providing the pill-popper with poor sleep, if any. Physicians and hospitals often prescribe them unnecessarily, to the patient's detriment. In a large number of cases a bit of exercise, some protein, or a little sex would be more effective, less dangerous, and certainly less costly.

A large proportion of insomniacs are actually suffering from "pseudoinsomnia"—they *think* they cannot sleep, and thus experience what seems to be insomnia. Many are troubled by anxiety or depression; 20 percent need psychotherapy rather than medication. For these folks, pills are inappropriate and useless. Once assured that they can sleep and are "normal," they often overcome their insomnia.

Before rushing to the doctor, drugstore, or medicine cabinet, insomniacs might benefit from consultation with a professional sleep-disorder clinic, which may be able to prescribe a nondrug solution to the problem. For the name of one, write to the American Association of Sleep Disorder Centers, University of Cincinnati Sleep Disorder Center, Christian R. Holmes Hospital, Eden and Bethesda Avenues, Cincinnati, Ohio 45219.

If you and your doctor believe sleeping pills are the correct answer, it is important to understand what they can and cannot do. Some will, for the short term, offer relief from minor insomnia. However, most of the two dozen or so nonbarbiturate sleepers available become ineffective after two weeks of continuous use. Only one has done better than that in sleep-lab tests. A large percentage of the public mistakenly believes that sleepers can provide long-term effectiveness, despite the fact that recent tests indicate insomniacs using no medication at all sleep as well as those taking pills for extended periods. Still, many keep popping them until unexpected, ugly side effects appear.

The granddaddy of all hypnotic sleepers, chloral hydrate, was introduced medically in 1869. The drug is usually found in soft gelatin capsules and can be administered orally or rectally. Chloral hydrate combined with alcohol—the movies' famous "Mickey Finn"—can knock you out or even kill you. Along with paraldehyde, another popular drug with an equally unpleasant taste and odor, chloral hydrate fell into disfavor when barbiturates were later developed. Because chloral hydrate has an irritant effect on the gastrointestinal tract, addicts often suffer from extreme stomach disturbances.

The most popular and safest prescription sedative today is Dalmane, a member of the benzodiazepine substance group which is related chemically to tranquilizers such as Valium and Librium. Dalmane legally sells for 10 to 20 cents per pill.

By comparison, barbiturates cost about a penny each. What does one get for this high price? For some, as many as twenty-eight nights of insomnia relief. For others, not much at all. When it works, effects begin in about twenty minutes, with sleep lasting seven to eight hours. Dependence is uncommon unless the drug is taken for an extended period of time, more than three months. A small percentage of users experience various adverse side reactions to Dalmane and other sleepers, including dizziness, loss of coordination, euphoria, headache, nausea, coma, diarrhea, irritability, constipation, fear, palpitations, flushes, loss of appetite, sweating, hallucinations, blurred vision, and even hyperactivity. Because sleepers are central-nervous-system depressants, users should avoid alcohol, as the combination can be synergistically dangerous. Driving or operating complex heavy equipment should be avoided. Indications are that suicide, accidental or planned, is possible with sleepers, particularly when combined with other drugs.

In addition to Dalmane, other popular nonbarbiturate sleepers are Doriden, Placidyl, Valmid, Noludar, Sopor, and Quaalude (see Methaqualone), paraldehyde, and the chloral hydrates, Noctec, Somnos, Aquachloral, and Kessodrate. All fall within the same price range, yet none is medically effective for more than two weeks, if at all. Generally, these drugs produce results within fifteen minutes to an hour, providing some users with four to eight hours of sleep. Doriden and Quaalude top the abuse list. Abusers usually seek these drugs out not as a cure for insomnia, but rather for a cheap, euphoric boozeless drunk with an accompanying loss of inhibitions. To a much greater degree than Dalmane, and to a lesser degree than barbiturates, they can be habit-forming.

Withdrawal after heavy abuse can produce mental and physical symptoms similar to those seen in cases of barbiturate addiction, including hangover, delirium tremens, convulsions, and death. Severe dependence requires professional, closely supervised medical attention. Treatment may include step-by-step withdrawal, or substitution of a barbiturate equal to the quantity of nonbarbiturate sedative taken each day. Withdrawal from the barbiturate then follows. Psychiatric help may also be required.

People with liver, kidney, and heart problems should seek advice from their physicians before using hypnotic-sedatives, as should those taking anticoagulants. The depressed and suicidal should use sleepers with caution.

Nonbarbiturate sedatives are regulated under the Comprehensive Drug Abuse Prevention and Control Act of 1970. Penalties are provided for illicit possession, manufacture, and sale.

Less abused, but also capable of producing mild psychological dependence, are over-the-counter sedatives, available without prescription. Many brands are aggressively marketed, the most popular being Nytol, Sleep-Eze, Sominex, Compoz, and Sure-Sleep. These preparations are a combination of ingredients usually containing salicylamide, an aspirin-like agent capable of producing minor calming action, antihistamines, and, in some cases, scopolamine. Some claim scopolamine, when taken in larger than recommended doses, can cause adverse reactions including loss of memory, hallucination, reduction of academic performance, and a general look of stupidity. Although recently judged unsafe by a Food and Drug Administration panel, scopolamine can still be purchased at will by the unwary.

The best bet for insomniacs: Avoid sleepers completely, if possible. Most will not help for more than a couple of weeks and many will actually interfere with sleep beyond that point. Seek information about insomnia remedies from a sleep-disorder clinic or discuss other nonmedicinal approaches to the problem with your physician.

SPANISH FLY

If you expect Spanish fly to send you and your lover into spasms of sexual delight, watch out! A most unpleasant surprise awaits those who toy with this famed "aphrodisiac."

Scientifically, Spanish fly is known as cantharides and is actually produced from the crushed wings of the *Lytta vesicatoria* (also *Cantharis vesicatoria*) beetle. The thought of eating beetle parts may not seem particularly appealing, but that's not the worst of it. This is one drug that not only fails to live up to its reputation as a sexual mood enhancer, but will also prove to be a real bummer.

Cantharides are used legally as a method of inducing farm animals to mate. The drug doesn't make bulls feel sexy or conjure up images of bovine Linda Lovelaces, however. What it does is to severely irritate the urethral passages during urination. The resulting burning sensation in the genitals creates a false sense of sexual excitement in the animal.

People have long believed the myth that Spanish fly will cause them to have superhuman sexual capacity and desire. Wrong! Even a tiny dose will more often cause a combination of fever, painful urination, extreme irritation of the genitals, and a bloody discharge. If that's not enough to scare you away, consider the fact that cantharides can permanently damage the kidneys and genitals. Maybe you can get a kidney replaced in this modern age of transplants, but go try to find a new set of genitals. Even worse, in a great many instances, use of cantharides by humans has resulted in death. Not much fun at all.

Don't be fooled by phony ads or head-shop products that offer "real" Spanish fly. Thankfully, they are not selling the real thing, but only cayenne pepper, a substance that gets fun seekers nowhere sexually.

Let a word to the wise be sufficient: Leave Spanish fly to the farm animals. The aphrodisiac benefits in human use are simply a lot of bull.

STP

COMMON NAMES: *DOM, serenity tranquillity peace*

STP burst onto the psychedelic scene in the form of five thousand high-dosage tablets given away on June 21, 1967, at the Summer Solstice Celebration in San Francisco's Golden Gate Park. Resulting tales of madness mingled with those of euphoria to create the legend of STP.

Even the origin of the letters STP contributes to the paradoxical nature of this hallucinogen. A synthetic amphetamine-related psychedelic similar to DMA, MDA, MMDA, and TMA, its actions are both stimulant and pseudo-hallucinogenic. Does STP stand for the motor-oil additive—the speed side of the drug—or is STP short for "serenity, tranquillity, and peace"—the hallucinogenic property? "Yes" is the answer to both.

STP, or 2,5-Dimethoxy-4-methylamphetamine, is more correctly referred to as DOM. Like LSD, it may be taken orally, dissolved on tablets, sugar cubes, or stamps, or injected. An average dose of tasteless, odorless white crystalline powder is 1–5 mg. As psychedelics go, the trip is usually long and intense, beginning in about one hour and lasting from eight to twenty-four hours. Some have claimed trips of several days, but such reports are rare.

A dose of less than 1 mg acts as a euphoriant, while larger doses produce trips similar to those from LSD or mescaline. Physical responses are similar to those of amphetamines, as it stimulates the sympathetic nervous system and causes increased heart rate, blood pressure, reduction of appetite, tremors, sweating, and pupil dilation. Amphetamine-like effects are less pronounced than psychological responses.

As with LSD, set (the user's psychological frame of reference) and setting (his physical surroundings) profoundly affect the course of the trip. Visual perception is altered; colors create a new world of brilliance and clarity; shapes and forms evolve and change. Time and space interweave while the self stands apart and observes it all. Mood changes may vacillate between sadness and joy; confusion and anxiety may ensue.

An unusually high percentage of bummers have occurred with STP

because of the trip's duration and intensity. Thorazine is a controversial treatment; disagreement exists as to whether the drug alleviates
or potentiates effects of a bad trip. Tolerance develops rapidly if STP
is frequently used. Physical dependence has not been proved and the
drug does not create withdrawal symptoms. Lethal dosage has not
been determined.

STP is presently under the Drug Abuse Control Amendment with
one convicted of possession liable to a fine up to $1,000 and/or im-
prisonment for a maximum of one year.

STRYCHNINE

Contrary to rumors circulating among street drug users, there is no reliable evidence that strychnine has ever been used in the preparation of LSD or other psychedelic drugs.

Strychnine is the alkaloid found in the seeds of the *Strychnos nux vomica* tree, native to China, India, Australia, and Burma. Used properly, the drug can be a valuable medicine capable of providing short-term relief from ailments such as neuralgia, constipation, dyspepsia, and impotence.

Curiosity has been aroused over the years because of strychnine's reputed aphrodisiac qualities. Actually, it is not an aphrodisiac at all. What it will cause is a potent but painful erection in impotent men, one that remains even after a series of orgasms, accompanied by a high level of body heat and profuse sweating—far from a sexual turn-on.

Strychnine can kill. Just a bit too much (more than 2 mg) makes the heart rate start racing at dangerous levels, causing convulsions and possible delivery to a funeral home.

Because tolerance varies widely from person to person, strychnine should be used only by skilled, professional medical personnel. A drug experimenter would be wise to add it to his list of no-no's.

SUGAR

You might wonder why a book about drugs would include mention of an everyday food such as sugar. Since we are writing about substances often abused in our society, we would be remiss if we omitted sugar, which has to be near the top of the list. In addition, because some drugs create a desire for sweets, one should have basic knowledge about the dangers of sugar before heading for the candy store to satisfy those cravings.

Refined sucrose, $C_{12}H_{22}O_{11}$, comes to us courtesy of the chemical laboratory, which processes almost all the fiber and protein out of sugar cane or beets to leave us with a product that is nutritionally valueless.

In the United States today, we find sugar not only in our coffee and candy but in virtually every manufactured food we eat. Manufacturers start our habits early by putting sugar into baby food and cereals. Even bacon and tobacco are sugar-cured to satisfy the sweet tooth. The average American today consumes roughly 100 pounds of refined sugar each year—enough to make more than six hundred cherry pies! Sugar has become a national addiction, a definite threat to health, and the habit seems to be growing.

When Marco Polo first brought sugar back from India in the thirteenth century, he had no way of knowing he was introducing the Western World to a substance that, when ultimately abused, would be a cause of problems such as pimples, diabetes, tooth decay, migraine, overweight, and heart disease. These facts have now been thoroughly documented by the scientific community, and it is time for us to recognize this killer, a major part of our national diet, for what it is.

We are not only talking about the white stuff either. "Raw" sugar is just as worthless in terms of nutritional value, and brown sugar is white sugar with a bit of molasses thrown in for coloring.

We will not go into a long discourse about sugar in this volume. Many other books are available that discuss this subject in depth. One current interesting and informative work is *Sugar Blues* by William Duffy.

Read food labels so you can be fully aware of those products containing sugar. If you cannot completely kick the sugar habit, try to keep it under control. The best method is to substitute natural sugar for the refined variety whenever possible. And, when the yen for a sweet hits, have a piece of fruit instead of a candy bar or cola.

SYRIAN RUE

COMMON NAMES: *African rue, rue, wild rue*

Syrian rue (*Peganum harmala*), another of Mother Nature's legal hallucinogenic plants, contains seeds rich in harmine, harmaline, and harmalol. This perennial, woody, 12-to-16-inch member of the caltrop family, unrelated to any American or European rues, is native mainly to India, the Middle East, and the plains of Spain. In some Mediterranean marketplaces Syrian rue is sold commercially as a spice.

Only small doses of Syrian rue should be used when experimenting, since it is an unusually powerful drug whose effects vary widely from person to person. Suggested starting dose is ⅓ ounce of seeds, chewed thoroughly before swallowing. Depending upon the user's reaction, dosage may be slowly increased to a maximum of 1 ounce of seeds.

Small doses of Syrian rue (25–50 mg) act as a mild stimulant and produce feelings of drowsiness and dreaminess for about an hour or two.

Larger doses (300–750 mg) may cause hallucinations. The drug acts upon the central nervous system and users often feel highly stimulated, experiencing wild visions. In the Middle East, Syrian rue is sometimes mixed with other psychoactive plants such as datura (rich in belladonna alkaloids) or *Banisteriopsis rusbyana* (loaded with DMT), for extra kick and potency, since these types of drugs potentiate each other.

Syrian rue should be ingested on an empty stomach. Under no circumstances should a novice take more than 250 mg of this or any other substance containing harmine. Users who do may well rue the day, as the drug can depress the central nervous system. Harmine and related alkaloids are MAO inhibitors, which means that if combined with the wrong things they can result in troubles ranging from headache to heart trouble to death. Keep away from tranquilizers, amphetamines, antihistamines, alcohol, avocados, ripe bananas, broad beans (pods), pickled herring, yeast extract, sedatives, mescaline, nutmeg, aged cheeses, excessive caffeine, canned figs, chicken liver, excessive amounts of chocolate, cocoa, narcotics, sauerkraut, ephedrine, macromerine, licorice, and oils of dill, parsley, or wild fennel.

THC

For all practical purposes, pure recreational THC does not exist. You can't buy it, you can't make it, you can't eat it, you can't smoke it, and no one's quite sure what it would do to you if you could.

This is one drug that has not made it from the pharmaceutical companies to the underground labs to the street. It is still under the researcher's lock and key, and, so far, there have been very few security leaks. That doesn't mean no one has heard of it. On the contrary, many "knowledgeable" drug users swear they have bought guaranteed, genuine THC at one time or another, but then they probably also believe in Tinker Bell.

THC is the primary active ingredient in every cannabis preparation, from marijuana to hashish to hash oil. Its chemical name, delta-9-tetrahydrocannabinol, defines its status as one of the chemical substances called cannabinols found in the hemp plant. These cannabinols share a similar chemical structure, but thus far only THC has been isolated as the mind-flexing, high-producing agent that makes the *Cannabis sativa* plant unique.

THC was first synthesized in 1966. The extremely delicate and costly equipment needed to manufacture it has left THC solely in the hands of professional laboratories under regulated contract to a limited number of bona-fide drug researchers.

These researchers only dispense pure THC for their marijuana experiments. In synthesized form, THC dosage and quality can be carefully controlled.

Though this may be a boon to much-needed scientific research, it leaves the street user high and dry amid rumors of THC's miraculous qualities. Since it is the substance that produces marijuana's effect, the offer of a "pure" dose is understandably appealing to cannabis devotees. Unfortunately, nine times out of ten, the unsuspecting consumer will buy a dose of the more dangerous drug PCP, and the other time a combination of whatever leftovers his dealer can scrape together—LSD, mescaline, or occasionally amphetamines.

An average marijuana joint has about 1 percent THC content, while hash oil, at the other end of the scale, may have as much as 30 percent THC. PCP has no THC content, but has some other properties that aren't nearly so harmless (see PCP). To give you an idea of its danger, it is only legally available as an animal tranquilizer, since its use by humans was banned years ago for having created too many unpredictable side effects, such as convulsion and death. PCP is an extremely tricky drug to use, even once, since a low dose may send you on a scary, totally confused, mental mystery tour, with numb limbs and sweaty palms. A high dose can lead to coma. The tricky part is that you can't predict your dose, since the stuff is usually in a capsule or tablet of indeterminable mixture and quantity.

Real THC is a clear resin or sometimes a translucent, buff-colored goo. It has also been produced as a soluble white powder to be mixed with water. However, it is unlikely that you have ever seen THC, unless you've been in the deep freeze all winter along with the ice cream. THC is such an unstable substance that it must be kept below freezing, in sealed glass vials, to retain its potency.

The drug causes the same effects as marijuana and hashish: up to three hours of a dreamy, euphoric state with intensified perceptions, a bit of confusion, and short-term memory loss. Occasionally the user may mildly hallucinate. THC causes an increased heart rate, reddening of the eyes, and a dry mouth resulting from reduced saliva flow. It is not physically addictive, nor do regular users develop a tolerance. Overdose potential has not yet been determined.

At $1,000 an ounce, or about $15 to $50 a dose, it is not likely that the pothead can afford THC, anyway. Besides, chances of scoring the real McCoy are somewhat akin to winning the Irish Sweepstakes, and when you lose, the PCP bummer you risk hardly makes it worth the gamble.

TOBACCO (NICOTINE)

If you are a smoker, you probably have a dim recollection of the first time you ever tried a cigarette. Remember how you coughed and choked? Perhaps your body was trying to send you a simple message: *Don't smoke!* If you listened to your lungs and rejected smoking, you are much better off now than the millions who are cutting days off their lives each time they light up.

We live in a topsy-turvy society. We have drug controls, yet the law permits the Western World's two biggest killers—tobacco and alcohol —to be used as often as desired by young adults. When it comes to drug use, tobacco is one of the worst choices of all.

There is virtually nothing that is appealing or pleasant about tobacco smoking. Your first experience generally produces a sickening feeling. You cough, sputter, feel nausea, and may even vomit. Tobacco does not make your head feel good, nor does it produce psychic entertainment. About all it does is make your breath, furniture, clothes, home, and the air around you smell foul (to the increasing annoyance of others). Consider those little burn holes in clothes and furniture, the discolored fingertips, the tobacco in pocket linings, and that chronic cough in the morning, then ask yourself: Why smoke at all?

The answer is simple. You are hooked, and hooked good, just as a junkie gets hooked on heroin. In fact, tobacco is the most habituating, addictive over-the-counter drug currently used by man. If you don't believe it, think back to the time you ran out of cigarettes and had to get dressed at one a.m. on a cold, rainy night to search for an all-night store or vending machine. If you didn't, you might have started looking for long butts in the ashtray. It's frightening what addiction will do to otherwise sane, responsible people, but cigarettes will do it every time. Next time you take a plane flight, watch the action in the smoking section when the No Smoking sign goes off. You can practically hear forty matches striking simultaneously! It may be pathetic, but remember you are dealing with addicts, nothing less.

Make no mistake about it. Tobacco is an addicting drug, not just an annoying bad habit, as many claim. It has a powerful hold on its slaves, who refuse to recognize it as serious and deadly simply because it is legally obtainable.

Consider some of the statistics:

In the United States, 54 million smokers consumed 620 billion cigarettes in 1976, 84 billion more than they did in 1970, at a cost of $15 billion.

Since the 1964 Surgeon General's Report, which presented a devastating picture of cigarette smoking, only 13 percent of male and 3 percent of female smokers have quit.

Between the years 1970 and 1975, 870,000 new adults started smoking.

A few cigarettes can hook a potential addict. Studies indicate that 85 percent of adolescents who smoke *more than one cigarette* become tobacco addicts.

According to the American Cancer Society, 70,000 Americans will die of tobacco-induced lung cancer this year, twice as many as ten years ago.

The national lung-cancer rate among women has doubled in the past ten years, and continues to spiral upward because of increased smoking among teen-age girls.

In America, 27 percent of teen-age girls are steady smokers. Oddly, they believe smoking is sophisticated and a form of liberation. Many assume they will be able to stop without difficulty at some point in the future. They may be in for a big surprise, however.

The surprise is this: Of the 61 percent of all smokers who have seriously tried to quit, 57 percent will still be smoking five years from now. Tobacco use is a tough habit to break—one of the toughest.

If you have not already started smoking, read on. Perhaps we will tell you enough to discourage you from ever doing so. Even if you already smoke, read on. Perhaps we will mention something that can start you on the road to quitting.

Tobacco has a long and colorful history. When Columbus landed here, he found Indians peacefully puffing away on the cured leaves of the *Nicotiana tabacum* plant, native to our shores. He, and others, brought the stuff back to Europe, where smoking quickly became all the rage. By the early 1600s, thousands of tobacco shops could be found in London. Cultivation of the plant spread rapidly, too. Once Europeans became addicted, they found life without tobacco so difficult they planted seeds wherever they landed.

Although tobacco smoke consists of nearly five hundred compounds in its particles, it is nicotine, an alkaloid in the plant's leaves, that causes most of the acute effects of smoking. Extracted nicotine is a colorless, acrid, oily liquid. It has no medical use but has been used as an insecticide (it is, after all, one of the most powerful poisons known). The drug is named after Jacques Nicot, who introduced smoking to France while serving as ambassador to Lisbon.

Cigarette tobacco contains about 1.5 percent nicotine; the smoke from an average cigarette yields about 6 to 8 mg of the drug. Cigars contain appreciably more nicotine, averaging 120 mg each, twice the amount needed to kill a normal human adult if he chose to eat it.

In addition to nicotine, a variety of other toxic substances can be found in cigarette smoke, including cyanide, "tar," and carbon monoxide. None can be completely removed or isolated, and all can do significant damage to the smoker. Cigarette smoke contains about 1 percent carbon monoxide—cigars about 6 percent—by volume . . . the same foul stuff your car exhaust emits. Some medical experts would like to see carbon-monoxide content listed on cigarette packages, since it varies from brand to brand, as do "tar" and nicotine.

Tobacco can be chewed, snuffed, or smoked in cigarettes, cigars, or pipes. Smoking is today's preferred method, although chewing and snuffing have been popular in times past, particularly before the invention of the automatic cigarette-making machine early in this century.

What prompts us to smoke tobacco in spite of the fact that it tastes terrible, irritates our throats and lungs, and may even kill us? Again, addiction is the reason. Tobacco addicts must constantly provide their brains with nicotine. One cigarette produces only a thirty-minute supply. It is then time for more, and the cycle goes on and on. Most smokers consume fifteen to twenty-four cigarettes per day, a minimum of one each waking hour. No other drug is taken with such frequency. Yet if you called a smoker an addict, he would respond with a sense of indignation. Don't allow that to keep you from delivering an occasional sermon, though, for even though the law permits him to damage himself, you have an obligation to raise his level of consciousness to the point that he can face up to his tobacco problem.

Facing up is not easy, so be understanding. Realize that the smoker-addict who tries to quit will experience withdrawal symptoms. Though not as bad as those faced by a heroin addict, they will cause a good deal of suffering in many cases. Among the effects of nicotine withdrawal are irritability, headache, cramps, anxiety, insomnia, nervousness, diarrhea, sweating, palpitations, impatience, energy loss, drowsiness, dizziness, fatigue, lightheadedness, constipation, loss of concentration, tremors, depression, and a feeling of emptiness and hunger.

Several stories are told about people who have tried to quit smoking. Perhaps the most famous is about Sigmund Freud, the father of modern psychology and a twenty-cigar-a-day smoker. Even after he developed cancerous sores on his palate and jaw he could not break the habit. When doctors removed part of his jaw as a result, they told him continued smoking would cost his life. The best he could do was quit once for twenty-three days before reverting back to his foul smoking habit, which continued until he died of cancer.

Another tale comes out of Synanon, the famed drug-rehabilitation facility. In 1970, to instill complete self-discipline among the two hundred heroin addicts in residence, a strict no-tobacco-smoking policy was put into effect. The end result: One hundred addicts left the program because they could not handle the loss of nicotine. Some said it was tougher to give up than heroin.

Rather than recognize nicotine as the addictive culprit, smokers often believe the "act of smoking" (holding the cigarette, putting it in the mouth, etc.) is the most important part of the habit. Not true. Those who use other smokables, such as opium, hashish, or marijuana, still keep smoking tobacco. Smoking is no more than a method for the smoker-addict to ingest nicotine. The old nonsense "I just light them up and let them burn down in the ashtray" is just that—nonsense! A smoker sneaks in puffs because he has to get his fix, even at the cost of losing his sense of smell or taste. He also continues in spite of the myriad physical dangers of tobacco use.

What are these dangers, specifically? First and foremost is the threat of death. Each year, in the United States alone, a quarter of a million people die prematurely as a result of tobacco use—more than four times the number of Americans killed in the Vietnam war, enough people to fill the stands at the Super Bowl for the next four years, and ten times the number of people killed annually in auto-mobile accidents.

Even before it kills, smoking can make your life a miserable affair. Not long after you begin smoking, such problems as a nagging cough, shortness of breath, and elevated heart rate will be experienced. Production of saliva will be increased, lung tissues dangerously irritated, and bronchial secretions noticeably elevated. Constricted blood vessels, increased blood pressure, slightly enlarged pupils, and a generally overstimulated central nervous system may also result. Increased smoking can cause tremors, stroke, paralysis of breathing, heart damage, visual impairment, kidney dysfunction, reduced appetite, cancer of the lungs, mouth, esophagus, pancreas, urinary bladder, and larynx, or even emphysema, where the lungs lose elasticity and retain abnormal amounts of air.

Even if you escape illness, you face the risk of burning or asphyxiating yourself and loved ones by smoking in bed or being careless with a lit cigarette. It happens all the time—just ask your local fire department.

Pregnant women should avoid smoking. Smokers' children may weigh less at birth than those of nonsmokers, and when babies are under 5 pounds at birth, mortality rate rises. Babies may also be nutritionally deprived, since absorption of food through the gastrointestinal tract is noticeably reduced by smoking. Smokers experience a higher rate of premature births. Those planning to breast-feed should cut out cigarettes, as nicotine can be passed along to a child through its mother's milk.

Now that we have made you aware of tobacco's dangers (maybe you have even lit up a couple while reading this), you may be curious about how to deal with your addiction. The truth of the matter is that we can't offer much encouragement. But although statistics show that breaking the habit is extremely difficult, that does not mean you shouldn't try in earnest.

All kinds of plans have been suggested for reducing tobacco use. Some say federal subsidies to the nation's 400,000 tobacco growers should be ended. Though that is something to consider, it is doubtful it would reduce smoking. Others advocate banning models in cigarette advertising (we tend to pattern ourselves after models) or a ban on cigarette advertising completely. In fact, 40 percent of current smokers surveyed said they would favor a prohibition on all cigarette advertising, currently budgeted at about $300 million annually. That might help future generations, but would do little to help existing addicts left with their nicotine cravings, advertising or no advertising. Another plan calls for reduction of tar and nicotine in cigarettes by 50 percent. Although this sounds good in theory, if the craving prevails, smoker-addicts will probably double consumption.

One plan that makes sense for future generations is school education about smoking and the dangers of tobacco addiction. Such educational efforts must be undertaken at an early age, in kindergarten or first grade, when children are taught about illness and germs. All romance should be stripped from smoking. It should be stressed repeatedly that smoking is a no-no, as we presently do with addictive drugs such as heroin. (Heroin takes fewer lives than tobacco.) Unless we successfully stigmatize tobacco, it will continue to appeal to many. The business of selling cigarettes is big business indeed, and, as we witness so often, the best interests of our population are often subordinated to the desire for profits.

If you want to stop, you can attend a smoking clinic. Although they have not been around long enough to document any long-term success, first results seem to indicate that they do help some people.

New products being tested include nicotine chewing gum and high-nicotine-content cigarettes, which may cut down the amount of smoke inhaled—a halfway measure at best.

Cutting down is a common route, but often it does not work. Believe it or not, the most effective way to stop smoking is to stop in a "cold-turkey" (complete withdrawal) fashion. Although we don't claim it is easy, it requires less willpower than cutting down. A little preparation will help if you try this method. First, make up your mind you are never going to touch another cigarette. Tell friends and co-workers about your plan, asking for their help and support. Warn them you will be more irritable than usual, but ask them to bear with you. Ask fellow addicts not to smoke around you. Do not keep cigarettes in the house or let yourself sneak one when you go out to walk the dog. Do not let outside pressures influence you to start smoking again. Hospital waiting rooms are full of healthy people chain-smoking because some friend or loved one is ill down the hall.

If you fail, don't give up. Try again . . . and again. It is worth it. You can add years to your life and prevent pain and suffering if you succeed.

If you are unable to stop completely, try some halfway measures to minimize potential damage. Switch to a low-"tar"/low-nicotine cigarette. Death rates for smokers of these cigarettes have dropped 16 percent. Don't smoke a cigarette past the halfway point. Use a filter that partially blocks out "tar" and nicotine, such as One-Step-at-a-Time or Aquafilter.

If you have not started smoking, don't. If you do smoke, try to quit. Tobacco never created heroes or movie stars—just slaves to its addiction.

TRANQUILIZERS

Stress is not an invention of the twentieth century. We have suffered from its effects since man first dodged dinosaurs. Fear, guilt, and worry accompany our passage through life, and over the centuries we have sought various means of alleviating our mental anguish.

Tranquilizers *are* an invention of the twentieth century, the latest means of dulling our minds to pain. Use of these mood-changing, mind-altering drugs is not only accepted but often encouraged by the public and the medical community alike. As a result, one out of six Americans is a regular tranquilizer user. Anti-anxiety drugs account for 250 million prescriptions a year, over sixty doses for each man, woman, and child in the United States. Only alcohol, nicotine, and aspirin rank higher than tranquilizers as "abused drugs." Almost 30 percent of all American women, with highest consumption in the age bracket from thirty to fifty-nine, attempt to erase their problems with mood-changing drugs. Tranquilizer misusers far outnumber abusers of illicit drugs, with minor tranquilizers accounting for 15 to 25 percent of annual hospital admissions. In spite of this, some doctors still scribble prescriptions for a "panacea" rather than investigate other avenues of treatment, perhaps in response to patients' demands or to the expensive, effective, and misleading advertising by drug companies. Undoubtedly helpful to those with genuine psychiatric problems, tranquilizers are too often prescribed for hypochondriacs and normal, healthy people.

A central-nervous-system depressant, tranquilizers may be divided into several categories: benzodiazepines, meprobamate, methaqualone, phenobarbital, phenothiazines, and tri-cyclic anti-depressants.

Benzodiazepines, which include Valium, Librium, Dalmane, and Serax, are considered minor tranquilizers. Safest of the anti-anxiety agents, they are long-acting, thereby necessitating less frequent use. Potential for overdose and addiction is small, but possible, with heavy, prolonged use. Pharmacologically similar, Valium and Librium are the most widely prescribed drugs in the United States.

Meprobamates include Miltown and Equanil. The first of the minor tranquilizers when marketed in 1955, it was considered a mild, safe, nonaddictive anxiety-reliever. Users discovered its euphoric, barbiturate-like effects and "Miltown" became a household word. The high addiction and overdose potential of the drug was not realized until later.

Methaqualones include Quaaludes, Sopors, Mandrax, Parest, and Somnifac. A nonbarbiturate sedative-hypnotic like meprobomate, it was once considered safe and non-habit-forming. Methaqualone's high addiction and overdose potential has now been established (see Methaqualone).

Phenobarbitals include tranquilizers such as Luminal. It is less expensive than most tranquilizers and has a low overdose and addiction potential when used for short periods. The drug acts as a muscle relaxant without the sedative effects of other barbiturates. Long-term use may result in barbiturate withdrawal (see Barbiturates).

Phenothiazines include Thorazine, Stelazine, Compazine, and Mellaril—all considered "major" tranquilizers or anti-psychotics used in the treatment of schizophrenia and other psychotic states. While addiction potential is low, overdose potential is moderate. Jaundice and Parkinson-like symptoms may appear as side effects. Some feel these drugs are overprescribed and should be used only in severe cases. Controversy also exists concerning their use in the treatment of bad trips caused by drugs such as LSD.

Tri-cyclic anti-depressants such as Elavil and Triavil are anti-depressant mood elevators with a moderately high overdose potential and low addiction rate. Although widely prescribed, some say they are generally ineffective and should be used only for severe psychiatric disorders.

The distinction between "minor" and "major" tranquilizers is a chemical one; it does not indicate differences between their degrees of potency. Most users of minor tranquilizers feel their use is therapeutic, rather than recreational, helping them smooth out the rough edges of life. Availability of tranquilizers further adds to their acceptability. Whether ingested in tablets or capsules every three to six hours, or injected as part of a medical procedure, tranquilizers are considered legitimate pharmaceutical aids.

Tranquilizers are indicated for sedation in the fields of dentistry, neurology, cardiology, obstetrics and gynecology, orthopedics, pediatrics, dermatology, plastic surgery, and psychiatry. Controversy exists over their use in the treatment of alcoholism and in amphetamine, heroin, and barbiturate withdrawal, although they have been effective in many cases. When used judiciously, they are valuable as a sedative, anti-anxiety agent, anti-convulsant, muscle relaxant, and sleeping aid.

Acting on the limbic system of the brain, tranquilizers depress the central nervous system by affecting the connection between the sensory and motor pathways. As the skeletal muscles relax, anxiety and tension disappear into a peaceful, calm state. The resulting euphoria may affect coordination, speech, libido, and attention span, reduce aggression, and induce sleep. Depending on tranquilizer, dosage, and the attitude and personality of the patient, this sedative effect may be short-term, lasting a few hours, followed by deterioration into a state of agitation or depression. This can create a cycle of sedation-agitation and may lead to psychological dependence.

Tranquilizer effects, both adverse and therapeutic, are generally less extreme than those of barbiturates. Tolerance may develop within a few weeks if the drug is continually kept in the bloodstream by three-times-a-day ingestion. Side effects may include apathy, low blood pressure, blurred vision, rashes, disorientation, confusion, muscle weakness, headaches, upset stomach, fainting, lack of coordination, dizziness, menstrual, bladder, and ovulary irregularities, anxiety, and hallucinations. Some users experience stimulation rather than sedation, which results in hyperexcitability, insomnia, hostility, and rage. Large doses can lead to tremors, loss of muscular coordination, and convulsions. With time and heavy dosage, habituation, psychological dependence, and withdrawal symptoms may occur.

Tranquilizers can kill when potentiated by other central-nervous-system depressants such as alcohol, barbiturates, opiates, hypnotic-sedatives, and synthetic narcotics. Accidental poisoning or suicide is almost impossible with a tranquilizer unless the drug is combined with another depressant.

Alcohol and tranquilizers have a synergistic effect on each other, creating an additive result when they are taken together. Since the liver processes alcohol first, the tranquilizer must wait its turn, circulating through the system many times over, damaging organs with each visit. Body functions, including breathing, heartbeat, and sensory and reasoning powers, slow down and may eventually stop, causing death.

In addition to alcohol, minor tranquilizers should not be used with anti-depressants or antihistamines and may decrease the effectiveness of birth-control pills. Major tranquilizers should be avoided when using anti-depressants, antihistimines, barbiturates, other tranquilizers and sedatives, blood-pressure medication, or diuretics. These substances, along with anti-convulsants, anti-coagulants, and MAO inhibitors, should also be avoided in combination with tri-cyclic anti-depressants, which remain in the system for two weeks after their use is discontinued. All drugs should be temporarily avoided after the user has stopped taking tri-cyclics.

Since tranquilizers depress the central nervous system and relax muscles, they cause the user's reaction time to increase. Operating machinery or power tools, driving a car, or riding a bike in traffic may all be hazardous to the health of the user, as alteration of vision and time and space judgment greatly multiplies the chance of accident.

Pregnant women should avoid use of tranquilizers, which penetrate the placental barrier. Birth defects, fetal death, congenital heart disease, and skeletal abnormalities have all been attributed to use of the drug, which also infiltrates the mother's milk. The most publicized case of tranquilizer danger to fetal development was that of Thalidomide, a nonbarbiturate sleeping pill, originally thought harmless, which resulted in severe birth defects. Tranquilizers are also ranked third among drugs causing damage to the stomach lining, trailing only aspirin and alcohol.

Street tranquilizers are even more dangerous, since they are sometimes cut with unknown substances, or crudely manufactured in amateur laboratories, adding to the unpredictability of an already unpredictable drug. Tranquilizers' shelf lives vary, with some pills becoming impotent while others become more toxic with the passage of time.

Addiction, both physical and psychological, may occur with prolonged heavy use. Self-medication is often the culprit when tranquilizers are abused. The need to increase dosage to achieve the same effect signifies tolerance has set in.

An addictive personality may find the drug to be a "legitimate" source to feed his habit, not realizing that withdrawal from tranquilizers may be as difficult as from alcohol, opiates, or barbiturates. Sedative users should take precautions. Do not use tranquilizers for minor temporary problems or refill prescriptions without consulting your doctor. Do not use the drug over long periods of time, follow directions exactly, and do not self-medicate.

Prolonged medication should not be stopped abruptly. Tranquilizer use must be gradually discontinued to avoid unpleasant withdrawal symptoms. A dependent user may experience such symptoms within four to eight hours after cessation. Hyperexcitability and anxiety, insomnia, respiration and pulse reductions, coordination impairment, slurred speech, nausea, vomiting, tremors, and convulsions may occur, depending on the drug's potency, the victim's metabolism, and the length and frequency of use.

Medical supervision is necessary for safe withdrawal from tranquilizers. Get the overdoser to a hospital, or, if he is conscious, induce vomiting. Do not force an unconscious person to throw up, but turn him on his side in case he does. Do not give him amphetamines or coffee. Keep him awake and walking. Find out exactly what he took, how much, and what it looked like, if possible.

Tranquilizers are regulated under Schedule IV of the Controlled Substances Act. Prescriptions are not refillable more than five times within six months, and the drug's production and distribution must be recorded and supervised by manufacturers. Physicians and pharmacists are expected to keep records, and security precautions against theft must be taken.

One of the first tranquilizers was Sedobrol, a cube which made a sodium-bromide broth. Research on the drug rauwolfia produced many of the pioneer sedatives, followed by barbiturates in the thirties and nonbarbiturates in the 1950s. Discovery of the benzodiazepines revolutionized the tranquilizer industry. Unlike their predecessors they relaxed users without sedating. Librium was discovered in 1960, instantly becoming the world's most widely prescribed drug until the introduction of Valium in 1963. Today, Valium remains the top-selling drug, indicative of our obsession with anxiety (see Valium).

Less dangerous and sometimes more successful alternatives to tranquilizers are available, from massage and exercise to alleviate muscle tension, to nondrug means of falling asleep. Depression is suppressed, not solved, by the use of tranquilizers; the anxiety problem still exists.

Rather than being the panacea of our time, tranquilizers should more likely be considered a psychiatric Band-Aid.

VALIUM

Are we a nation of neurotics? Can a pill-popping populace function as well as one which copes with stress through other means? Or is it true, as Huxley writes of the future panacea, Soma, in *Brave New World,* that "a gramme is better than a damn"?

To many of the thirty million Americans who consume three billion tablets a year, Valium means a tranquillity trip. Whether ingested in the form of a 2- or 5- or 10-mg pastel-colored tablet, or injected in liquid form, the benzodiazepine tranquilizer Valium is the best-selling prescription drug in the world, followed closely by its chemical cousin Librium (see Tranquilizers). In one recent year, these two top "tranqs" grossed $250 million for their manufacturer, Hoffman-LaRoche, which plowed back $12 million for elaborate advertising aimed at further increasing the popularity of its products.

Although one in ten Americans uses Valium, the United States ranks behind Germany, France, and Japan in per-capita sales. Of the sixty million Valium prescriptions written in the United States each year, the majority have been prescribed for nonspecified medical complaints—anxiety which manifests itself in physical problems such as queasy stomach, nausea, or tremors or, as the ads proclaim, "for relief of psychic tension and its somatic symptoms." Females outnumber male users by 2.5 to 1.

Used medically as a muscle relaxant, anti-convulsant, and psychotherapeutic aid, Valium is a central-nervous-system depressant containing desmethyldiazepam, 3-hydroxydiazepam, and oxazepam. It is five to ten times stronger than Librium, though less potent than barbiturates or major tranquilizers such as Thorazine. The drug is thought to work on the limbic system of the brain, creating the sedative, tranquilizing, muscle-relaxing effect which peaks about ninety minutes after ingestion and disappears twenty-four to thirty-six hours later.

Valium is used by psychiatrists, anesthesiologists, cardiologists, neurologists, orthopedists, pediatricians, and obstetricians for its sedating and relaxing properties. Valuable in the reduction of spasms, it is used to control the convulsions of grand mal seizures and cerebral palsy and the contractions of tetanus, in addition to its preoperative use as a sedative. The drug is intended for short-term use only, not for chronic emotional problems, and should not be considered a substitute for psychiatry.

Standard therapeutic dose is usually 5 mg taken three times daily. Over an extended period of time, tolerance will set in; higher doses will be required to achieve the same effect, and 30 mg a day can escalate to 100, 200, or even 300 mg a day, at which point the user is addicted and will experience withdrawal symptoms if he stops suddenly. Even with normal dosage, the drug should not be used continuously for longer than a month. Proponents of Valium contend that addiction occurs only if it is used at six to twenty times the prescribed dose for a period of months, or if 400 mg is taken daily.

Overdosing on Valium is difficult, although it has been implicated in 10 percent of all drug-abuse emergencies requiring medical attention, particularly when it had been combined with alcohol or other central-nervous-system depressants. Controversy exists over the use of Valium in combination with methadone, administered by some drug programs which believe that the ingredients in the two do not affect each other. Others insist that Valium and alcohol or methadone create a potent "doper's cocktail," leading to further addiction and possible death.

As with most other drugs, overuse, misuse, and careless prescription—and not the drug itself—are to blame for deaths from Valium. The victims are mostly multiple-drug users who are not aware of the potent result of combining a seemingly innocuous drug such as Valium with other substances. Valium is potentiated by alcohol, phenothiazines, narcotics, barbiturates, anti-depressants, and MAO inhibitors.

Adverse reactions may include drowsiness, headache, constipation, fatigue, rashes, tremors, incontinence, vertigo, blurred vision, nausea, change in libido, confusion, blood changes, and depression. Some feel the regular user may evolve into a depressed personality with extended use. Paradoxical reactions include anxiety, hallucinations, insomnia, rage, increased muscle spasticity, and hyperexcitability. Since respiratory functions are not affected by the drug, suicides rarely find success with Valium alone. Withdrawal from heavy use should be attempted only under medical supervision.

Valium is regulated under Schedule IV of the Controlled Substances Act, with prescriptions refillable up to five times within six months.

WILD FENNEL, PARSLEY, AND DILL

An oral dose of five to twenty drops of oil taken from the seeds of wild fennel, parsley, or dill, familiar and useful kitchen spices, can provide users with hallucinations. But there are serious dangers to consider.

Those who ingest any of the three may may suffer epileptic-like convulsions along with their hallucinations—not much of a fun trip. In addition, while they are safe when used in normal cooking and flavoring proportions, the active ingredient that gives these plants their psychotropic kick will, because of the quantity needed, do serious damage to the user's kidneys and liver.

Our advice: Keep away from the use of these as drugs. Otherwise, you might ruin your recipe for a long and healthy lifespan.

YAGE

COMMON NAMES: *ayahuasca, caapi, drug, jungle drug, natema, tiger drug, yaje, yake*

Indians of Brazil and Colombia call it caapi; in Peru, Bolivia, and Amazonian Ecuador it is referred to as ayahuasca. Known as yage in the Andes and North America, it can be pronounced *yah-HAY, YAH-hay*, or *ya-hee*.

Whatever one chooses to call it, claims made for the woody *Banisteriopsis caapi* vine are many.

Pleasure: Yage supposedly provides great relief from the hardship and strain of daily native life.

ESP: Some believe yage increases ESP ability and use the drug to predict future events (the most active alkaloid in this plant is harmine, once known as telepathine because of this phenomenon).

Aphrodisiac: Yage may act as a sexual stimulant.

Hallucinogen: The drug can produce brilliant flashes of light in the mind, illusions of objects becoming larger or smaller, vivid hallucinations, and an exceptional ability to see well in the dark.

Yage is prepared by boiling fresh caapi bark in water. Natives often add other psychoactive plants to the brew, such as datura (rich in belladonna alkaloids) or *Banisteriopsis rusbyana* (containing DMT), for an extra kick.

After it has been boiled for several hours, a cup of the strained native concoction will contain about 400 mg of harmal alkaloids. However, that is a "native" dose and natives are used to this stuff. Experimenters should take no more than 100 mg. Those planning to try yage should be careful about dosage, as too much can be poisonous.

If yage tea is not your bag, and fresh caapi is not available, pure harmine can be snorted in the form of harmine hydrochloride. Since this drug can irritate the nose and throat for several days, users often place 50 mg under the tongue and between the lips and gums for easy absorption. Results are almost instantaneous.

Yage should be taken on an empty stomach, for immediately after ingestion the user will vomit. Once he has gotten past that, the trip begins.

First sign is a slightly drunk feeling, during which hallucinations may occur. Sleepiness, slurring, lack of coordination, and dizziness may accompany purple or blue light flashes, said to be common to the yage experience.

As the user gets higher, he begins to hallucinate to an even greater degree, feeling a burst of psychic energy as well as sharpened night vision. Sexual senses heighten, but care is advised. Too much yage can turn the mind into a nightmare of visions accompanied by disturbing psychoactive feelings.

Pure harmine produces sensations and effects similar to those of mescaline, along with an inebriated buzz.

Under no circumstances should a novice ingest more than 250 mg of harmine. More can depress the central nervous system. Moreover, since harmine and related alkaloids are MAO inhibitors, combination with the wrong things can result in headache, heart trouble, or death. Keep away from tranquilizers, amphetamines, antihistamines, alcohol, avocados, ripe bananas, broad beans (pods), sedatives, mescaline, nutmeg, aged cheeses, any quantity of milk products, cocoa, narcotics, sauerkraut, ephedrine, macromerine, yeast extract, excessive caffeine, canned figs, chicken liver, excessive amounts of chocolate or licorice, pickled herring, and oils of dill, parsley, or wild fennel.

YOHIMBE

COMMON NAMES: *lizard tail, yerba del pasmo, yerba mansa*

Watch out, Messrs. Lipton and Tetley—the Bantu natives of West Africa have come up with a stimulating, aphrodisiac tea that has a lot more going for it than flo-thru flavor.

The recipe: Boil 6 to 10 teaspoons of shaved bark from the tropical *Corynanthe yohimbe* tree in a pint of water for about five minutes. Adding 1,000 mg of vitamin C will strengthen the brew, speed up its action, and reduce any possibility of nausea. Use honey or sweetener to cut the unpleasant taste. Strain the resulting two cups of tea and sip them both slowly. You now have an hour or so to find yourself a willing partner before experiencing the drug's first effects.

Yohimbe bark contains a number of alkaloids, of which the most powerful is a substance called yohimbine (also produced synthetically as yohimbine hydrochloride), which can be used as a snuff for more rapid results. Although there are some clouds relating to their legality, both forms are presently available in the United States.

Those with sensitive stomachs may experience a few minutes of nausea after sipping the brew. In about a half-hour you will begin to feel warm shivers up and down your spine along with mild restlessness and anxiety not unlike the early stages of an LSD trip. Quickly following will be a pleasant, euphoric, tension-free state with a somewhat intoxicated feeling.

Yohimbe is generally used for sexual purposes. The drug's action, lasting from two to four hours, causes a change in the user's peripheral blood flow while, at the same time, it stimulates the spinal ganglia which control the corpus spongiosum. What all that simply means is that it will help to produce a strong male erection for men suffering from problems of psychological impotence.

Both male and female users claim that coitus and orgasm are greatly heightened as a result of ingesting yohimbe. The drug causes pelvic tingles, mild perceptual changes, and psychic stimulation, but will result in hallucinations only if taken in extremely high and potentially toxic doses. While chemically similar to both psilocybin and LSD, it is usually used for its stimulant effect rather than because of any hallucinogenic properties.

Yohimbe is not physically addicting, nor does it have any known unpleasant aftereffects (except for a possible runny nose for a couple of hours after tripping). It can, however, become something of a psychological sexual crutch if used too often. The drug definitely should not be considered by those suffering from hepatitis, hypoglycemia, or blood-pressure disorders. If you have any trouble with your kidneys, heart, or liver, stay away from this one, too. These organs can have difficulty in handling yohimbe and failure can occur if large doses are ingested. An important caution is that yohimbe should not be used by anyone who has taken antihistamines, diet pills and other amphetamines, tranquilizers (except for Librium), or narcotics. Keep away from alcohol when using yohimbe; the combination is very toxic.

THE AUTHORS

Lawrence A. Young is a graduate of Columbia Grammar School and New York University. Founder of one of New York's best-known corporate communications consulting firms, Mr. Young has served as an adviser to many of the nation's leading corporations for more than a decade. He has lectured at the United Nations, Pratt Institute, and to major business groups across the country. He now resides in Miami, Florida, with his wife, Linda.

Linda G. Young attended Syracuse and New York Universities, where she received her master's degree and lectured. Ms. Young taught urban-disadvantaged, educable mentally retarded students in the New York City public school system for fourteen years. Mother of two teenaged boys, she has served as an educational advisor to three of the nation's leading universities. In her spare time she tries to recover from writer's cramp by exercising her green thumb in the garden.

Marjorie Miller Klein has been an investigative reporter and articles editor for *Miami Magazine*. A native of Washington, D.C., Ms. Klein began her writing career when she served as editor in chief of *The Old Line*, the campus humor magazine at her alma mater, the University of Maryland. Prior to collaborating on *Recreational Drugs*, she authored a series of short stories and now has a first novel in manuscript form. Mother of two pre-teenagers, she has taught in the public school system and at Miami-Dade Community College. What little spare time she has is devoted to bicycling, quilting, and painting.

Donald M. Klein, a practicing attorney in Miami, Florida, graduated from Harvard College and the University of Miami School of Law, where he later taught. While at the U. of M., he served as editor of that school's prestigious *Law Review*. He and Marjorie have been married for fifteen years.

Dorianne Beyer is a native of New York City who has also lived in London. Ms. Beyer has worked close to the drug scene for the past several years as a criminal attorney for The Legal Aid Society and is now in private practice. A graduate of Hunter College and Rutgers Law School, she is currently serving as co-publisher of a popular new magazine.

LIST OF COMMON NAMES

Since many recreational drugs are known by their common names,
consult the section or sections in parentheses.

A (Amphetamines)
Acapulco gold (Marijuana)
Acid (LSD)
Afghani (Hash Oil)
African rue (Syrian Rue)
Amies (Barbiturates)
Amoeba (PCP)
Amys (Amyl Nitrate)
Angel dust (PCP)
Angel hair (PCP)
Anhalonium (Mescaline; Peyote)
Animal tranquilizer (PCP)
Areca nut (Betel Nuts)
Ashes (Marijuana)
Asthma weed (Lobelia)
A stick (Marijuana)
Ava (Kava Kava)
Awa (Kava Kava)
Ayahuasca (Yage)

Badoh negro (Morning-glory Seeds)
Bador (Ololuiqui)
Banewort (Belladonna)
Barbs (Barbiturates)
Barrels (LSD)
Beans (Amphetamines; Mescaline)
Beast (LSD)
Beautiful lady (Belladonna)
Bennies (Amphetamines)
Benz (Amphetamines)
Benzies (Amphetamines)
Bernice (Cocaine)
Bernies (Cocaine)
Betel morsel (Betel Nuts)
Bhang (Marijuana)
Big C (Cocaine)
Big D (Dilaudid; LSD)
Big H (Heroin)
Biscuits (Methadone)
Bitter grass (Calea)

Black beauties (Amphetamines)
Blackbirds (Amphetamines)
Black mollies (Amphetamines)
Black oil (Hash Oil)
Black Russian (Hashish)
Blanks (Heroin)
Blockbusters (Barbiturates)
Blotter (LSD)
Blow (Cocaine)
Blue acid (LSD)
Bluebirds (Barbiturates)
Blue cheer (LSD)
Blue devils (Barbiturates)
Blue heaven (LSD)
Blue heavens (Barbiturates)
Blue mist (LSD)
Blues (Barbiturates)
Blue star (Morning-glory Seeds)
Bombida (Amphetamines)
Bombido (Amphetamines)
Bombita (Amphetamines)
Boo (Marijuana)
Bottle (Amphetamines)
Boy (Heroin)
Broccoli (Marijuana)
Brother (Heroin)
Brown (Heroin)
Brown dots (LSD)
Browns (Amphetamines)
Brown sugar (Heroin)
Buddha sticks (Marijuana)
Bumblebees (Amphetamines)
Burese (Cocaine)
Bush (Marijuana)
Businessman's trip (Amphetamines;
    DMT)
Butter flower (Marijuana)
Buttons (Mescaline)

C (Cocaine)
Caapi (Yage)

LIST OF COMMON NAMES

Caballo (Heroin)
Ca-ca (Heroin)
Cactus (Mescaline)
Cadillac (PCP)
California sunshine (LSD)
Candy (Barbiturates)
Carrie (Cocaine)
Cartwheels (Amphetamines)
Cecil (Cocaine)
Chalk (Amphetamines)
Cherry leb (Hash Oil)
Cherry top (LSD)
Chicken powder (Amphetamines)
Chief, the (LSD)
Chinese red (Heroin)
Chiva (Heroin)
Chocolate chips (LSD)
Cholly (Cocaine)
Christmas trees (Barbiturates)
CJ (PCP)
Clearlight (LSD)
Coast-to-coasts (Amphetamines)
Cobics (Heroin)
Cobies (Morphine)
Coffee (LSD)
Coke (Cocaine)
Colombo (Marijuana)
Columbian (Marijuana)
Columbian red (Marijuana)
Contact lens (LSD)
Co-pilots (Amphetamines)
Corine (Cocaine)
Courage pills (Barbiturates)
Cranks (Amphetamines)
Crap (Heroin)
Crossroads (Amphetamines)
Crystal (Amphetamines; PCP)
Crystal joints (PCP)
Cube (Morphine)
Cubes (LSD)
Cupcakes (LSD)
Cyclones (PCP)

D (Dilaudid)
Deadly nightshade (Belladonna)
Dead on arrival (PCP)
Death's head (*Amanita muscaria*)
Death's herb (Belladonna)

Demis (Demerol)
Devil's apple (Jimson weed)
Devil's testicle (Mandrake)
Devil's trumpet (Jimson weed)
Devil's weed (Jimson weed)
Dexies (Amphetamines)
Dillies (Dilaudid)
DOA (PCP)
Dollies (Methadone)
DOM (STP)
Domes (LSD)
Doojee (Heroin)
Dope (Heroin; Marijuana; Morphine)
Dots (LSD)
Double-cross (Amphetamines)
Double-trouble (Barbiturates)
Downers (Barbiturates)
Downs (Barbiturates)
Dream (Cocaine)
Drug (Yage)
Dry high (Marijuana)
Dust (Cocaine; PCP)
Dynamite (Cocaine)

Elephant tranquilizer (PCP)
Emsel (Morphine)
Eye-openers (Amphetamines)

Fifty (LSD)
First line (Morphine)
Fives (Amphetamines)
Flag root (Calamus)
Flake (Cocaine)
Flats (LSD)
Flea powder (Heroin)
Flower of the virgin, the (Ololuiqui)
Fly agaric (*Amanita muscaria*)
Flying saucers (Morning-glory Seeds)
Footballs (Amphetamines)
Forwards (Amphetamines)
French Quaalude (Methaqualone)
Funny stuff (Marijuana)

Gage (Marijuana)
Gag root (Lobelia)
Gainesville green (Marijuana)
Gangster pills (Barbiturates)
Ganja (Marijuana)

Gas (Nitrous Oxide)
G. B. (Barbiturates)
Giggles-smoke (Marijuana)
Gin (Cocaine)
Girl (Cocaine)
Glory seeds (Morning-glory Seeds)
Gold (Marijuana)
Gold Columbian (Marijuana)
Gold dust (Cocaine)
Goods (Heroin; Morphine)
Goofballs (Barbiturates)
Goof butt (Marijuana)
Goofers (Barbiturates; Sleeping Pills,
    Nonbarbiturate)
Goon (PCP)
Goric (Paregoric)
Gorilla pills (Barbiturates)
Grass (Marijuana)
Green (Ketamine Hydrochloride)
Green dragons (Barbiturates)
Greenies (Amphetamines)
Griefo (Marijuana)
Griffo (Marijuana)
Gunk (Inhalants)

H (Heroin)
Happy dust (Cocaine)
Hard stuff (Heroin; Morphine)
Harry (Heroin)
Has (Marijuana)
Hash (Hashish)
Hawaiian (Marijuana)
Hawk, the (LSD)
Hay (Marijuana)
Haze (LSD)
Hearts (Amphetamines)
Heaven dust (Cocaine)
Heavenly blue (LSD)
Heavenly blues (Morning-glory Seeds)
Hemp (Marijuana)
Herb (Marijuana)
Hikori (Mescaline; Peyote)
Hocus (Morphine)
Hog (PCP)
Hombrecitos (Psilocybin)
Honey oil (Hash Oil)
Hooch (Marijuana)

Horse (Heroin)
Horse tranquilizer (PCP)
Huatari (Mescaline; Peyote)

Idiot pills (Barbiturates)
Indian hay (Marijuana)
Indian oil (Hash Oil)
Indian tobacco (Lobelia)
Instant zen (LSD)

J (Marijuana)
Jay (Marijuana)
Jelly babies (Amphetamines)
Jelly beans (Amphetamines)
Jive (Marijuana)
Joint (Marijuana)
Jolly beans (Amphetamines)
Joy powder (Cocaine; Heroin)
Juanita weed (Marijuana)
Jug (Amphetamines)
Jungle drug (Yage)
Junk (Demerol; Dilaudid; Heroin;
    Morphine)

Kaif (Marijuana)
Ka-ka (Heroin)
Kauii (Marijuana)
Kava (Kava Kava)
Kawa (Kava Kava)
Kawa kawa (Kava Kava)
Kif (Hashish; Marijuana)
Killer weed (PCP)
King Kong pills (Barbiturates)
KJ (PCP)

L.A. turnabouts (Amphetamines)
Lady (Cocaine)
Laughing gas (Nitrous Oxide)
Leaf (Cocaine)
Leaf of God (Calea)
Lidpoppers (Amphetamines)
Lightning (Amphetamines)
Little children (Olouiqui; Psilocybin)
"Little men" (Psilocybin)
"Little women" (Psilocybin)
Lizard tail (Yohimbe)
Locoweed (Jimson weed; Marijuana)
Love drug (MDA)

LIST OF COMMON NAMES

Loveweed (Marijuana)
Lucy in the sky with diamonds (LSD)
Ludes (Methaqualone)

M (Morphine)
Mach (Marijuana)
Magic mushroom (Psilocybin)
Mandragora (Mandrake)
Mandrakes (Methaqualone)
Mariguana (Marijuana)
Marshmallow reds (Barbiturates)
Mary (Marijuana)
Maryjane (Marijuana)
Mary Werner (Marijuana)
Mauii (Marijuana)
MBD (Pemoline)
Medicine (Methadone)
Mellow drug of America (MDA)
Mellow yellow (Banana Skins)
Mellow yellows (LSD)
Mesc (Mescaline)
Mescal (Mescaline; Peyote)
Mescal buttons (Mescaline; Peyote)
Meth (Amphetamines)
Mex (Marijuana)
Mexican (Marijuana)
Mexican calea (Calea)
Mexican mud (Heroin)
Mexican reds (Barbiturates)
Mezz (Marijuana)
Microdots (LSD)
Minibennies (Amphetamines)
Miss Emma (Morphine)
Mist (PCP)
Mohasky (Marijuana)
Moon (Mescaline)
Morf (Morphine)
Morphie (Morphine)
Morpho (Morphine)
Morphy (Morphine)
Moto (Marijuana)
Mu (Marijuana)
Mud (Morphine)
Muggle (Marijuana)
Mujercitas, las (Psilocybin)
Mushroom (Psilocybin)
Mutah (Marijuana)

Natema (Yage)
Nebbie (Barbiturates)
Nemish (Barbiturates)
Nemmies (Barbiturates)
Nimbie (Barbiturates)
Nimby (Barbiturates)
Ninos, los (Psilocybin)
Nitrous (Nitrous Oxide)
Noble princess of the waters
    (Psilocybin)
Nose (Cocaine)
Nose candy (Cocaine)
Nose powder (Cocaine)
Nuggets (Amphetamines)

Oil (Hash Oil)
One, the (Hash Oil)
One-hit grass (DMT)
Orange mushrooms (LSD)
Oranges (Amphetamines)
Orange sunshine (LSD)
Orange wedges (LSD)
Owsley (LSD)

Panama red (Marijuana)
Paper acid (LSD)
Paradise (Cocaine)
Parica (Epena)
Peace pill (PCP)
Peaches (Amphetamines)
Peanuts (Barbiturates)
Pearls (Amyl Nitrate)
Pearly gates (LSD; Morning-glory
    Seeds)
Pearly whites (Morning-glory Seeds)
Pep pills (Amphetamines)
Perks (Percodan)
Peyotyl (Peyote)
Phennies (Barbiturates)
Pig tranquilizer (PCP)
Ping lang (Betel Nuts)
Pink and green amps (Amphetamines)
Pink ladies (Barbiturates)
Pinks (Barbiturates)
Plants (Mescaline)
Pod (Marijuana)
Poison (Heroin)
Poppers (Amyl Nitrate)

Pot (Marijuana)
Pukeweed (Lobelia)
Purple haze (LSD)
Purple hearts (Barbiturates)
Purple microdot (LSD)

Quacks (Methaqualone)
Quads (Methaqualone)
Quarter moon (Hashish)
Quas (Methaqualone)

Rainbows (Barbiturates)
Rat root (Calamus)
Red (Marijuana)
Redbirds (Barbiturates)
Red and blues (Barbiturates)
Red devils (Barbiturates)
Red oil (Hash Oil)
Reds (Barbiturates)
Reefer (Marijuana)
Rhythms (Amphetamines)
Roach (Marijuana)
Rock (Cocaine)
Rocket fuel (PCP)
Rope (Marijuana)
Roses (Amphetamines)
Royal blue (LSD)
Rue (Syrian Rue)

Satan's apple (Mandrake)
Sativa (Marijuana)
Scag (Heroin)
Scar (Heroin)
Schmeck (Heroin)
Schoolboy (Codeine)
Scuffle (PCP)
Seccy (Barbiturates)
Seeds (Morning-glory Seeds)
Seggies (Barbiturates)
Seni (Mescaline; Peyote)
Serenity Tranquility Peace (STP)
Seven barks (Hydrangea)
714s (Methaqualone)
Sheets (PCP)
Shit (Demerol; Dilaudid; Heroin;
    Marijuana)
Sinsemilla (Marijuana)
Sister (Morphine)

Skag (Heroin)
Skinny (Marijuana)
Skyrockets (Amphetamines)
Sleepers (Barbiturates; Sleeping pills,
    Nonbarbiturate)
Sleeping pills (Barbiturates)
Smack (Heroin)
Smash (Hash Oil)
Smeck (Heroin)
Smoke (Marijuana)
Snappers (Amyl Nitrate)
Snop (Marijuana)
Snorts (PCP)
Snow (Cocaine; Heroin)
Snowbird (Cocaine)
Soapers (Methaqualone)
Soaps (Methaqualone)
Soles (Hashish)
Soma (PCP)
Son of one (Hash Oil)
Sopes (Methaqualone)
Sparkle plenties (Amphetamines)
Speckled birds (Amphetamines)
Speed (Amphetamines)
Speedball (Cocaine)
Splash (Amphetamines)
Splim (Marijuana)
Star dust (Cocaine)
Stick (Marijuana)
Stinkweed (Jimson weed; Marijuana)
Straw (Marijuana)
Strawberry fields (LSD)
Stuff (Demerol; Dilaudid; Heroin;
    Marijuana; Morphine)
Stumblers (Barbiturates)
Sugar (LSD)
Sugar lump (LSD)
Summer skies (Morning-glory Seeds)
Sunshine (LSD)
Supari (Betel Nuts)
Superblow (Cocaine)
Supergrass (PCP)
Super Quaaludes (Methaqualone)
Super soper (Methaqualone)
Superweed (PCP)
Surfer (PCP)
Sweet calomel (Calamus)
Sweet flag (Calamus)

LIST OF COMMON NAMES

Sweet Lucy (Marijuana)
Sweet lunch (Marijuana)
Sweets (Amphetamines)
Synthetic Marijuana (PCP)

Tea (Marijuana)
Tecaba (Heroin)
Tens (Amphetamines)
Texas tea (Marijuana)
Thai sticks (Marijuana)
Thing (Heroin)
Thorn apple (Jimson weed)
Thrusters (Amphetamines)
Tiger drug (Yage)
Tlitiltzén (Morning-glory Seeds)
Tooies (Barbiturates)
Toot (Cocaine)
Truck drivers (Amphetamines)
Turnabouts (Amphetamines)
Turnsole (Heliotrope)
25 (LSD)
Twist (Marijuana)

Unkie (Morphine)
Uppers (Amphetamines)
Ups (Amphetamines)

Viper's weed (Marijuana)

Wake-ups (Amphetamines)
Wakowi (Mescaline; Peyote)
Water (Amphetamines)

Wati (Kava Kava)
Wedding bells (Morning-glory Seeds)
Wedding bells acid (LSD)
Wedges (LSD)
Weed (Marijuana)
West Coast turnarounds
    (Amphetamines)
Wheat (Marijuana)
White (Cocaine)
White girl (Cocaine)
White lightning (LSD)
White man's plant (Jimson weed)
Whites (Amphetamines)
White stuff (Demerol; Dilaudid;
    Heroin; Morphine)
Wild rue (Syrian Rue)
Window pane (LSD)
Woodpecker of Mars, the (*Amanita muscaria*)

Yagona (Kava Kava)
Yaje (Yage)
Yake (Yage)
Yellow jackets (Barbiturates)
Yellows (LSD)
Yerba (Marijuana)
Yerba del diablo (Jimson weed)
Yerba del pasmo (Yohimbe)
Yerba mansa (Yohimbe)
Yopo (Epena)

Zen (LSD)